VC10

Dedicated to Sir George Edwards and his band of brothers at Vickers. Long may their excellence and exploits be remembered. Their spirit lives on at the Brooklands Museum. Also to the artist Valerie Shirley (Sale), SWLA, who taught me so much and who loved VC10s.

Also by the Author:

Secret Wings of World War II: Nazi Technology and the Allied Arms Race
Secrets of the Spitfire: The Story of Beverley Shenstone: The Man Who Perfected the Elliptical Wing
Vickers VC10
Saab Cars: The Complete Story
Saab 99 and 900
Citroen: The Complete Story
Long Haul
Heavies
Jetliners
The New Illustrated Encyclopedia of the Automobile

VC10: Icon of the Skies

BOAC, Boeing and a Jet Age Battle

Lance Cole

Pen & Sword
AVIATION

First published in Great Britain in 2017 by
Pen & Sword Aviation
an imprint of
Pen & Sword Books Ltd
47 Church Street
Barnsley
South Yorkshire
S70 2AS

ISBN 978 1 47387 532 6

A CIP catalogue record for this book is available from the British Library

Typeset in Ehrhardt by
Mac Style Ltd, Bridlington, East Yorkshire
Printed and bound in the UK by CPI Group (UK) Ltd,
Croydon, CRO 4YY

Pen & Sword Books Ltd incorporates the imprints of Pen & Sword
Archaeology, Atlas, Aviation, Battleground, Discovery, Family History,
History, Maritime, Military, Naval, Politics, Railways, Select, Transport,
True Crime, and Fiction, Frontline Books, Leo Cooper, Praetorian Press,
Seaforth Publishing and Wharncliffe.

For a complete list of Pen & Sword titles please contact
PEN & SWORD BOOKS LIMITED
47 Church Street, Barnsley, South Yorkshire, S70 2AS, England
E-mail: enquiries@pen-and-sword.co.uk
Website: www.pen-and-sword.co.uk

Contents

The time will come, when thou shalt lift thine eyes
To watch a long-drawn battle in the skies,
While aged peasants, too amazed for words,
Stare at the flying fleets of wond'rous birds.
England, so long the mistress of the sea,
Where winds and waves confess her sovereignty,
Her ancient triumphs yet on high shall bear,
And reign, the sovereign of the conquered air.

Translated excerpt from Gray's
Luna Habitabilis (1737)

Acknowledgements

This book has taken years of research to create and I am indebted to many people. I was fortunate enough to know and be tutored by the great (late) E. Brian Trubshaw – 'EBT' – and it is to him and his memory that I offer thanks and respect. He kindly wrote some further words for me to include herein. At Brooklands, the Vickers veterans, museum staff and members, have been of great help and kindness and I offer thanks to them. I was lucky enough in earlier days, to talk to Sir George Edwards to whom I, like so many, am indebted.

I would particularly like to thank Jelle Hieminga, the Dutch KLM-trained pilot, engineering graduate and VC10 enthusiast of VC10 website fame, 'A Little VC10derness' (www.VC10.net), for his kind sharing of information and perspectives about the VC10. Jelle, a regular supporter at Brooklands Museum, is a true chronicler of the VC10 story in a reliable and detailed perspective and has kindly agreed to some of his content being referenced herein.

Others who have helped with my research and views include: Dr N.A. Barfield, N.W. Boorer, Group Captain John Cunningham, Christopher Orlebar, Ronald Ballantine, Blair Shenstone, Peter J. Davis and Wing Commander Kevin Brookes, as Officer Commanding 101 Squadron. Also, friends at West London Aero Club, the British Airways Archive, Qantas PR, Boeing PR, the RAeS, The Brooklands Museum Trust and Allan Winn and Julian Temple.

A donation from the proceeds of the sales of this book will be made to Brooklands Museum Trust.

Introduction

VC10: An Elegance of Function

*'The VC10 had to be better than the 707, not just different, and we succeeded that
requirement in many ways.'*

Sir George Edwards, OM, CBE, FRS, FRAeS

This is the story of not just an airliner, but also the airline industry, an
airline and the nation and society it served. The Vickers VC10, the British
Overseas Airways Corporation (BOAC), the geopolitical and social
history of Great Britain and the British Empire are all interwoven. Other national
airlines have served political, as well as passenger needs, but the circumstances
surrounding BOAC, the end of an era, and government edict to a national, yet
State-supported carrier, are circumstances unique to BOAC and the VC10.

Throw in the legacy of Imperial Airways, the British class system, the remnants
of The British Raj, African independence, and a curious narrative of attitude and
paradox emerges in this airline and airliner story. Somehow, the VC10 became the
culmination of several decades of African and colonial aviation adventure by the
British and their airline. For Africa is not just an essential part of the VC10 story,
but the origination of it.

The sleek VC10 was *not* a triumph of form over function, but rather a triumphant
engineering-led elegance of function. The VC10's function dictated its form and
on the subsonic side of Concorde, that form happened to be the most beautiful
airliner ever made. Most people agree with such sentiment. So, reflecting the
late Dr Ing. Ferry Porsche's wonderful phrase about his cars having 'elegance of
function' seems to be a great way of capturing what we are talking about in this
aeroplane. And if we are to make an automotive analogy, I suggest that the VC10
would be a V12 Aston Martin; power and handling being to the fore. If the VC10
had been German, it would have, of course, been a Porsche 911 930-series Turbo
– with everything hung out the back.

There have been many things said about the VC10, its main British civil operator,
BOAC, and about the rival 707. Some such tales are lies, some manipulations, and
some are stated in truth. Even today, there remain differing versions of certainty.
It is vital that a rational and evidence-based opinion is framed. We need to put
aside national egos and agendas, and reach a view of the VC10 – and the great
BOAC battle with the Boeing 707 – that understands that we cannot always make

direct or fair comparisons between the two competing airframes; because they were designed differently for differing requirements. Boeing's 707 was originally smaller, less oceanic-capable, the Vickers VC10 was also originally smaller and not targeted at ocean crossings; both designs 'grew' until they were bigger. One – the 707 – lacked runway performance by design; the other – the VC10 – had runway performance, but lacked ultimate ultra-long-range ability – at the request of its specified operator.

Many years ago, I wrote a technical history book on the VC10 which was well received by enthusiasts and by the men who made the VC10: I tried to pay tribute to their incredible work as best as my then younger mind could. Some readers objected to my claim that if you were to design a specific 'hot and high', runway dedicated airframe, it still ought to be T-tailed and rear-engined. Critics said that as since the VC10, there have been nothing but conventionally shaped airliners with wing-mounted engines – I was wrong. But this was a claim of perceived wisdom, rather than pure fact. For the T-tail and rear-engined layout does *remain* the choice for regional and business jets needing ultimate performance – the Citation X proves the point. Bombardier's CRJ 200, Embraer's Phenom, Fokker's 100, Gulfstream's G650, all seem to have proven my 'clean wing' point – T-tails and rear engines are *still* an effective configuration for delivering lift in a specific application. Boeing's C17 is T-tailed too, as is the A400M; true, they both have wing-mounted engines – but use high wings to avoid the foreign object ingestion problems and roll-angle limitations of low wings with pyloned engines dangling

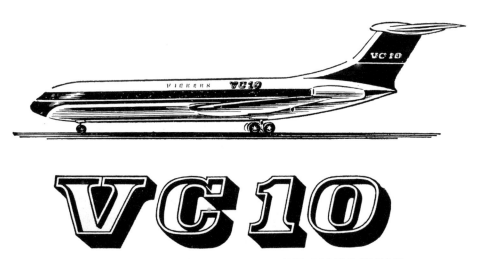

POWERED BY FOUR **ROLLS-ROYCE** CONWAY TURBOFAN ENGINES

VC10 advertising by Vickers.

off them a few inches from the ground. So the VC10-type layout is still viable and does have benefits. Oh, and T-tailed, rear-engined 727s and DC9/MD80s (reflecting their manufacturers faith in the configuration) are still flying.

Coming back to the VC10 and its wider airline story has been a long-held ambition and I am fortunate enough to have known and been previously tutored by the late Brian Trubshaw, the man who knew so much about the VC10 and what happened to it.

I still cherish my childhood memories of flying on VC10s to and from Africa. I will never forget my first sight of that wonderful dark blue BOAC VC10. My grandfather, himself a pilot and a member of West London Aero Club at White Waltham (scene of a famous 1977 low-level VC10 flypast), took me to London Heathrow. Then, I saw what was to be my airliner bound for Africa. There it was, a BOAC VC10, with its 40ft high, whale-tailed empennage jutting proudly out in a line-up of blue and golden 'Speedbird' tailfins at Terminal Three, London Heathrow Airport. There were VC10s everywhere: VC10s roaring at full power, or nose-up clawing into the sky, with the sense of energy from a distant tail. Other VC10s arrived with the eerie howling sound from the engines as thrust reverse was cancelled on the landing roll out. Once on board, the voice of the gold striped captain, reassuring in its silken tones, the glimpse of a stewardesses elegance, the murals on the cabin bulkheads; the fleeting flash of dark blue and gold hues, all added to the sheer sense of the VC10 occasion; such things made a mark on a child.

When I returned to a British school, before Concorde was launched into airline service, the fact that I had flown in on a BOAC VC10 was something special, even my teachers asked me about it and I flashed my BOAC 'Junior Jet Club' souvenir book as if it was a passport to identity. It carried with it a certain cachet. Schoolboys drooled over Ferraris, Jaguars, Aston Martins and Porsches, but they also drooled over blue and gold VC10s and Super VC10s. Just as in the old days of the Imperial flying boats, to have flown in on a VC10 and arrived from afar, really was something, it *meant* a lot – less about the passenger – but more about the sheer style and brilliance of the machine itself. There was a real sense of adventure in having flown on the VC10. And coming home on an East African 'Super' VC10 was, for jealous schoolboys, akin to arriving from the moon.

As a child and as a man, I was, like so many, utterly enthralled by the VC10, it was at least, a healthy obsession. Later in life I was lucky enough to fly a VC10, and spend a few precious hours with the RAF machines at Brize Norton. I still recall sitting in the 'jump' seat behind the commander as we rocketed upwards, thundering up, nose high, the Conways crackling and the VC10 steeply attacking the sky. That old cliché about climbing like a homesick angel suddenly seemed so apt. Then we burst out of the clouds like a cork out of a bottle and into the blue and levelled off, seemingly coming to a standstill as the power was pulled back and silence ruled. You could not get that thrill in a 707 or DC-8. Only taking off from a winch-launch in a super-sleek glider was to later rival the sensation of climb angle and speed.

Flying to and in Africa, has remained a draw to me. In the 1990s I was fortunate enough to be a brief part of the story of the Catalina flying boat owned by Pierre Jaunet that operated from the Zambezi. We moored that Catalina, registered as 'Z-CAT', at the old Imperial Airways flying boat pier that could still be found upstream from Victoria Falls. From there we set off across Africa, tracing the old Imperial route. I even got to fly Z-CAT from the left hand seat – and made a bad job of it. But I know how lucky I was to be part of that re-enactment of a past glory. The Catalina was so slow that we were overtaken by an eagle that flew alongside us, eyeballed me in the cockpit, hunched its wings and dived ahead of us. The ghosts of Imperial's C Class flying boats were surely watching. It was from, and for Africa, that the C Class, the Comet and the VC10 were all conceived. I first thought of writing about that history there and then, moored on the banks of the Zambezi where once, elite passengers took a small launch out to a giant silver flying boat that rested like a metallic dragonfly lapped by Zambezi waters, glinting in the sun and emblazoned with the legend 'Imperial Airways London'. It was a link with home, or a tumbrel to ride afar.

At the other end of the Imperial route lay Rose Bay, Sydney. I spent a few brief, yet wonderful months there, in paradise, spending every day on the harbour, right next to the old flying boat base on Sydney's magical inlet. Today, small float planes buzz about Rose Bay and the superb *Catalina* restaurant reminds us of those great days of the weekly aerial link between England and a cove on Sydney harbour, one brushed by a warm, light breeze, as C Class flying boats jostled at their moorings. A small memorial and a few hints of a grand past mark the place at Rose Bay where history was made. You can take a ferry from Circular Quay to Rose Bay, and if you are lucky an ancient de Havilland Beaver floatplane will alight upon the water in front of you. Just imagine what it would have been like if it had been a giant C Class depositing itself with one last heave after the long journey from England and Singapore.

As a child I also flew on Boeing 707s, DC-8s, Caravelles, 727s and even Nigeria Airways Dakotas, and other types, before adult experiences on 747s and the tri-jets. I can visualise now the view of barnacled, podded, wing pylon-mounted engines nodding on their mounts as Mr Boeing's 707 was rocked and twisted by heavy turbulence over Texas, and as the glamorous Pan American (Pan Am) flight attendants in their tight, blue, figure hugging skirts, bustled about making the cabin secure, while the grey-haired, utterly dependable gold striper in command up front in the Boeing's small cockpit drawled over the cabin PA system, reassuring us that there was: 'Nothing to worry about folks, Boeing builds them strong.'

It was the sight and sound of the VC10 that inspired me and many others to devotion and it was the VC10 men that did it – Messrs, Edwards, Hemsley, James, Lawson, Marshall, McElhinney, Petty, Salisbury, Stevenson, Walsh, Wilmer, and Zeffert. BOAC's Ballantine, Bristow, Stoney, Todd, and many more contributed to the VC10 affection too.

British Formula 1 Grand Prix driver, Innes Ireland was another VC10 fan, and over a single malt (bottle not glass), Ireland, who lived up the road, recounted to me his tale of returning from the South African Grand Prix at Kyalami, on a VC10, when the crew invited him to the flight deck for take-off from Johannesburg (and Salisbury). Ireland said he could not believe the take-off performance.

'The thing went up like a bloody rocket, nose nearly vertical old boy!' Ireland, more used to Comets and 707s, had never experienced anything like it, adding: 'Whatever BOAC management said, the pilots and crews loved their VC10s. That machine had real performance like a sports car, and it was *so* stylish. It just oozed class. I have an Aston Martin in the garage, it's just the same, do you want to see it? Oh, would you like more *Glenmorangie?*'

The battle between the VC10's main operator, BOAC, and its boardroom – of the VC10 versus the Boeing 707 – has become the stuff of legend amongst enthusiasts; a battle perhaps not dissimilar to that about the Spitfire, the Hurricane, and the Messerschmitt Bf 109, in terms of aviation debate. British opinion versus American opinion has become a fulcrum of perception, but there remains an internal British argument about the merits of the VC10 and BOAC's role. It is suggested that the evidence of numbers indicates that the thousand-plus 707s sold, prove its superiority over the fifty-four VC10s and Super VC10s sold, but the analysis and opinion needs to be much more sophisticated than such numerical basis might suggest, or allow. After all, as an analogy – we would not say that the Ford Escort or Volkswagen Beetle were 'better' cars than a Rolls-Royce, Aston Martin, or a Ferrari – just because the Ford and the VW sold in their millions compared to the tiny numbers of British or Italian exotic cars. Comparing apples with pears has never really been fair, has it? But there are many aspects to the debate.

Surely it is unfair to attack the Boeing 707 on grounds of emotion or ego, just as it is unfair to attack the VC10 on similar or other grounds. The VC10 was not perfect and the 707 was not flawed; the two were different – designed for different tasks at different times. The VC10 was an expensive engineering solution to a unique specification, but the fact remains that the VC10 did offer aspects of design and application that were more advanced than the 707.

This text is an attempt to take a good look at the past of Imperial and BOAC, and at events which then centred our attention on the VC10 itself. I have tried to deliver the full story, but nothing is definitive. In my books I am sometimes accused of being too wordy or too detailed. This may be true, but surely it is better to have provided all the evidence in detail and be criticised for that, than the alternative.

There is far more to the VC10 story than meets the blinkered eye of perceived wisdom. I often find that people of certainties, rely on others acquiescence not to challenge their pronouncements – or then frame any such questioning, as heresy or insult. It is an intriguing trick. To me, the VC10 has suffered at the hands of such people, and herein I offer my view, and the evidence to support it, *you* are free to disagree and go away and write your own VC10 book – which would be more constructive than whingeing on the web.

We need to go back to the Edwardian era and thence to the 1920s flights of Imperial Airways in order to fast forward to BOAC, to understand the reasons for the VC10 and all the issues around it. I make no excuse for a detailed examination of Imperial and BOAC, for without them and their needs and actions, the demands of BOAC's routes, the demand for a machine (the VC10) to meet such needs would not have transpired. So a lengthy look backwards is the perfect antidote to the current clichéd mantra of ignoring events by 'going forwards' and therefore omitting the lessons that might be learned. Just like an air crash investigation, history requires that we do indeed look backwards to find out what happened. Verdicts require *all* the evidence, not just what certain parties presume to be a so-called truth stated upon the certainties of pre-decided outcomes.

The potential of the VC10 and its possible variations was overshadowed and affected by politics and other factors. Much of the technological lead that the Vickers designers created for the VC10, and its planned variants, was thrown away – but not by Vickers. The lack of realised development was such a waste – as with the hovercraft, the work of Sir Frank Whittle, the Rover car company, and so much more – Britain failed to develop or market these developments, or simply sold them off to a foreign bidder in an apparent ideological attempt to dispose of the nation's engineering base.

We should also recall the VC10's excellent safety record in the context of the accident-strewn era in which it flew. The airline business was not as safe in 1970 as it is today. Big jets branded with big airline names often fell out of the sky after prior warning events that could have precluded the final fatal outcome.

Brian Trubshaw the VC10 and Concorde test pilot was kind enough to write the Foreword to my earlier VC10 technical history book. Prior to his death, he supplied the following words about the VC10 and BOAC and this text, which I include here:

Note from the late 'EBT', Brian Trubshaw, MVO, CBE, FRAeS:

'The full and forensic story of BOAC's involvement should be charted alongside that of Vickers, Sir George and the team of which I was part. It is clear that the passage of time, and a broader view, will deliver a record of what actually occurred across all the issues.

'There is no doubt that with the VC10, BOAC got what it asked for, but went on to criticise its own child. Other factors were at play, many political. Like too many great British products, the VC10 became immersed in politics and changing attitudes of various BOAC chairmen. Other events in global aviation, not least the lengthening of the runways the VC10 was designed to tackle, moved the goalposts. However, the facts are that the VC10 was a design triumph that eradicated many of the issues associated with the first generation of jet airliners on both sides of the Atlantic

'The great reserves of power, lift, and overall performance, designed and built into the VC10, gave it the possibility of being developed in a manner that the rival Boeing 707 could never have been, and such development was laid down by Vickers/BAC and its team of brilliant designers. That such potential was lost was not their fault. The blame lay with others. I was there; I was intimately involved as test pilot and then chief test pilot of Vickers-Armstrongs after I succeeded Jock Bryce in that role. We flew and proved the great VC10 design of Sir George Edwards, Ernie Marshall and the men of Vickers at Weybridge. We launched the giant airliner as the biggest ever built in Europe at the time, actually lifting off in a distance of just over 2,100ft on the 3,800ft runway (plus a short run–up extension) from Brooklands. This was not something a 707 or DC-8 could ever have managed.

'Other factors influenced what happened next and Vickers advanced work was forfeited. A 24,000lbs thrust development of the Conway engine, a 30ft fuselage extension for over 200 passengers and more fuel tankage, could have created a whole new market for a developed VC10. The various cargo handling designs were also ahead of their time.

'How odd it was that BOAC should have undermined their airliner, yet also subjected it to a significant marketing campaign the likes of which had not been seen before. VC10 and Super VC10 made many friends at, and for BOAC, and in the RAF and other airlines. BOAC and the RAF never lost a VC10. At the moment, VC10's are still flying with the RAF, which seems fitting.

'To have the design story and the operational, political, and commercial story of the VC10 brought together, should wipe away a few false trails and the misconceptions that have grown with time.'

Trubshaw was clear about the VC10: BOAC surely did get just what it asked for in the ultimate subsonic airliner of its era, and it seems, beyond.

As Trubshaw stated: 'The commercial battle of the airlines and their airliners in the 1960s is an intriguing and important tale that deserves to be told. Too many of our great British inventions have suffered the tragedy of wasted development.'

Trubshaw also made reference to first generation jet airliner design issues on both sides of the Atlantic; there he was also framing the Comet's issues. The Comet 1 was small, and used four engines to transport less than forty passengers. The revised Comet 4 was moderately stretched; meanwhile patriotic fervour framed the Comet as the great hope of British-is-best design, despite its known limitations. It might pay the reader to recall that even the ultimate Comet 4 was smaller than a Lockheed 1649 Super Constellation. Except in speed, Comet was a step backwards in passenger capacity, payload and range. Sheer speed was to prove not to be enough.

Admitting that the Comet, as the world's first jet airliner, was an unfinished and flawed work, was never going to happen in 1950s Britain and such a statement will infuriate those who, today, are still certain of their certainties. And how dare anyone suggest that de Havilland's were anything but perfection in everything they did. De Havilland's were of course brilliant, but not infallible.

But at least the Comet 4 had decent runway performance at 'hot and high' difficult airfields; early 707s did not have such capabilities. African Governments, scared of losing US investment, paid for their own runways to be lengthened – thus removing part of the VC10's advantage and handing access and market share to the 707 and DC-8. Even after such runway work, 707s and DC-8s were heavily compromised in payload range terms from such airports. Yet the VC10 answered the separate problems of the 707, Comet and more. At one stage in the late 1960s, *Flight* magazine pontificated that the Super VC10 would end the sales run of the mighty 707. *Flight* also opined on just what an all-VC10/Super VC10 mixed passenger and cargo fleet at BOAC would have done. As we know, neither scenario became a reality.

Sir George Edwards knew from the innovative Viscount (400+sales), and then the less well received Vanguard (less than fifty sold), that there was no point in building a new airliner design that matched, or mirrored, existing or planned competing airframes. In his 1973 RAeS lecture he revealed an underlying truism, one applicable to the thinking behind the VC10: 'It is never any good doing something that is either level with, or behind the state of the art, merely because the operating costs are low.'[1]

From Viscount to Valiant to 'Vanjet' studies and to VC10 first-flight, this is a great story of design triumphing, despite fluctuating corporate and political events. All these years on from the VC10 days, there is still something about the VC10 and the life of a supposedly inanimate lump of finely hewed metal. Here, was true industrial design and engineering legend, a machine like no other. At one brief stage of a glamorous 1960s history, the Super VC10 was the biggest airframe in Europe, and the strongest, most stylish, fastest, and most powerful civil airliner built and flown anywhere; a true second generation airliner. Did any subsonic aeroplane ever look so good? BOAC's rich, dark blue, with the shinning golden 'Speedbird' glinting on that stunning sculpture of a tail, just added to the emotions of the VC10 moment.

That this aircraft should engender such affection remains an interesting aspect of human behaviour. Maybe it was the shape and stance of that amazing tail that captured so many hearts, for here was the proof that great design can deliver so much. That further VC10 and Super VC10 potential was designed for, yet cast aside by the decisions of idiot politicians, seems a tragedy, and one that can still be felt at Weybridge, where the Vickers veterans still gather at their Brooklands Museum home at what must be the greatest enthusiasts' altar of winged and wheeled worship on the planet. They still feel raw at what was lost, and who can blame them.

I hope I have managed to meet the design target for this narrative; hopefully we are only slightly over-specified in weight, in the act of proving the point. The men of Vickers might have made the rare occasional mistake, but this is my record of their genius and the genesis of the airliner that BOAC procured from them, and the resulting design – the incomparable VC10.

Perhaps it is time to set the tailplane incidence, arm the stall warning and stick pusher, check the flap and slat settings. Then sit up straight and release the brakes, spool-up the Rolls-Royce engines, then launch, hit V1 and Vrotate, and climb steeply away to VC10 skies amid the sound of crackling Conways and a howling upon the ruffled airs of flight. Here, lies the sheer engineering and design brilliance of the VC10. Vickers called it, 'the shape of the future', and it was.

Lance Cole
Downderry Cornwall, Arcturus Zimbabwe, Rose Bay Sydney

Chapter 1

Icon of the Skies: The VC10 Legend

"BOAC got what it had asked for."
Brian Trubshaw, MVO, CBE, FRAeS,
in conversation with the author

Iconic is an overused word, all too easily applied to too many objects, but the VC10 was (and remains) a true icon of not just industrial design, but also of airline life, and of world travel as it opened up the mass market. People loved, truly loved, the VC10 as an icon of the air. Pilots, passengers, and small boys and girls the world over, adored the sight and the sound of the VC10 and its enlarged variant the Super VC10 – which really was super in every respect.

To many, the VC10's most important customer was the RAF, and the VC10's military transport and flight refuelling story is one that, although not intimately linked to civil operations, cannot be ignored in the story. The RAF's transport needs were, like BOAC's, also wrapped up in the end of Empire, yet then lasted into the second decade of the new millennium. The story of the RAF and its own Transport Command and Tanker squadron VC10 deployments spanned fifty years.

There is no over-sentimentalised gushing in saying that the VC10 was utterly, devastatingly, beautiful (perhaps in pure engineering terms, unnecessarily so), and remained stunning in the metal and in the mind long after it had passed by. Every line of the VC10 'works', it is as though the thing was styled – like a great car design from Pininfarina, Bertone or Michelotti, or more appositely, Sir William Lyons, Malcolm Sayer, or a Sir Nigel Gresley locomotive.

The VC10 was shaped not by Italian sculptors, but British engineers – men not given to artistic or emotional over excitement, but just as with aircraft, even Concorde, the engineers and designers behind such great shapes, would hate to be associated with a suggestion of 'styling'. But have you ever met *anyone* who is not moved by the shape of the VC10?

So the VC10 was a supreme piece of industrial engineering design. In its lines, it was wonderfully sculpted, but not 'over-designed', or a fashion victim.

Even the shape of the VC10's cockpit windows has a distinct form as a design motif that sets a mood, a face, one that seamlessly draws the eye into the lean fuselage that itself then arcs back into that great, swept 'whale tail' of a fin. The VC10's nose-to-tail Saville Row tailored style simply reeks of great design that has never dated. Unlike certain 'exotics' underneath that stylish skin, lay great engineering integrity.

The VC10, in the sum of all its parts, was a perfect blend of form and function; it was indeed a marker to the beauty of Concorde – upon which many of Sir George Edwards VC10 engineers and designers worked, and which many ex-VC10 pilots flew as a supersonic elite. It was *the* sleek, sweptback aerodynamic sculpture of the 1960s, instantly recognisable anywhere in the world – as was the BOAC blue and gold livery and the 'Speedbird' emblem. The VC10 seemed to gel with James Bond and his sharply tailored suits, elegant watches, lean women, fashion couture and an impression of style and speed, above all – speed – in a quintessential 1960s design evocation that lived long beyond that decade and never aged. Sean Connery's James Bond would look good in a VC10, but so too would that more contemporary Bond, Daniel Craig; somehow, VC10 sits amid the design names of the 1960s and still looks fresh and perfect over fifty years later. We might say the same of the original Cunard liner the *Queen Elizabeth II*, the Supermarine Spitfire, Concorde, or the Blackburn Buccaneer and the Avro Vulcan. Making an automotive analogy, the Aston Martin DB6, Porsche 911, Jaguar E-Type, Ferrari 365 Daytona, all are similarly timeless. In fact, if you park an Aston Martin DB6 next to a VC10, the view is wonderful, although Sir George Edwards might have preferred to equate the VC10 with a Bentley – *his* personal car of choice – but now, it would have to be a Bentley Continental GT.

Perhaps ultimately eclipsed in sculptural terms by Concorde, the VC10 was and remains a massive statement of British industrial design brilliance. There are other VC10 emotional ingredients – such as that haunting sound of Rolls-Royce Conways howling as they decelerate as the VC10 taxies past, the engine pods, the raked main undercarriage, the upswept elevators, the wing shape, the slight nose-down stance upon the wheels. *Surely,* none of this elegance was by accident.

The BOAC VC10 interior design and the revised Super VC10 cabin design, created a new standard of style, safety and comfort for all airliners. An 'architectural' look was used for the cabin wall and ceiling mouldings. New materials and patterns were used to trim the cabin. The 707 and DC-8 had reiterated old prop-liner style designs for their cabins, the VC10 created a new interior design fashion for airliners.

The Economy Class seats were the strongest made, had a forward support spar keeping it away from the legs of occupants seated behind, and achieved a 13.6g impact rating, much safer than the old 9g rating. Special cushions and webbing made the seat the most comfortable standard-class airline seat in the world. Concealed cabin lighting was a first in the VC10. The Super VC10 saw revised colours and panels in a more contemporary look. Overall, for both machines, better comfort, fresher air and more room amid new colours, all set new international standards in Economy Class and interior designs.[1]

'Ah but,' say the Boeing men, 'it only sold a few, whereas Boeing's seven-oh-seven warhorse sold into four-figures. So what did exquisite design, inside and out, achieve?'

The answer to that is not a simple response. As the acclaimed Scottish industrial designer Dawson Sellar, always opined, 'what on earth was the point of bad or boring design when good design cost no more, and made things sell and achieve a place in peoples' affections? Good design earned money and more, in marketing terms. So, an often ignored tangent of the VC10 is that of its place in the annals of global industrial design.' 'Old school' engineering purists of course, might be horrified at such words, but earning a place in peoples affections *is* what the VC10 design did.

The VC10 influenced airliner design and brought new techniques and standards that are now commonplace. So the advance of design was the VC10 achievement beyond its airline service.

Even if it was a subconscious act, the VC10 design team and aerodynamicists, surely also created a piece of stunning engineering design. For the conservative British to turn out something so 'designed' as the VC10, was in fact, quite a shock in a drab, grey and beige austerity world of post-war Britain. The men of British

VC10 Climb Out.

'safe' design might have expected the French to go all arty with their sexy-looking Caravelle jet liner, but an English design should surely be staid, square, redoubtable and upright in its angles – like a Morris Minor or a Vickers Vanguard! Nothing flashy (like a Caravelle or a Citroën DS) would be allowed – surely? Well, not until the VC10 and the Malcolm Sayer-styled Jaguar E-Type, both arrived in a blast of 1960s British style that was beyond even the Italian stylists. Britain, however conservative, however stifled, *could* turn out the best designers and engineers in the world.

Beige gave way to blue and gold.

The VC10 was the epitome of expensive-looking, designer-stylist couture in alloy, yet it was made and shaped by men immersed in old-school engineering. Yet their attitude was different – outward looking – and they gave us the perfect lines of the Viscount and the V1000, and finally, Concorde itself. They imagined beyond the constraints of the old, British conservative design psychology.

The State's Carriage: Imperial to BOAC

Inherent within the VC10's airline life, was the whole theatre of British civil aviation, its history, and the BOAC story. BOAC was born from Imperial Airways, which itself was birthed from the strands of early British privately owned airlines; Imperial and its successor, BOAC, were both State funded organs, not just of national transport, but also of colonial will.

BOAC then straddled that old world, and the new world of social change and end-of-empire, yet it was the child of many attitudes that were decidedly 'imperial' in outlook. Both airlines were subject to the vagaries of government, the Civil Service, overseeing boards, and the personal issues and egos of various leaders, MPs, ministers and transient political figures. Transient political appointees perhaps being the most lethal and potentially toxic risk of all to any business, especially a nationalised airline – or Britain's railways. In matters of transport and defence, the arrival of a clueless new minister of such a department of responsibility can cause great concerns and harms to airlines, air forces, or to armies and navies. Experts in their respective fields make much better appointees. Advising civil servants might also have their own agendas. All the themes of politics and corporate game playing contributed not just to Imperial Airways and BOAC, but to the ethos and practices that resulted in BOAC's route network and its airliner procurement. The VC10 was a child of such circumstances, yet few authors have investigated such influencing genesis.

A factor so often overlooked by aviation enthusiasts and purists, were the social science issues – after the Second World War, British society changed. Previously stuck in a perceived wisdom of class, social hierarchy, deference to royalty, and defined social rules, Britain was a society ripe for social revolution – if not actual revolution. Imperial Airways had been the instrument of a ruling class and an Empire administration. All that was to change and BOAC was cast between the two differing worlds of old and new. As British society changed in the 1960s, so too did travel, notably air travel upon the wings of the national airline that was BOAC. Such ingredients provide a sub-plot to the story and, in the political and corporate machinations that affected BOAC we see certain evidence of the issues suggested herein.

Britannia Rules the Air?

Britain had previously dominated the seas and the building of the ships that traversed the seas. Britannia ruled the waves, and it assumed it would rule the skies, which was an assumptive error of costly arrogance. Somehow, despite the engineering and design brilliance of British boffins, the British threw away the chance to rule the skies and the airliner market of the mid-late twentieth century. The reasons for the failure lie deep within the psychology of the British elite who ran affairs at the time. As the high flying Douglas DC-2 and DC-3 came into being in their modernistic monoplane, alloy monocoque streamlined design, the British were turning out wire-braced, wood and steel-built aerial yachts of biplane configuration and achieving stately progress in the lower airs. Devices such as the Handley Page HP42 and the Short S-17 Kent Class (generically known as the 'Scipio'), sailed the foetid lower altitudes of the Empire's airways as the new world rushed ahead in cooler airs many thousands of feet above. It really was a bizarre set of circumstances. We have to wonder, how on earth it transpired.

Looked at from the hindsight of today, we can suggest that aspects of BOAC and of Imperial Airways were very messy indeed, with a great deal of questions hanging over certain decisions and policies – and they are truly a crucial part of the VC10 and BOAC story. A very large amount of money has been swallowed up across the decades.

After over four decades of flying, the RAF's VC10 story has only just ended, and left many hardened military men in tears when it closed that final chapter. The VC10 flew for just over fifty-one years – a significant achievement.

Before that occurred, there were the decades of a very British story.

Chapter 2

Empires in the Sky: From Comet to V1000

'The slaughter of that beautiful babe in the bulrushes was an act of defeatism that will come home to roost'

> Aviation writer, Stanley H. Evans, on the
> termination of the Vickers V1000/VC7.
> (Private correspondence to B.S. Shenstone in 1956)

'One of the most disgraceful, most disheartening and most unfortunate decisions that has been taken in relation to the British aircraft industry in recent years ...

'From a national point of view that will be a tragedy when here, in almost completed form, we have a potential world-beater.'

> Mr Paul Williams, MP (Sunderland South), the
> House of Commons. 8.51pm, 8 December 1955, speaking
> on the cancellation of V1000. (Hansard, Vol 547, cc665–670)

Despite the travails of the Second World War, British and American minds took time out from military strategy to consider the world in a more peaceful, post-war environment. Paramount amongst such considerations, were the expected airline transport needs of the world powers and their peoples, notably of the west. The Brabazon Committee, under John Moore-Brabazon, who had flown with Geoffrey de Havilland at the dawn of aviation, was the 1940s British body that performed the act of soothsaying to the future of British civil aviation; uppermost in its mind were the needs of the Empire, of mail, and of elite passengers travelling to their positions of colonial authority and importance. Mass travel was *not* what things were about.

The Americans had a wider vision of the new world order, and that vision served them well.

The Atlantic axis and the rising need for fast travel to Asia and Africa to serve old and new worlds, would be the key driving factors in years to come, yet there would be paradoxes and contradictions inherent within the debates and the application of the instrument of national policy via Britain's airline – Imperial – and then its offshoot as the British Overseas Airways Corporation (BOAC). Some of the British failed to grasp that the war would end their Empire, they thought that there would be a return to flying boats and First Class travel. Such people, locked into their insular certainties, did not envisage mass travel, the tourist-class market, and an emerging world that would desire jet airliners and new airways.

While – circa 1943–1945 – the British toyed with their wartime Brabazon Committee looking at military and civil airframes for a post-war future, America developed, often-superior, military aircraft that could very easily be re-purposed as airliners for the new era and the new world market. Urgent wartime developments in airframe and powerplant technology soon gave us the DC4, DC6, DC7, Lockheed Constellation range, and Boeing's bomber-derived airliner such as the Stratocruiser – all based upon wartime airframes. Military budgets had 'free' knock-on effects for civil airliner design and development, but the British were slower than the Americans to make the most of the opportunity. Converted British types like the Argonaut, Hermes, and Lancaster bombers were stumbling steps – ineffective anachronisms all.

However, a huge leap forwards in piston and turbine-engined, large, long-range airframe design did take place. Meanwhile, cash-strapped Britain was, despite the brilliant Viscount, still toying with elitist behemoths such as the Bristol Brabazon and the Saunders Roe Princess flying boat – 'First Class' affairs for the British and the very class system and empire mindset that would continue as a pre-war airliner psychology. While the troubled British four-engined Avro Tudor (surely a blot on Avro's record?) seated less than twenty passengers, the four-engined American DC-4 could seat forty-five and a DC-6 over sixty. The economic arguments were obvious, yet ignored in London. But soon a prop-turbine Viscount and a four-jet Comet 1 that would seat thirty-six passengers in recumbent luxury, with no thought to the possibility of passengers who were not VIPs, was upon us. The British had woken up, a bright future hailed. Then came the Comet disasters, and the men of set minds wagged fingers and said; 'I told you so'.

But *was* Comet really the answer? As an example, consider some other foreign airline chiefs and their airlines – such as Albert Plesman. He and his KLM did *not* rush to order Comet 1s, and there was a very sound reason why, and it was *not* about the Comet's structure. Neither did TWA or American Airlines order the Comet 1, even if Pan Am were so enamoured of a Comet variant. Some people say that Comet 4 should have been sold by the hundreds; others understand why it was not.

Were these the circumstances of how aviation framed the moment the new world across the Atlantic realised that the old world in London, with all its blinkers, passed the baton to a quicker thinking society?

In Britain in 1949, realising the error of design psychology, certain, more internationalist British designers stunned the world with the propeller powered Vickers Viscount as a British design conceived not just for British airline needs, but one that met the new demands of airlines worldwide, who, ordered it by the hundreds.

Then came that brilliant, but flawed, step into an uncertain future that was the de Havilland Comet 1 and a mistaken belief (perhaps even a delusion) that a decade later, a post-disaster, re-framed Comet 4 could compete in a world that had moved on.

Despite DC-7Cs and even larger L.1649s as prop-liners, jet airliner design concepts moved to 150 seat, six-abreast, swept-winged airliners with large underfloor cargo holds. Comet may have been brilliant in 1949, but by 1959 it was, despite a 'stretch', still small, relatively uneconomic, and was soon eclipsed. Indeed, de Havilland's own advertisements for the Comet 4 stated in 1959–'60 that: 'The Comet's size fits the available traffic' – surely an admission that it could *not* meet the size of future growth in traffic that lay inevitably just around the corner: change and changing of minds, was to be resisted in the 'here and now' school of 'we know what we know'.

The British should, when bathed in patriotic fervour, always recall that their original Comet 1 used four, thirsty turbo-jets to transport just thirty-six luxury-seated passengers and a small amount of mail freight. Four jet engines for thirty-six passengers, looked at with detachment, was, in airline accounting terms, not exactly the triumph so often touted. But with no competition of any kind, the small cabin was a factor that was not argued over. It was a feature that became an acceptable abnormality, an invisible issue. This was the first jet airliner and, although under developed and small, that was that – it was *all* that mattered. Yet, even as an enlarged Comet 4 variant, the Comet remained small and narrow in the cabin, with about eighty, two-class passenger seats in mainline configuration; it also had limited freight capacity. After just a few years' service, BOAC 'dumped' its still-fresh Comet 4s, which rather proved the point that Comet 4 was a hope too far as a 1960s premier airliner. After a brief BEA existence and few overseas operations, the upper crust Comet was relegated to a life of one-class tourist and charter life with Dan-Air's clever Comet reincarnation.

A Defining Formula and Trident Tribulations

By the late 1950s, 130–150 seat, true 'airliner' generic design concept had eclipsed Britain's thirty-six seat Comet 1, forty-four seat Comet 1A and sixty to eighty seat Comet 4/4C, or the ninety-two seat short/medium-haul 4B. A later four-engined jet airliner, the Convair CV-880, with its 105 seats and short, heavily loaded wings, would also be similarly eclipsed by the drive for seat per mile operating costs in an ever increasing airline accountants' battle of the skies.

The vital calculation of an airliner's ability to lift its weight, the weight of its passengers, cargo and fuel, and to fly a known distance – the 'maximum-payload range' – became the defining operational and sales formula; this coalesced on both sides of the Atlantic around an airframe that would lift 130–150 long-haul route sector seats, with four jet engines and a 3,000 mile range. But the issue of how long a take-off run – on a hot, high altitude or short-length runway – such an airliner might require, or its need to off-load weight to get safely airborne, seems to have been less visible in certain quarters.

Despite the Viscount's international success, after it and the Comet 1, there came from Britain the cancelled V1000/VC7, the delayed Bristol Britannia, and, the prop-driven Vanguard for both BEA and Vickers favoured customer, Trans-Canada Airlines (TCA), the precursor to Air Canada. The Vanguard was strong and highly economical, but service introduction was delayed until 1960 due to problems with the Tyne engine; and designed to a narrow BEA specification. Vickers lost money – a lot of money (cited at £16million) – on the Vanguard, but the orders did keep the factory going at a difficult time.

The long-range, larger, prop-turbine Bristol Britannia 312, was a machine designed by other British minds that had not yet realised that the days of the prop were numbered, even if turbine-driven. It seems that the Bristol Company and many in British aviation seriously believed that the Britannia 312 could compete against the jet-engined 707 into the 1960s – an utterly bizarre managerial deployment of strategic irrationality that even the brilliant Peter Masefield (ex-BEA) stated to be 'fact'. Meanwhile, Comet 1 carried a very few elite passengers in a series of very fast, short hops across the British Empire hued map, but such limitations were invisible to many observers. But Boeing and Douglas were investing nearly one billion US dollars between them in their late 1950s, true jet liners, as the 707 and DC-8 respectively.

So the clever, but myopic British school of airliner design, suffered from quickly dating appeal, delayed development and in the case of the Comet, tragic errors. Comet was brave, and in many ways clever; it cruised beautifully, but it was flawed nearer the ground, and structurally compromised at the hand of current knowledge and practice. But principally, and as so often overlooked, it was too small and too thirsty for its payload range and seat per mile figures and no amount of patriotic flag waving was ever going to alter those facts.

American designers at Boeing and French designers at Sud Aviation proved the point when they came up with different ideas – the 707 and the Caravelle respectively. At first, such designs were dismissed by the British as the wrong choice, or nationalistic flights of fancy. The British attitude to the daring Caravelle was hostile.

Yet the British, in an act of hypocrisy, would on one hand publicly criticise the Caravelle for being an exotic French design, by the French for the French (failing to realise that such a concept was a winner and a trend setter in a new world order), but *then* the British sold to the Caravelle's manufacturer, complete Comet nose sections and Rolls-Royce engines to power it!

You cannot help but wonder why the British did not just order the Caravelle for BOAC and BEA and be done with pride? SAS, Iberia, Alitalia, Air France, Swissair, and a host of American and other airlines bought Caravelles and got on with the job, using the then ultimate short-medium haul jet tool.

Ah, but the antiquarian prop-driven, British, BEA-specific Vanguard was better old boy …

Then, realising that jets *were* the answer, the British would demand a four-engined jet and go and turn the original design for a capable short-medium-haul jetliner – the superbly proposed Rolls-Royce Medway-powered DH121 concept – into the cut-down and constrained Spey-powered Trident, a device useful only to the airline that demanded its original *larger* design be curtailed down to their revised and short-term edicts based on a small and temporary pothole in passenger traffic numbers circa 1959–60; it was the 'available traffic' argument again. Thus did BEA ignore world markets and growing demands for capacity, range, and take-off performance, and so hobble de Havilland and the Trident to BEA's own blinkered mindset. The resulting cancellation of the Medway engine also impacted vital military airframe projects.

Ironically, BEA then spent the next ten years demanding that the Trident be made *bigger* – resulting in the addition of a (fourth) booster engine to the tri-jet; add in the auxiliary power unit, and arguably the Trident 3 was five engined, certainly it was four-engined for thrust purposes! Poor old de Havilland's were stuck between a rock (BEA), and the proverbial hard place that was the mess that was British aviation amid the effects of the Sandys Report and the amalgamation of small independent aviation companies into larger manufacturing entities.

Via exchanges with de Havilland, Boeing had had sight of the original, much more competent, Rolls-Royce Medway engined Trident proposal, the DH121 with its new wing. The 727 was to ape that idea – not the smaller, stubbier airframe that de Havilland's subsequently created for BEA as the Trident 1 – as BEA twisted de Havilland's arm behind its back. BOAC's actions meanwhile, killed off Vickers V1000 four-engined jet airliner project with no comment at all upon the fact that the 707s BOAC would subsequently quickly order within months, would *not* be runway and payload competent on BOAC's key revenue earning routes of tropical, Empire and Commonwealth service. What a strange and paradoxical omission in management strategy.

Calamity and the Sclerosis of British Airline Attitude

So ended British internal design competition that might have produced a world beating tri-jet airframe, and a big long-haul four-engined jet before anyone else did it – both probably worth 2,000 orders in total. So began more single, airline-dictated demands, and to hell with wider, international sales appeal and financial viability for the airframe manufacturer. To make matters worse, the two dictating airlines concerned (BOAC and BEA) were tax-payer subsidised corporations. Vickers and other British aircraft manufacturers only became part of a nationalised, State-supported 'British Aircraft Corporation' amalgam as BAC a decade later.

Even top British airline men were speaking out, and not at just procurement decisions, but at the poor quality of some British aircraft manufacturing practices. Beverley Shenstone, the ex-Supermarine Spitfire aerodynamicist, and BEA's 1950s chief engineer, got himself into a lot of trouble, when just before Christmas in 1953, at an Institute of Engineers lecture in Southampton, he criticised what he thought were sloppy practices in aircraft factories – he said he had seen wings dragged across floors, poor workmanship, and metalwork damaged. American practices and build quality were better, said Shenstone. He woke up to find himself plastered all over *The Times*, *Flight*, and facing MPs and Trade Union leaders' opprobrium. But some in the industry felt he had been making a point worthy of discussion. And were the workers under good or bad management?[1]

In 1955 the British airline and airframe procurement structure looked like something designed to go wrong. It was a political, corporate, and psychological sclerosis shielded by vast sums of public and private money and an arrogance of attitude. We might ask if it was a vignette of a strange period of post-war British social and political disorder shaded both blue and red.

Boeing meanwhile, never blinked and created the 707, and latterly the superbly capable 727 which aped the rear-engined design trend from Britain and Europe and was a viable future-proof airframe that would meet the demands of the new age that BEA had refused to consider. The BEA-optimised DH Trident would sell 117 examples – mostly to the State-sponsored carrier BEA and a few overseas operators. Boeing would sell 1,832 of its 727 around the world, simply because the 727 – the high-lift hot-rod – was better in every vital respect, even if once airborne, the ground-hugging Trident flew with true de Havilland panache; cracks in the wings latterly staining its reputation a touch.

Incredibly, despite the lessons of the Vickers Viscount's international appeal and over 400 sales, the British airlines carried on with the view that a British airline could, and should, demand an airframe tailored to its own specific needs and that any export sales potential in the design was not that airline's concern. Propellers were touted as the answer for the 1960s.

Of the past? Who could forget the wire, fabric and alloy concoction that was the Handley Page HP42/43 biplane airliner design – created for Imperial Airways at exactly the time others, such as Junkers, Boeing, Fokker, Lockheed, and Ford, were creating the world's first monoplane, all-metal, true airliners. The HP42 seemed to be no more than an update of the HPW.8, which in 1920 became the world's first 'proper' airliner in that it was not a conversion based upon a pre-existing military bomber airframe (as the Vickers Vimy Commercial had been). As the latter HP42s wcre mooted, the Americans took to their metal Ford Tri-motors with the same alacrity as Germans did to their Junkers JU52s. The British decided to sail on upon the wings of their biplane behemoths – such as HP42. We might have expected Imperial, and the British, to have learned their lesson, but not a bit of it. The British airlines, locked into their views, could not face or accept the temerity of change or advance – unless of course *they* thought of it – now *that* would be different.

As we know, Viscount distanced Vickers from the herd. So the men of Vickers were *not* afflicted by British 'Civil Service' and corporate myopia and parochial arrogance, and thus created airframes like the Viscount and V1000/VC7 as machines with global performance attractions and sales potential, but which were then sadly swayed by the demands of a British airline and British Governments that ruled the financial roost.

Across the Atlantic, the likes of Boeing and Douglas had long since stopped designing airframes tied to the specific need on just one airline, however illustrious an airline's history. Meanwhile, the Convair jetliners failed because *they* were too closely tied to one-specific operational theory and utterly bankrupted their manufacturer.

Empire Expectations

The British and their Empire had a lot to answer for – good and bad – and in 1946 the close-minded attitude still pervaded in aviation. How else could one explain the bomber conversions that were the Avro Lancastrian and Tudor, the HP Halton, and the Avro York, as opposed to the far more viable and capable Lockheed Constellation, or the Douglas DC-4 and its progeny?

Prior to the Second World War the British Empire had dictated its needs for transportation to its masters. Post-the Second World War, would not the British just carry on doing the same thing whatever the advances of aviation created by war? A self-serving design psychology ruled the British mind and mandate. Meanwhile, more open minds across the Atlantic had, pre-war, already created the revolutionary Douglas DC-2 and its DC-3 development, and then the DC-4, DC-6, DC-7, all were being designed and then sold, not just to national American carriers, but also to overseas airlines such as the likes of Koninklijke Luchtvaart Maatschappij (KLM) known globally as Royal Dutch Airlines, an airline which would make great strides using and promoting such equipment.

German Science and a Secret Legacy

In post-1945 global aviation design practice, a great change in knowledge took place at a fast pace and it informed a change in direction for military and civil aircraft design. The basis of the knowledge came from Germany and the legacy of that nation's rapid development of glider wing design and technology in the 1920s and 1930s that stemmed directly from the post First World War *Treaty of Versailles* and its enforced limitation upon German powered aircraft design and development. From advanced German glider design, came advanced German swept-wing, all-wing, delta-wing, and jet engine technologies. All this, and rocket science too, was part of the great lode of aerodynamics science seized by the Allies from the spring of 1945 onwards as Germany collapsed.

In April 1945, *before* Hitler's death, American experts were racing across Germany and seizing advanced aerodynamic research and the men that created that knowledge of future vision. By June 1945 the British were at it too – the Fedden Mission, under the lead of Sir Roy Fedden of the Bristol company, was scouring German research units for war-prize advances. The revered de Havilland Company managed to get an aerodynamics expert into Willy Messerschmitt's Oberammergau design office and from there stemmed much knowledge of advanced, swept-wing design and high speed flight. Alongside the Fedden Mission, there could be found the other 'F' mission – the Farren Mission – that of William Farren (later Sir William) who, with various aviation and RAE experts, was also scouring Germany for advanced aeronautical knowledge. Inside the Farren Mission there could be found a man by the name of George Edwards (from 1957 Sir George Edwards). With Edwards was Captain A.J. Nannini, the Vickers weapons and armaments expert. Test pilot Captain Eric Brown was also present. After touring Germany, the Farren Mission men did, after visiting BMW in Bavaria, arrive at Messerschmitt's Oberammergau design bureau. Of significance, Edwards also interviewed wing design expert W. Voigt. The similarly named, R. Vogt, the German aerodynamicist and swept-wing specialist, was also interviewed and both men were soon found to be working in the American aircraft industry, with Vogt at Boeing working on swept-wings. The Farren team recruited Dr Dieter Kuchemann – a man who would soon contribute to Vickers, RAE research and ultimately, the VC10 and Concorde wings. Also scooped up was Dr K. Doetsch. Both these men would contribute to the development of British supersonics, and George Edwards would work with them in the 1950s and 1960s, notably on Concorde.[2]

George Edwards would, like other British wartime investigators, wait many years before admitting that the point of the British presence in Germany was to gain as much knowledge as possible about high-speed wing design from the core of the most advanced collection of techniques then known in Germany. The

Americans, so keen to secure German rocket experts, would take longer to either admit – or continue to deny – the contribution of German expertise to aerospace and aerodynamic developments under the American flag.

Indeed, in Germany, there could be found American experts sifting through the swept-wing and jet airframe research, including men from Boeing and the Bell Aircraft Corporation's chief designer R. Woods. Even a certain C. Lindbergh pitched up; men from General Electric were also in Germany and T. von Karman of the California Institute of Technology (CALTECH) was also sniffing out research clues in Europe. Shorts and Avro also scooped up research into swept, delta, all-wing design and transonic technology. Indeed, Shorts chief designer, D. Keith-Lucas (a supporter of all-wing or 'flying wing' themes), was also in Germany. G. Lee at Handley Page was one of the most able British experts who had access in Germany to the practical details of sweep-back and sweep-forward effects in wing design.[3]

As we know, Vickers also had access to the German high speed aerodynamics research and it is safe to assert that the Allies secured an incredible cache of advanced German aerodynamic knowledge and feasted upon it. Britain's new Labour Government seemed unbothered by the opportunity and let the Americans, French and Russians race ahead with State funding to develop such findings – notably in the transonic compressibility aerodynamic arenas. So it was *private* British industry, *not* the British State, that itself explored the knowledge for post-war British projects. The British Government also gave away to the USA the supersonic secrets of the Miles M.52, and to this date, no convincing explanation as to this act has ever been given.

Back in 1945–47, the swept-wing experts, the works of Prandtl, Lippisch, Horten brothers, Multhopp, Voigt, Vogt, Heinkel and many more, were absorbed into the Anglo-American academic base – and reinforced by Operation Paperclip, which, contrary to some perceptions, was not just about securing rocket propulsion knowledge. At the Royal Aircraft Establishment (RAE), Drs D. Kuchemann and J. Weber contributed great learning and much more from the 1930s pre-Nazi era Gottingen school of design. George Edwards had access to many of these people and under the Farren Mission interviewed them. Latterly, he agreed that the Germans had been far ahead in aerodynamic terms and how fortuitous it was that the RAE's Morien Morgan had been on the Farren Mission to Germany in 1945 – from which had stemmed great strides in swept-wing, delta-wing and supersonic knowledge that finally manifested in Concorde itself.[4]

The Allies grabbed so much advanced aerospace science from Germany that the US Military Government of Germany, at the request of the Secretary of State for Occupied Areas, actually had to redraft the post-war peace treaty and invoke legislation protecting the USA from any claims by German designers who felt that their intellectual property had been stolen. Even later British commentators described Allied actions as a looting, or legalised seizure.

From tailless, delta, crescent wings and suction aerofoils, to jet design and rear mounted engines, from pylon engines, swept-wings (forward as well as rearward), T-tails, slats, flaps, ejection seats, composite structures, low–drag all–wing and variable sweep calculations and beyond, to the world's only truly supersonic wind tunnel (Mach 5.5), which was quickly shipped to the United States of America: the German aircraft designers were decades ahead, just as were the rocket men of Peenemunde, soon to be the rocket men of Huntsville, Alabama, and then NASA and the Apollo projects.

From this cache of genius, America seized a re-branded future where such technology was remade and in many senses provided the underpinnings of the jets of the Cold War, and the airliners of the 1950s and 1960s. Inside the American aerospace industry were many German names who had, shall we say, 'arrived' in the United States soon after the summer of 1945. Until very recently the true nature of the knowledge transfer of Nazi funded and pre-Nazi German advanced aerospace science, has neither been admitted nor appreciated. By 1947, inside the American and British aviation establishments, were German experts who would go on to inform the design database of the major military and civil airframes of the next four decades, and to frame the aerial vehicles of the Cold War and the space race respectively.

The Americans (and the Russians) embraced the German knowledge and the designers, whereas much of the British political and academic establishment, so shocked to have discovered that they did *not* know it all, were slower to accept such advanced science into their thinking. However, belatedly, they would try to catch up, and the swept, delta-type, and all-wing research plundered by British experts in Germany circa spring 1945, gave rise to an Air Ministry specification for a large bomber – the Vulcan, Victor and Valiant were the resulting competing proposals to such 'official' specification. So German technology influenced the Vickers Valiant; and thus Vickers consequent Vanjet and VC10 ideas. One might argue that the DH Comet and the Avro Vulcan, to name just two examples, were proof of British brilliance and its golden era. That these aircraft contained German wing science, is rarely admitted, but to cite Avro's exact words, the German delta-wing works of Alexander Lippisch, were, in the design of the mighty Vulcan, categorically stated as: 'Of assistance'. A lovely euphemism from the British establishment.

Lippisch in London

We should recall that as early as 1930–1931, Alexander Lippisch flight tested unpowered and then powered, delta-winged airframes with great success at the

Wasserkuppe, and publicly at Berlin Tempelhof. So revered was Lippisch (and his delta discoveries), that as late as December 1938, a few months before the Second World War became real, Lippisch was the invited guest lecturer at the Royal Aeronautical Society in London. There, assisted by his former research colleague, the engineer-aerodynamicist Beverley Shenstone (who spoke fluent German), Lippisch revealed his unique test findings and designs for his wing planforms. Lippisch was the only man in the world researching delta and swept-wing airflow using advanced German slow-motion camera (Zeiss *Movikon*) technology in smoke-lance equipped high-speed wind tunnels. The RAeS even published a translation of his findings at the time; the American NACA also re-published such German research as a series of 'Memorandums' in the late 1930s.

To this day, the British still insist that the delta-wing itself was Roy Chadwick's actual invention as some kind of act of British genius. While not in any way wishing to offend him or his legacy, this is utter rubbish. Chadwick did indeed design the Avro Vulcan, Britain's first true delta-winged jet, but he did not conceive the delta configuration and did not test or fly the first delta-wing aircraft. And as more knowledge was gained, the Vulcan's straight, wing leading edge became curved. But it was Lippisch who flew the first Delta-type wing – in 1930–31 (Butler and Edwards had sketched such a thing decades previously and H. Junkers, and J. Dunne, may have been edging that way with their respective all-wing designs). However, even as late as 2015, experts appearing in the media and on the BBC were still claiming that the delta-wing was 'invented' by Chadwick and waving a sketch on a newspaper to apparently prove it. We can only excuse them upon the grounds of their ego, ignorance, or laziness.

Of significance, Richard Vogt the German aerodynamicist who had worked on wing sweep, including forwards sweep, and advanced wing design and airflows, had been scooped up under Operation Paperclip and taken to the USA. There, he would find employment at Boeing where he contributed to swept-wing research in the 1950s across Boeing's output. Vogt knew all about the issue concerning applied degrees of wing sweep. Other 1930s German experts, men like Adolf Busemann, who under Operation Paperclip also soon found himself working for NACA and, by 1951, was a professor at the University of Colorado, had determined prior to 1945, that a 35° sweep angle provided the best trade-off between drag, lift, and attainable transonic Mach number. Boeing had grasped the importance of German research as early as 1946. And what of Rudiger Koisin and the cranked or aero-isoclinic wing? Would not the Handley Page Victor provide proof of concept?

Many people know that under Operation Paperclip, over 1,500 German experts were shipped off to the USA (notably the Peenemunde rocket men), but less well known is the fact American experts went the other way – into Germany. During 1946–48, teams of academics, scientists and designers toured Germany under Joint

Intelligence Objectives Agency (JIOS) remit and under the remit of the Office of Strategic Studies (OSS) – the precursor to the Central Intelligence Agency (CIA) – and swept up a vital lode of science, inventions and expertise across numerous disciplines; notably aerodynamics and propulsion. A Technical Industrial Intelligence Committee (TIIC) was one of these search groups in Germany and had over 380 members, with translators, transport and accommodation laid on at US taxpayers expense.

A United Nations remit that phrased seizing science as, 'the advancement and improvement of production and standards of living', cited the 'proper exploitation' of German and Nazi technology. Therefore, private American companies (major industrial concerns) were allowed access to Germany and its industrial secrets under a Field Intelligence Agencies/Technical (FIAT) remit. Over 500 employees of US companies scoured the German research base. So, just as the British companies de Havilland and Vickers had managed to get experts into Willi Messerschmitt's Oberammergau design office in the summer of 1945, Boeing too, soon had an expert touring German research institutions and aviation companies.[5]

Boeing's Chief of Design, George Schairer, is officially said to have accompanied one of the American research teams into Germany and reviewed the aerodynamic research. There, he too realised that 35° was the ideal wing sweep angle. Four years later the Boeing B-47 deployed the new knowledge and five years from that date, the Boeing B-52 and then the 707 had 35° swept-wings. The reason why, lies in German research and the seizing of it for re-framing as the product of American brilliance: an American chorus of denial and shouts of 'rubbish' always follow such claims, however well evidenced, to which it is best to just respond with the names of 'American' citizens – like von Braun, Multhopp, Lippisch, Vogt, etc., etc.

The British, the French (and the Russians), were all part of this great scientific game. Soon, placed into British industry were expert German designers, many of whom, like some of those who went to America, had been deemed *not* to be Nazis, and some who had.

The names of German (but non-Nazi) experts also included the previously cited Dieter Kuchemann and another German, one closely associated with Kuchemann's work, a Dr Johanna Weber, who also played a role in post-war British wing design development at the RAE and touched the Super VC10 wing design work. The fact that Dr Weber was a woman in an all-male preserve is often overlooked.

The first designs for the DH Comet 1, were also of a 35° swept 'flying wing' – more correctly an all-wing – this directly reflected German research findings. Few observers realise that the 'advance' of the production design Comet 1 was in fact a reverse-engineered step backwards from the original proposals for a high payload capacity, long-range, all-wing device of great futurism, which was refined from a tail-less all-wing into a highly swept, tail-equipped design that made even the later V1000 look tame. The all-wing Comet idea had speed, range, lift, payload and style, in fact it was simply too futuristic, it was too much for British minds, and Comet became the moderately swept, conventional planform shape that we are all so familiar with. Boeing's first airliner thoughts of 1949 were also of delta and all-wing iterations.

However, swept-wings, delta-wings, high-lift devices and a rash of airframe developments, including of true significance, the T-tail and pylon mounted, and rear-mounted engines, were all pursued from seized wartime German research.

Significantly in the 707 story, and contrary to many claims made then and now, neither America nor Boeing pioneered wing-pylon mounted jet engines – German designers did so before any American wing-pyloned jet engine types. The 1944 dated Junkers Type 287, and the 1946 Type 140 of Professor Baade, and the Arado 234 of 1944, categorically evidenced that jet engines hung from pylons were a German idea, not a Boeing B-47 invention of 1949! The French did not 'pioneer' rear-mounted jets in their Caravelle either – they had the idea after the Focke-Wulf 294 Athodyd design by Hans Multhopp with its stub wing-mounted rear jet pods.

Military aviation advanced very quickly off the back of such works. Such findings soon percolated into civil aviation. At Boeing and at Vickers Armstrongs, there were swept-wing, jet age experts at work on advanced airframes, some of them had German names and had come from the ruins of Hitler's nasty little experiment upon the world and its people. Those who wish to fulminate and deny these facts as 'rubbish', only serve to undermine their own so-called 'expert' credentials. History as written by the victors, is not always a reliable guide to factual reality, it takes time for the truth to come out.

Curiously, despite seizing so much knowledge, the Americans did not initially develop leading edge high-lift devices for their airframes. Lack of leading edge devices, allied to a lack of aerofoil development, also afflicted the Soviet airliners, this, despite a large number of German experts being seized by the Soviet Union in 1945. The British seem to have made more of the leading edge lift-enhancing qualities of the leading edge slat, or the drooped leading edge. Even Comet 1 had originally had small outboard slats (soon to be so unwisely deleted). In fact early British knowledge of leading edge lift devices came from the German emigré aerodynamicist and engineer Gustav Lachmann who worked for Handley Page Ltd in the 1930s and whom had patented such a device early on in his career.

The wartime science, seized and accrued post-1945, was a huge and vital reserve of knowledge that was developed between 1945 and 1955. It would not be wasted, notably in America.

Random Research

Reeling from the travails of war and near-bankruptcy, the British fired off research arrows into all sorts of aerospace arenas. A large cast of British aviation companies began to churn out all types of aircraft. And, it seemed, nobody could really decide whether to embrace the jet age or persevere with propeller powered flight. The new de Havilland Comet was one thing, but the Saunders Roe Princess was of another prop-persuasion, as was the new great hope the Britannia as a prop-turbine egg-beater-driven device. Even the behemoth that was Bristol's Brabazon crept quietly away to a forgotten corner of design thinking.

The creation of the post-war operations of BOAC led to an airline that was not just an airline, but a nationalised, semi-State controlled, de facto national instrument of political will upon a new world still beset by old boundaries of the Empire. This situation created strategic management confusion and conflict for, and by, BOAC as a British airline transport entity: such themes would manifest in the VC10 story itself. Social change was afoot, and BOAC was initially too big and too encumbered to move at the pace of others such as the Americans, Boeing, and the airlines it served. BOAC supported the Comet 1, but showed only temporary interest in Vickers idea for a large long-haul jet airliner in that company's studies for V1000/VC7 and then, finally, after procrastinations, went with the propeller-driven future of the Bristol Britannia in two bites – the original version and then a longer-range '312' variant.

In America, the revived post-war Pan American Airways (PAA), would have a clearer commercial remit (as would Australia's national airline Qantas), yet PAA, or 'Pan Am' too, would serve as a national flag carrier in more than the expected sense. The power of the American industrial and political lobby would secure a far less insular design direction than the confused and diffused British needs and aims of a declining power clinging to its pre-war psyche and geopolitical position.

Boeing's brilliant big beast of a 707, and latterly the class-leading 727 (surely to all but the most clouded of minds, the best-designed, most proficient short-medium-haul jet airliner ever created), would soon shatter the myths of those British beliefs. Boeing military jet transports and bombers – as B-52 and B-47 – were being designed, built, tested and made into successes in record time. Why reinvent the wheel creating some exotic airliner design when you could re-purpose and rebrand a tried and tested, part-part paid for piece of kit into a very fine airframe? It was obvious, and the 'it' in question had to be the superb Boeing 'Dash 80' – the 707.

The Comet's failure re-opened the door to American opportunity, and the 707 story was born, but before that happened the men of Vickers Armstrongs had in fact, designed and nearly completed the build of a sensational, new long-range,

V1000 RAF Transport.

four jet turbofan-engined airframe that could be used by the military and by airlines as a transport device par excellence, not just on the Empire routes but on transatlantic routes and global operations. This was the highly advanced V1000.

V1000: A Massive Loss

V1000 was far more than a Comet – even more than one in 4C guise could ever be. V1000 was in effect a second generation jet airliner *before* that era arrived. This aircraft represented a new, international outlook and design psychology, and it came from the genius and future vision of the men of Vickers led by George Edwards and the company's Advanced Projects Office under Ernest Marshall's design leadership – the men who had brought you the Viscount and its eventual 400 sales around the world. The new aircraft was the V1000, and with the first airframe eighty-five per cent complete, it was to be killed off by an insane decision taken by idiot politicians aided by BOAC's stance. That decision must be proof that the British politicians 'attitude', and their inability to see beyond what they knew in the short-term, and that they did not *want* to know anything else, still pervaded. Paradoxically, it was British men, engineers and designers at Vickers, who threw off such conventions and saw into a brilliant internationalist future. Ironically, it was their own countrymen who killed off the chance to actually dominate the world's airline fleets by merit for the next decade and beyond. As so often happens, the men of British heavy engineering and British industrial design were the victims of British politics, and poor State management.

The V1000 and its planned commercial, airline-specific derivative, the VC7, had it all – advanced design in structural and aerodynamic terms, a cranked swept-wing, four turbofan power plants, long-range, decent payload capacity, and a runway performance that made it usable not just on long straight runways near sea-level, but on shorter and more difficult fields on global airways. The V1000 was big, a real 'heavy' jet in its context.

Only in its 'buried' wing root engine installation was the V1000 in any sense structurally different from the similarly shaped airframes that followed from Boeing, Douglas, and ultimately Airbus. Burying the engines in the wing root was highly aerodynamically efficient (as was the cranked wing), and a fashionable design choice in the early jet age – doing so offered significant aerodynamic benefits in comparison to having the engines hanging off the wing as pyloned 'barnacles', where they tended to cause unwanted turbulence and loss of lift by affecting the aerofoil's span lift distribution efficiency; not to mention the leading edge performance by interrupting the slats or droops and doing the same to trailing edge flaps. These factors created design issues for the pylon-wing behaviours. Low hanging, wing-pylon engines, also sucked up foreign objects from dirty runways and created a roll-angle limitation due to the risk of ground striking the pods if a wing was too low in a crosswind landing. Yet such pylon-mounted engines were said to be safer, kept fuel, fire, and noise away from the fuel tanks, main fuselage and cabin – according to theorists and many American designers.

This contentious theory was *not* proven in a number of accidents, including decades later in crash testing- using a retired 707. And if this theory was so true, how come Boeing built the rear-engined 727 or Douglas the DC-9? How come the wing-engine mounted Boeing 737 suffered so badly in accidents when the engines caught fire? But back in 1955, Boeing and other American design teams favoured the wing-pylon mounted engine theory. Wing-pylon engines were, however, certainly much easier to work on, to remove, and are easier to accommodate in the airframe, and have structural 'relief' qualities. In the Vulcan, Valiant, Victor, and in the Comet, the British trend for wing root buried engines manifested – offering lower drag, and easier roll angles – against the complex, but solvable wing-box/spar structural and safety issues extant, and which correct armour plating and designed-in reinforcement could address.

V1000 – Genesis and Cremation

Kicking off in 1951, and running through beyond 1954, George Edwards, Ernest Marshall, Basil Stephenson, Ken Lawson, Hugh Hemsley, John Hay, Maurice

Wilmer, and others, as key figures of the Vickers engineering team, began studies for a post-war military and civil long-range jet type. They were requested to frame the V1000 project by the Ministry of Supply (MoS) under MoS Specification C.123D in 1952, as a new RAF type to replace the piston-powered post-war types such as the Handley Page Hastings. Post-war, post-Berlin airlift of 1948, and with a huge British military network to serve the world over in the yet-to-end British Empire, a fast new RAF transport was needed, in fact it was an urgent essential. Could the new transport type share features in common with the new Vickers Valiant bomber in order to ensure not just compatibility in operating regimes and schedules, but maybe in actual design and shape in order to provide 'decoy' capabilities in any 'Cold War', radar-related scenarios? Such strangeness had to be considered by airframe suppliers to Her Majesty's Government and its Ministry of Supply (MoS).

Even at this stage BOAC were invited to contribute to the specifications, as an airline transport derivative was obvious – the VC7. The RAF's V1000 could have been in service by 1958, a VC7 perhaps by late 1959. The then Minister of Supply, Reginald Maudling, was originally keen on both, and on Vickers as a company. After all, the V1000 was *not* (contrary to some latterly published claims) Vickers first big jet – it had already learned much with the Valiant.

The reason why the V1000/VC7 was so needed was also obvious – the old British Empire and Commonwealth airfields were often 'hot' in terms of local temperatures (30°-35°C), and also 'high' in terms of altitude (5,000ft+), and sometimes both. Throw in an aircraft's weight, and you had the 'WAT'-formula of 'Weight, Altitude and Temperature' as one that defined if an airliner could get off the ground in the conditions and runway length available. Such routes had runways of 5,000ft or 6,000ft in length (as well as elevation), or rarely perhaps 8,000ft, and often dangerous local terrain. In contrast, New York and Los Angeles would soon offer 11,000ft-14,000ft runway lengths at near-sea level. London Heathrow offered 10,500ft.

Any machine required to service the shorter tropical runway airfields needed to be quick off the mark and able to climb properly – with decent payloads. And the same factors applied to the RAF's end-of-Empire transport uplift airframe requirements. The conditions applied across BOAC's route network, except for the North Atlantic routes, which were not then the principal focus of operations or earnings. Kano, Nairobi, Gan, Karachi, Singapore, Salisbury, Tripoli, Hong Kong and tropical points east, were the RAF and BOAC 'Empire' mindset. London Heathrow's main 1960s runway, at low altitude, seemed innocuous compared to the narrow, short, hot runways at, for example, Lusaka, or the lift sapping tarmac at Salisbury (now Harare), Entebbe, Karachi, or some in Asia, or South America.

So a machine for serving the military on the Empire and commonwealth routes, could obviously serve the civilian airlines on the same medium-range routes. Here was a large sales opportunity for an aircraft maker.

Work on the project at Vickers Wisley base – as 'V1000' – started in October 1952, and as soon a December 1952, Vickers had forty-five draughtsmen working on the V1000 with planed basic weight of around 100,000lb. By 1953, sixty-three men were at work on a prototype – first a wooden mock-up, then an in-the-metal pathfinding airframe. Of note, much of the work already done for the Vickers Valiant bomber was transferable into the structure and design of the V1000. The military procured Valiant begat the V1000, just as the Boeing B-52 and B-47 military studies led to the B-362, B-367-80 for the USAF, and thus gave birth to a B-717 KC-135 military specification (with twenty-nine as initial order) that then delivered a civil derivative as the Boeing 707 itself. The RAF ordered six V1000s as a starting off point, so both nations were using military subsidies to underpin civil development, but on differing scales.

The Vickers modified Valiant idea was for a 90–100 seat, four-jet airframe, with a range of 2,100nm at a take-off weight of 126,500lbs, topped off with a 664kt high altitude cruising speed. From this early iteration came a longer range specification that would take-off at 155,700lbs weight, have a true North Atlantic, all-weather capable, 3,650nm range at a service ceiling way up at 40,000ft. Rolls-Royce Conway engines were proposed – with 13,500lbs to 15,500lbs thrust per engine being the early figures in 1952 – not dissimilar to the thrust ratings of the 1959 launched Boeing 707's with Pratt and Whitney Turbojets. But Conway was an early pioneer of the 'bypass' turbofan design and clearly capable of massive development to over 20,000lbs thrust.

Yet Edwards and Marshall soon realised that this machine was, still, effectively a re-invented Valiant – despite seating double the number of passengers a Comet might accommodate, and possibly too small for the new world mass travel market that they knew would soon dawn – 150 two-class seats laid out six-abreast from a single central main aisle had to be the target. George Edwards and his team had avoided insular British design psychology and designed an airliner for the wider world market, not a tailored, British airline bespoke device. So was born the true V1000/VC7 airliner. With its clean swept-wing, and vital cruise-rated low-wing loading (under 80lbs/ft^2), it had major aerodynamic advantages inherent within its operating performance (the later 707 and DC-8 would have planned wing loadings circa 100lbs.ft^2). As things developed to a less Valiant-based V1000, a few delays crept in – latterly to be cited by critics.

The specifications had coalesced around a 'Bluebook' draft design agenda framed as B 97948, but throwing off the design constraints of the mid-fuselage or 'shoulder' mounted Valiant wing had given birth to a new, low-wing airframe that was framed as specification B 98545. Range was now 4,580nm, take-off weight was 175,000lbs and the payload 30,000lbs, but upgrading the design to a true, new status would put the costs up. However, the benefits would be huge in terms of performance and consequent international market sales appeal. By late 1953, BOAC's lead engineer, Mr Dykes, and operations manager, Mr Jackson, were helping Vickers contribute to the airframe's outcome. BOAC senior management, in the form of Whitney Straight and Campbell Orde, oversaw the potential BOAC specification angle to the project. The RAF and the Ministry of Supply were behind the military version, but asking the State to fund a developed variant – the airline VC7 – was going to be difficult. George Edwards decide that a 'basic' military specification V1000 would have to be ordered by the RAF – six examples were cited as the contractual point, and that these State-funded orders would also meet the baseline standards of civil need and could lead to the refinement that would create the ultimate, long-range world-beating VC7 development of that starting point. A step-by-step approach in post-war austerity Britain was understandable.

Vickers also noted that advancing the design early, for a future civil VC7 outcome, would allow the earlier baseline military transport version to be improved, and, if the RAF version would need a cargo door and strengthened floor, the VC7 pure airliner might not, so extra fuel tankage could be installed instead. Or could an airline derivative pure-cargo-only, or cargo/passenger 'combi' variant, be produced for world markets? Vickers thought of it all, in 1955! That was years before its competitors produced such machines.

With six-abreast seating as a design specification in 1953, the V1000 was also years ahead of the Boeing 707. In a great piece of cost saving, the Valiant's mid and outer wing structures could still be used, so long as the mid-fuselage or 'shoulder' mounted wing configuration was discarded, and the noisy wing-root buried engines moved a bit further outboard from the cabin. In the Vickers design office, all sorts of permutations were toyed with before the defining V1000/VC7 layout and specifications were hardened up. One thing was for sure, here was a machine to lead the world, and it was British, and it was still not yet 1954 – a date well worth underlining in the context of other airframe developments.

The V1000 would have a low-set tailplane, swept fin, 32° main wing sweep, a higher sweep at the wing root to further reduce drag, solid milling of its metal structures and many structural reinforcements. Vickers would eschew de Havilland's ultra-light, speed-related construction techniques and deploy thicker gauges of metal at the cost of increased weight.

Vickers had first built a pressurised hull in a Wellington V and V1 derivative, and despite not knowing details of the Comet's inherent structural problems when they began designing the Valiant and the V1000, had put extra effort into refining a fail-safe, multi-load path pressure hull design. Experience with the Viscount fuselage also proved invaluable. Window and door apertures were ellipsoid and widely spaced, and metal panels were strong. Vickers pioneered airframe construction and in the V1000 used milled components from high-strength castings, and massive integral chassis reinforcing members or 'spines', as used in the Valiant's wing-to-fuselage construction, were deployed; strengths and gauges around door openings were scaled up. The V1000 was almost ship-built in true Vickers Armstrongs Tyneside tradition!

Large 'Fowler' flaps and a ventral under-fuselage flap panel all contributed to a low landing speed. At this stage leading edge devices were being designed for the V1000. Testing of a V1000 model by Saunders Roe in a water tank, for hydrodynamic studies and ditching, showed that the aircraft, with its long forward fuselage, might nose-dip if it ditched, so the idea of using the front undercarriage doors as a sort of emergency ditching hydroplane was invented and drawn up.

Of significance, the V1000 cranked wing sweep aped the German research of Koisin, and was mirrored by that of Handley Page. The Valiant had established a production cranked, or aero-isoclinic wing, for Vickers, with its 47° sweep at root easing out to a 20° sweep at the tip, with a cleanly curved leading edge mating the planform neatly together. Perhaps it was not as radical as the Handley Page HP 80 Victor isoclinic iteration, but it did explore aerodynamic advantages. The Vickers wing delivered some level of reduced aerodynamic compressibility onset at the wing root, and gave low sweepback with safe stall and spin behaviours at the tip: so combined root and leading edge and root-to-tip overall drag reductions were achieved. Low drag high-speed cruising at Mach. 80 was first explored by the Vickers design team via the Valiant studies and all this knowledge permeated down into the V1000/VC7 wing design – itself having some degree of aero-isoclinic cranked shaping.

Further aerodynamics work went into the V1000, including an advanced underbody wing-to-fuselage fairing designed to reduce localised drag over the wing root and undercarriage areas – a device later deployed on the Airbus A380. Photographs of the V1000 (as opposed to models), clearly show a very modern looking airframe, far removed from the 1950s industrial design motifs of the Comet or even the 707. At the tail, advanced metal fairings that were flexible helped seal the tailplane-to-tailfin junction.

Apart from those wing root buried engines, the V1000 looks for all the world like a 1970s later generation Airbus or Boeing machine – minus the barnacled engines.

The V1000 had advanced flying controls and an all-moving variable incidence tailplane and fully powered electro-hydraulic flying surfaces with individual sections to ensure 'fail safe' redundancy. The main structural components, such as the crucial wing box/spar and frames, were machined from solid billets of the relevant metals that were of a new quality never before manufactured. Alloys, extrusions, and machining, were advanced arts for the Valiant and for the V1000 – ensuring great strides in structural safety and the doubled-up 'fail-safe' principal. Of interest, the V1000 wing had that cranked leading edge, giving advanced aerodynamic efficiencies – smoother flows and less likelihood of shockwave formation along the inboard leading edge, and, spanwise, thence easing through sweep to the less-swept outboard sweep angle of 32°.

Vickers learned a lot about wing design very quickly from the Valiant's military design process. Meanwhile, de Havilland's were suggesting a reverse-engineered military design for a bomber, using the civil Comet airliner's wing and a new longer and deeper fuselage.

On 22 September 1954, the definitive framing of engineering frameworks for the V1000 took place – leading to the selection of structural specifications and more closely defined weights and performance expectations. By then, over 6,000 drawings had been produced and a mock-up of the shape considered. By January 1955, a first flight date of a sole, early prototype could be envisaged for late 1956, with a service entry for mid-1959 being perfectly rational.

By 1955, the V1000's design was significantly more capable than the forthcoming Comet 4, had a wing over fifteen per cent bigger than the suggested new Boeing 707 airliner, and was of greater sweep than a Comet, and had more power (Rolls-Royce were upgrading the Conway engine and ideas of water injection and reheat were even considered). At this stage, Boeing had *not* yet widened the 707s fuselage to rival the V1000's six-abreast layout. Later V1000 aerodynamic tweaks were to include aileron droop on take-off for more lift at hot and high airfields, and there was even some work on boundary layer control at the wing roots. The curved-top tail fin was replaced with a sharper styled fin design – with hints of later VC10 styling. The V1000 was set to become the largest, strongest, most technically advanced, longest range, airline transport airframe in the world. Airlines from all over the globe, even top American airlines, would have *had* to have ordered the V1000 as VC7 in order to remain competitive. National pride would soon have gone out of the window when the machine wiped the floor with future competing products – of which there were none – the 707 still being in military-to-civil airframe 'Stratotanker-Stratoliner' genesis at this time. And yet bizarrely, BOAC were to focus on the elegant, but ancient art of the prop-turbine Bristol Britannia, and to stick with Comet and its small cabin and freight capacity – even in redesigned the Comet 4 variant. The Comet 4 could not have competed, and the then to be launched Boeing 707 would not have matched the V1000/VC7 range and runway performance. Winter weather on the Atlantic 'Blue Riband' routes would have rarely caused a refuelling diversion into Gander, Shannon, or Prestwick for the

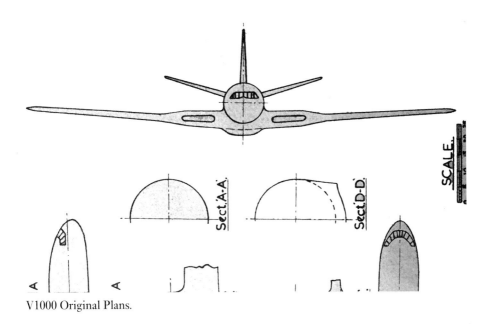

V1000 Original Plans.

V1000 and its variants – unlike the Comet or 707. Ultimately, V1000/VC7 was a *truly* oceanic, 3,500 miles-plus, winter capable machine.

Offering 120–150 seats and true long-range, with reliable payload uplift that would not be heavily constrained by the need to offload cargo, fuel, or passengers at tropical airports, or to add a headwind-related transatlantic fuel stop, long before the 707 stole the world market, was all within the V1000's max payload range grasp. And the V1000/VC7 could have been 'stretched' DC-8 style too, with 200 or 250 seats. The V1000/VC7 had a wing fifteen per cent bigger than the 707 – reducing wing loading, lowering landing speed and adding range and runway performance which would have swayed airlines towards it. Qantas could have had Pacific-capable VC7s *before* it asked Boeing to build it the unique 'one-off' ultra-short bodied 707-138.

Airframe Reality

By late 1955, the first V1000 prototype airframe was eighty-five per cent complete 'in the metal', and Vickers had briefed numerous airline executives on the stunning performance capabilities of their offering. The V1000/VC7 was in the same position as Viscount had been, in that it was a world-beating design that was far ahead of any competition anywhere in the world. At the same time, the Bristol Britannia, Lockheed Electra, and Vickers Vanguard (all troubled by varying design issues), and the argument over whether jet, prop-jet, or piston-prop powered airframes would be required equipment across the world's airline routes, were the focus of airline executives ruminations. It is recorded fact that Pan American Airways had shown close interest in the V1000/VC7. The old Vickers customer, Trans-Canada Airlines (forerunner of Air Canada), was a keen potential operator. BOAC should have been an ideal VC7 customer, yet said BOAC, the future lay with the exquisite Britannia; and if it did not, there was the Comet 4, whose limitations could, it seems, be ignored upon the mask of patriotism and past glories. Did BOAC really so naively believe that the Comet 4 could beat off the mighty 707? How could they – and did they not then quickly order 707s!

But massive changes were afoot in British aviation with the myriad small aviation companies all suffering, and a plethora of orders and types increasing costs notably for the RAF. Yet political considerations such as jobs in marginal constituencies and regional issues such as the economy of Northern Ireland would play hidden roles. Then would come the 1957 Sandys Report on British aviation and the nascent aerospace industries, from which came even more change and airframe confusion and forced collaborations.

Some people say that the VC10 was a natural progression of the V1000/VC7 story – via the Vanjet studies; others might argue that the VC10 was the bastard son of the V1000 and a post-Sandy's era cut-and-shut idea, amid a mess of State-influenced design, indecision and misdirection.

Meanwhile, in the 1950s, Super Constellations, DC-7s, and even the odd Stratocruiser, still strode the airways as queens of the skies. BOAC rushed out and bought second-hand DC-7Cs to meet its long-haul fleet shortage – spending huge sums to convert them to BOAC standards. Yet the V1000, as VC7, could and should have answered many questions, and perhaps sold one thousand airframes across a two decades life. The crazy policy decisions of successive British Governments, and the nation's own corporation of BOAC, were the British reasons why not, and denial of such can in the face of overwhelming evidence, only indicate some kind of issue in the believer.

Funeral Pyre

The V1000 story was killed off by government decree on 24 October 1955 (announced by the Ministry of Supply in November) and the men of Vickers left to walk away, the tooling soon to be junked and the chapter closed. It was not the first or last time British design brilliance would be sold down the river; the Miles M.52, and the TSR2 being other key examples of how the fiddlings of, 'here today and gone tomorrow', idiot politicians of whatever ideology, can impact national history, global design and the employment of working men.

Britain's Government had used (in great part, BOAC-framed) concerns over the V1000s engine power ratings and payload range contentions to end the programme for an RAF-based original V1000 contract, and thus the VC7 offshoot which Vickers had privately created. Vickers were less than twelve months behind schedule with the V1000 – which was nothing compared to the delays of other airliner airframes, then and latterly. Yet 'delays' were cited by enemies. But the RAF still needed a jet transport to keep up with its jet bombers and fighters – the problem was not going to go away; ironically and incredibly, five decades later the RAF would purchase ancient old Boeing 707 airframes re-manufactured for military surveillance duties! So, in a way, Boeing had the last laugh.

BOAC's 1955 claims of a so-called Conway thrust inadequacy and concerns over its growth potential were utter rubbish – because the same Conway engines of such Civil Service and BOAC concerns, were soon to be found in the BOAC Boeing 707s that the government (via the Ministry of Transport and Civil Aviation) authorised BOAC to purchase just months later. And did not the Handley Page HP. Victor use Conways – buried in its wings? The fact that the Conway had the potential to be uprated *during* the V1000 development process was known, as was its possible use in a developed Valiant nuclear bomber. There was even talk of a Conway re-engined Comet 4 (three decades later a re-engined Comet derivative-Nimrod would prove a point). So any claim that powerplant was a problem, seems hollow indeed. Yes, the V1000's weight went up as its abilities developed, but not to a degree thought unsolvable, and as weight went up, so too did the Conways thrust rating.

The V1000, near complete as a test airframe in 1955, was indeed the future.

We should never underestimate the effect of the death of the V1000 and its VC7 airline variant.

In the House of Commons, in November 1955, in an early V1000 cancellation related debate in Parliament, and imploring Minister Maudling to 'save' the V1000, Mr W. Robson Brown MP, stated that the V1000 was the only aircraft of its type in the world, and the only British machine, that could compete with American proposals. Mr John Peyton MP pointed out how much American competitors would relish the decision and the disadvantage to British aviation it would create. The Labour Party's Deputy-Leader, George Brown MP, also weighed in to frame the loss to Britain and the gain to America.

In response, Minister Reginald Maudling MP added that the Government could not support an aircraft (V1000) that would not, or could not, be ordered by overseas airlines if the national airline (BOAC) would not order it in the first place.

Surely the only conclusion of the meaning of his statement was that 'fault' must lie with BOAC or Vickers? The debate in Parliament continued up to a further point on the evening of 8 December 1955, when Mr Paul Williams MP called the cancellation of the V1000 not just 'disgraceful', but one of the most unfortunate decisions that had ever been taken for the aircraft industry. Mr Williams noted that criticisms of the V1000 as VC7, by detractors, had referred to it as a 'paper' aeroplane – i.e. just a concept, which was being economical with the actualité. But was not the then proposed DC-8 a 'paper' aeroplane too – opined Mr Williams. Yet such 'paper' status was being given as a reason to cancel the near-complete V1000/VC7. Arguments about V1000's weight increase had, said Mr Williams, utterly failed to note the increase in the thrust of the Conway engine, and confusion between basic weight and all-up maximum weights also existed in politicians comments.

Mr Williams noted that of the £2.3million already invested in the V1000, not one penny had been spent on the civil version (VC7) except by the firm (Vickers) itself. Mr Williams also noted that the V1000 had a lower wing loading than its American rivals – a key point in runway performance and in sales terms. Also noted were proposed British supersonic developments, how, if Britain could not deliver the V1000, would it deliver a competent supersonic airliner? And what would BOAC do if the V1000 died? 'Buy American', by the early sixties, said Mr Williams; little did he know that within *months*, not years, BOAC would do just that.[6]

V1000 advanced design.

As with George Edwards' statement that this was a national decision that we would regret for many years, and one confirmed by external commentators such as Mr Williams MP, who framed for public view just what potential loss was being realised. We can only say it was indeed a tragedy.

The slaughtering of the V1000 and any potential civil variant was another seminal moment in British industrial history and British political farce. It cost the British billions in lost revenue, jobs, and global prestige. There is no doubt that an aspect of British history turned upon the V1000's folded wings, yet few commentators outside aviation are aware of it.

The strangling in 1955, at near-birth of the V1000, did, as the great George Edwards (and others) observed at the time, hand the entire future world market for a large, four-engined, long-range airline transport, to America, on a plate. It was a madness that cost bankrupt Great Britain, so desperate for export earning commodities, great prestige and respect, as well as billions in lost income, earned yields, and global orders. In fact, in the cancellation of the V1000, we can see the beginning of the end for British civil jet aircraft manufacturing. It truly was a deliberate loss of historic proportions, and no fault lay with the men of Vickers at Weybridge for its occurrence. As with TSR-2, the original larger, Medway-powered DH Trident, the Vickers V1000 could have been the future.

Sir George Edwards stated publicly and to the author, that in his view the V1000 cancellation, and the short-term political decisions that framed it, was, 'the most serious setback that the British aircraft industry has suffered since the end of the Second World War'. He added the point that it occurred just as the great 1960s market for jet travel was to manifest on a global scale. Edwards might have been expected to blow Vickers trumpet, but he was right (he usually was), and he was right because of the sheer future vision that the V1000 represented – and MPs and others agreed with him. It was the Viscount all over again – only bigger, even better, and the world's first serious, large four-engined turbofan airliner design. As suggested, the proof lay in the scenario that surrounded the Viscount when Vickers and Edwards had produced the right aircraft at the right time and it sold worldwide – even to American domestic carriers and European carriers – even the Douglas Company's favourite customer, KLM!

The Viscount was, in the words of Gordon McGregor, ex-RCAF Battle of Britain and wartime fighter pilot and President of Trans-Canada Airlines: 'By a very wide margin, the best commercial aircraft of its class that has ever been built.'[7] The V1000/VC7 was the *same* thing – but a jet-age next-step and the biggest and best designed large airliner concept of its era and was well ahead of the early 707-120 concept. Indeed, it was McGregor who actually flew to London from Canada to try and save the V1000 with the promise of Canadian interest, alas to no avail, because, despite the urgings to BOAC of the Minister of Aviation,

Reginald Maudling MP, the airline still refused to support, or save, the V1000/ VC7. Did Maudling or McGregor know that in under a year BOAC would go on to order Conway-powered 707s? It is unlikely.

The Minister expressed 'regret' at the V1000's death and Geoffrey Ripon MP, the Parliamentary Secretary to the Ministry, called the cancellation a 'terrible tragedy'. Aircraft designer and famous aviation writer, Stanley H. Evans, stated in correspondence to BEA's Beverley Shenstone, that the V1000/VC7 was a world-beater, and that: 'The slaughter of that beautiful babe in the bulrushes was an act of defeatism that will come home to roost'.[8]

Evans was correct and the Americans must have been jumping for joy – as Brooklands wept.

As the V1000/VC7 died, BOAC quickly ordered those Conway jet-powered 707s – having ensured that no British jet competitor existed by ending the V1000 story! Yet then for BOAC's State masters to seek a British jet to serve the long-haul routes of the tropical climes of the world. And did not BOAC's own charter advise that it should seek British products to serve it? It was a management scenario that even the calmest of commentators might perceive as ill-conceived, if not astoundingly confused and utterly bizarre. What agendas were afoot? Did some conspiracy theory abound?

By avoiding the V1000/VC7 potential, notably as powered by advanced Rolls-Royce Conway turbofans and *not* Pratt and Whitney JTC3 turbojets, as found on the original 707s, BOAC had itself ensured that in 1956 Britain had no large four-engined jet airliner on its drawing boards. We should not blame BOAC for everything, but BOAC did essentially create the landscape that helped kill the V1000/VC7 within a political basis of claim.

BOAC would say that it had paid for and 'lost' its Comet 1s and Comet 2s; Comet 3, as Comet 4, was not ready, and that it had suffered the Britannia 312 delays and had had to pay out large sums on interim measures such as the DC-7C. Why, said BOAC, should it support yet another 'on-paper' project – the V1000/ VC7? The answer was, of course, that the V1000 and VC7 were very quickly 'real' and the V1000 was in the metal by 1955 and ideal for BOAC. Oh, but hang on, the prop-driven Britannia was at hand to answer it all!

Yet in October 1956, within months of the V1000's end, BOAC had indeed gone jet-minded and ordered the Boeing 707, and then to rub salt into the wound by specifying that its 707s should be Conway turbofan powered, despite BOAC's earlier citation of the Conway's supposed thrust issue as a reason to deny the V1000/VC7!

Were such outcomes accidents, or were they the result of the machinations of political and corporate games of smoke and mirrors? Or was it all just one great big foul-up by men paid very well indeed? And did BOAC, as alleged by some, seem to extend the delays surrounding the acceptance of the solving of the Britannia's relatively innocuous engine intake icing problem that Bristol worked to solve? Was it just a coincidence that the delay was of massive assistance to Boeing in its rush to get the 707 into the air as a viable airliner for sale? We can only assume that all this was the circumstance of accident and not some underhand game of power.

BOAC's Paradox of Internal Inconsistency

Why *did* BOAC effectively kill off the hope of a large four-engined British airliner in the V1000/VC7, but then say it 'had' to buy American Boeings because no British airliner existed! What of the statement that BOAC could not now wait for a British big jet to be designed – even though it had also said that the prop-turbine Britannia 312 would see it into 1960s competition with the 707.

There was more, and it was crucial: BOAC knew that the 707, either as a turbojet, or as turbofan, would not be capable in runway performance and maximum-payload range terms on BOAC's vital revenue-earning tropical routes with the very demanding 'hot and high' runways and equatorial weather route sectors.

Let us make the point clear.

BOAC was, with public money, ordering a big jet, as the 707 (fifteen of them), that could not, repeat not, adequately serve BOAC's main revenue vital (non-Atlantic) routes, and it was using £46million of precious British currency at a time of crippling national debt to do it!

BOAC was also, at the same time, expressing interest in the jet-powered de Havilland DH.118 four-engined large airliner proposal that was a sort of Comet 5, but with wing pylon-mounted engines! Paradoxically, BOAC also gave some encouragement to the Bristol 200 jet airliner proposal – that came in a suggested three and four rear-engined configuration. Not only was the V1000/VC7 killed off, but the 707's seal of international use (by Britain) was officially stamped at British tax-payers expense via BOAC's orders for it. BOAC's Boeing order for a 1960s intercontinental variant was built on hope, and promises of a not then fully developed airframe. But the V1000s airframe had been nearly complete in late 1955!

However incredible it seems from today's viewpoint, we should be clear that what happened was because the political and industrial consequences would have been so severe for cash-strapped Britain and for its workers.

Between BOAC and the British Government (which also needed to place jobs in Belfast at the Shorts factory in order to fend off economic crisis and political issues in Northern Ireland, and as orders for the Britannia failed to come in), Vickers and their V1000 would be sacrificed upon BOAC's suggestions and the RAF's forced withdrawal from a new Transport Command jet aircraft.

Here was BOAC screwing up its own future fleet and revenue earning choices!

The whole theatre seems like a farce, a psychiatric game, and open-season for conspiracy theorists to ask just what went on behind the scenes between BOAC's board and Boeing? There is little proof of such conspiracies, yet the BOAC decisions do seem internally inconsistent in terms of behavioural psychology.

Yet perhaps we should not forget, behind the British flag-waving, just how poorly some parts of British civil aviation (in its now termed 'golden age') had performed for British airlines. The Comet 1 disasters, the delayed Comet 4, the Airspeed Ambassador, the appalling Avro Tudor, the brilliant, yet troubled prop-turbine Britannia, the delayed Vanguard Tyne engine, the soon-to-be emasculated Trident; *all* had missed their targets and failed on the international stage. Only the Vickers Viscount shone as a true, global success and one that the V1000 could have built upon – the Vickers customer-base existed.

The repeating of the Viscount's story could, and should, have happened with the V1000/VC7 opportunity – as a jet age British success. Imagine if KLM, Lufthansa, Air France, Pan Am, TWA, Qantas and more, had used Viscounts at regional level to feed into their long-haul VC7 fleets. Imagine if they had then, for the 1960s, been offered a Vickers-built medium-route 120 seater twin-jet or tri-jet 'Vanjet' to complement their all-Vickers fleets and a V1000 on top! Vickers would surely have swept the airline order books in a manner beyond late 1950s comprehension. It was all there for the taking, yet it was all thrown away by others. Remember, the V1000 as a VC7, would, by 1957, have delivered the world's first, true four-engined, turbofan, long-range airliner with six-abreast seating, a large passenger and freight capacity, and a high-lift 'clean' wing to deliver decent uplift and performance in difficult operating conditions all over the globe. Airlines would have flocked to order it in 1956 – before the 707 in its early range-limited turbojet versions became the only real option for 1959 launch.

All this was a near-reality – yet a dashed reality. Can we be surprised at the tears and the anger shed and vented inside Vickers over such a loss?

Years later, the handful of VC10s, Vanguards, and BAC 1-11s sold, seem in comparison to the numbers of 707s, 727s, 737s, and DC-9s ordered, further proof of the madness that afflicted British decision making over the V1000, for it was not just the V1000/VC7 that was lost. The knock-on effects of its cancellation and of the Sandys Report, and the forced mergers within British aircraft manufacturing and the sales failures of the aircraft that resulted, all have origins in the decisions taken around the V1000's termination: TSR 2, Super VC10 265, Rolls-Royce Medway, and the first 'big-twin' British air-bus types, all are relevant in their loss. And what of the Shorts Belfast transport aircraft? No matter, the British Government could order the smaller Lockheed Hercules instead. Oh, and surely

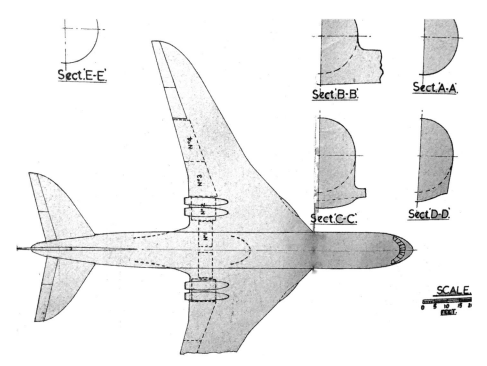

Sect.'E-E'.

Sect.'B-B'.

Sect.'A-A'.

Sect.'C-C'.

Sect.'D-D'.

SCALE.

V1000 Planform.

McDonnell Douglas F.4 Phantom fighters for the RAF was a good idea too. The F-111? Why not F-104 Starfighters? Better not …

What sway, what leverage did America have over Labour (and Conservative) British Government decisions at the expense of their own people and industry? The answer was that bankrupt Britain was utterly beholden to the United States of America and here was the proof. How 'special' was this relationship? Maybe it never existed, other than in the minds of those so conditioned? No matter, the Cold War and the airliner procurement wars would be perfect fulcrums about which to manoeuvre.

Perhaps this V1000 and related British procurement story was also the beginning of the end of the British engineering base – one which no amount of after-the-fact fiddling by Labour Governments could redress, nor a sometimes unwilling workforce change and, eventually, one which Mrs Thatcher's ruling Conservative Governments latterly failed to act to save, despite the veneer of flag-waving British patriotism – as they sold-off the nation's assets and undermined Britain's true-engineering culture and its myriad of manufacturers and employers. In *both* political cases, Left and Right, it seems that dogma and ideology were allowed to cost the nation its assets, and to cost the companies their livelihoods and the workers their employment. It is clear that politicians of all hues failed their countrymen.

Such claims can be reinforced by asking why else would two differing characters and opinion holders such as Sir George Edwards and Tony Benn, both work to together to try and save Britain's engineering base as they did. Both men were keen to ensure survival of British skills and British jobs. Both saw opposing political parties wreak havoc upon British engineering and British aviation. The 'sticking plaster' policy latterly applied to British aviation procurement strategy by various governments, somehow only resulted in a worse mess amid the scrabble for votes, influence, and ridiculous remedies. Tony Benn was adamant, he said (to the author): 'BOAC, Britannia, Boeings, and all that surrounded the V1000, VC10, BAC, and the Concorde affair, was a madness. Remember, at one stage, BEA asked us if it could order 727s! It was all utter lunacy of policy, pride, and power of all shades, and Britain suffered.'[9]

It was of course Benn (albeit wanting to nationalise aviation) who (in a political sense, and perhaps not in-part unlinked to Filton being in his constituency) 'saved' Concorde at a time of paradoxical Labour cuts to State funded aviation, amid the reality of Messrs Healey and Jenkins – and the political contradictions of their cosiness to American and European power bases despite being of Left leaning orientations. But no matter, Britain could always go, forelock-tugging and cap-in-hand to the International Monetary Fund (IMF) and the new European Economic Community (EEC) – known by some as the engineering emasculation confederation.

To prove just what we are dealing with, let us recall that after the V1000's funeral pyre, Roy Jenkins MP would, in the middle of the BOAC VC10 fracas, make the most uninformed of statements in Parliament by saying: 'It would be much better for our status to make a successful plane with the engines in the same positions as the Americans have theirs, than a less successful plane with the engines in a different position.'

Against the utter imbecility of such contention, Sir George Edwards and the men of Vickers had to work. Who on earth would have bought a British 'copy' of an existing 707 and why? BOAC would not have done so – it was 'married' to the 707!

Amid the 1950s political bun-fighting, lay the death of the V1000 and other subsequent decisions; such was the moment when the greatest ever prestige manufacturing and exchequer earning opportunity, was quite literally, thrown to the winds. So ended the V1000 story, but it did leave a legacy – the studies for Vickers jet airliner – the 'Vanjet' project as the machine that became the superb VC10 itself. And so, in defeat, began the VC10 story. Meanwhile, the astute

Americans raced ahead with their 707. They must have been smiling all the way to the bank, and who could blame them.

Against these fascinating backdrops of geopolitical and industrial policy stemmed the events from which the VC10 was born. That the resulting aircraft should have been so good, can only been cited as an outcome born of Vickers engineering brilliance. But then there was BOAC and its complicated story that began not in 1940 or 1946, but way back at the end of the First World War and an Imperial edict. To understand what happened to the V1000 affair in 1956, and then to the VC10, and why BOAC was structured as it was and behaved as it did, we have to go back to 1919.

Chapter 3

An Imperial Affair: Biplanes to Big Flying Boats

BOAC was born from the growth and amalgamation of some of the pioneer commercial air services that took to the air as early as 1919, when a certain Winston S. Churchill was Britain's first Air Minister. That was also the year that the world's oldest airline, K.L.M. Royal Dutch Airlines, officially began its existence under royal charter, which was just months before 'The Queensland and Northern Territories Aerial Services', as Q.A.N.T.A.S. (Qantas), came into reality. Ironically, BOAC's later transmutation into a branded 'British Airways' in 1974 revived a name of a British air service company from the early days of British civil aviation.

BOAC's roots actually go back to the First World War and the emergence of private British airlines which would latterly be forced to amalgamate into what became the grandly titled 'Imperial Airways (London)', which in 1939 became BOAC. We can thank Imperial Airways and the British independent airlines for setting up the routes and infrastructure that BOAC inherited – initially via domestic regional, European and then intercontinental services. There was, in 1917, a British Civil Aerial Transport Committee, and an Air Vice-Marshal named Sir Sefton Brancker became the key figure in promoting British aviation. The BBC's Lord Reith had been a somewhat unexpected figure of aviation – as a chairman of Imperial Airways and as first chairman of the new British Broadcasting Corporation (BBC).

On Hounslow Heath

Lord John Reith of BBC repute oversaw the amalgamation of Imperial Airways, and then the 1930s iteration of 'British Airway's into BOAC, a title which he claimed to have thought of as part of his belief in the British Empire and Commonwealth air arm that could earn a place in the nation's psyche in the manner of another great national corporation – the BBC itself. Reith was seen as an inspirational leader at Imperial Airways and his departure caused much unrest. A report into Imperial Airways operations by Lord Cadman in 1938 revealed several management and operational conflicts and we might see it as the stepping stone to the formation of the new corporation. Imperial's director and Reith's lifelong friend, Woods Humphrey, became a scapegoat for confused policy and confused government and governance. John Reith stepped into the chairmanship of Imperial in June 1938. Change came quickly under Reith and with orders from government, amalgamation of Imperial and British Airways led to BOAC being first framed in 1939, but delayed in terms of real commercial start-up by the Second World War it was originally the British and Commonwealth Empire Air Corporation, but became less of a mouthful for 1946. Interestingly, Canada vetoed a Commonwealth and Dominion-wide airline idea as it would restrict the likes of Canada from founding their own international carrier. South Africa and Australia adopted similar positions.[1]

Alongside the institution that was BOAC, we must cite Heston and its nearby Hounslow Heath (not Croydon) – once a scene of medieval life and Dick Turpin highwayman-style hijacks – as the origin of British civil airport and airline beginnings. The heath was a desolate and dangerous place, yet had been important in British history for centuries. Ancient man had built a cursus and a stone circle in an alignment that is mirrored by today's main, northerly runway. Julius Caesar built his first British camp on this alignment upon the heath. Curiously, a 'ley line' runs directly from the centre of London's significant sites and out along the London-Bath road, through Heathrow's main runway, Caesar's camp, the old circle, and beyond to Windsor Castle and westwards to further places of power. Little did ancient man know that the alignment upon the heath would become the world's busiest runway, teeming with metal monsters spewing thrust as they launched not just airliners across the world, but the airline of an empire. Today, Heathrow's main east-west runway also follows the line of the Roman road and tracks that coaches and horses took into and out of London, a fitting synergy indeed.

And of Heathrow's original 'third' runway that was aligned north-east-south-west into the prevailing wind? This has long been forgotten, even though it existed into the 1980s, only to be so short-sightedly sacrificed at the needs of buildings and money. Constructing Terminal Four, a new cargo centre and car parks so close to it – Heathrow's own ideal, short and medium-haul airliner-tailored third runway – ensured that its closure was enforced. We can now see how short-sighted such idiocy was. At Gatwick the new 1980s North Terminal was similarly built upon the potentially easiest alignment of a second runway, and avoiding the hill that a faltering American-operated 747, packed with passengers, came within 16ft (radio altimeter height recorded) of hitting in the 1980s after an engine failure on take-off – leaving burned grass in its wake.

Back in 1919, the heath at Hounslow became the take-off point for the first services of an 'aerial liner' to depart (Croydon aerodrome soon usurped it). Those who do not know why Heathrow is so named, need only to look back to the history of Hounslow Heath – the site of London Heathrow Airport and still known as

'LHR' on airline baggage tags and pilots documents. From Hounslow Heath, West London, British civil aviation was born, despite an understandable claim to fame from Croydon Airport in the 1920s.

So it was, on 25 August 1919, that a scheduled service from London Heathrow to Paris le Bourget was inaugurated as the first timetabled civil air service in Britain (a one-off flight had taken place six weeks earlier). The pilot was man named William Lawford, a man who had begun his aviation career in 1911. The first *ad hoc* civil 'one off' service from London actually took place on 15 July at Hendon aerodrome just over one month earlier when a pilot named Jerry Shaw, of Air Transport & Travel Ltd, flew a chartered flight from Hendon to Heathrow, thence to Paris and back. Shaw would soon fly a charter for a Dutchman named Albert Plesman and his own nascent airline – KLM. Shaw did not know it, but Shaw was the Briton who played a key role in the creation of Plesman's mighty KLM Royal Dutch Airlines. By late 1919, Hounslow Heath's new airport was witnessing four cross-Channel services a day.

Forgotten today, there were several London airfields in 1919 – notably Heathrow, Cricklewood and Edgware. They were surrounded by green fields. The point of customs exit and entry into Great Britain was solely based at Heathrow in a tented village, soon to progress to wooden sheds and wooden boards in the mud. In March 1920, the new Croydon Airport became the customs airport for London and a leading hub of airline transport development, but Heathrow would once again have its day. In the intervening period, a cast of small British airlines would flourish, and some die, as the survivors of 1920s aviation were forced together by act of political will, and a grant of capitol, and an overseeing committee.

A key player in this early 'air' arena would be Hillman Airways, which operated from Stapleford Aerodrome, close to Chigwell in London. From this unlikely base, Hillman flew services to Europe and to domestic British seaside towns. Flights to Liverpool and Blackpool were operated, and Hillman's were soon using de Havilland DH84 and DH90 Dragon and Dragon Rapides as the company became well established up to 1935; after which Hillman, along with smaller British independents, Spartan and United, was absorbed into the amalgamation that was the new British Airways. This incarnation of a 'British Airways', was then absorbed into Imperial Airways only, as we know, to re-emerge as a trading name in 1974 when Imperial's successor, BOAC, merged with BEA.

Before that occurred, a somewhat messy structure of British domestic independent airlines grew, operating a diverse fleet mix and *ad hoc* services. Yet 12,000 miles away the Australians, under 'outback' remote Queensland airline pioneers and backers W. Hudson Fysh, Paul. J. McGinniss, Fergus McMaster, and Arthur Baird, created and organised, Q.A.N.T.A.S. (latterly QANTAS and now, as the grammatically incorrect, but de facto 'word' of Qantas) and really got their act together to create on-demand flights from 16 November 1920. The obvious question was why couldn't British civil aviation be so efficiently framed? Qantas early *ad hoc* ferry flights in the remote bush became proper scheduled services on 2 November 1922 with a service from Charleville to Longreach with mail, and then onwards to Cloncurry (577 miles) the next day with one passenger. In its first year of regular services, Qantas carried 208 passengers, but by 1930 Qantas had flown one million miles and thousands of passengers.[2]

The early 1920s success of Qantas inspired Sir Samuel Hoare, who took over at the new Air Ministry in London in 1922; Hoare was forward thinking and needed hard evidence to convince the set minds in London that 'air' was the next great opportunity. Qantas provided the perfect lever to persuade the dull minds of Civil Service thinking and maritime preference.

It says something about the arrogance and the torpor of some of the British and their 'attitude' that their claims to excellence and superiority should have been usurped by 'upstart colonials' who were more mentally agile, better in adversity, and less constrained by class and society and the shackles of only being able to think within perceived wisdoms. The free-thinking Aussies, who had set up Qantas at Longreach, showed the British how to do it. The Deutsche Lufthansa and its Junkers JU52s, was also carving out a strong network throughout Europe, operating a route network of extensive reach. Air Union of France would soon build European and colonial roots. Societé Anonyme Belgique National d' Aerienne (SABENA) of Belgium would also begin its notable forays.

Although Imperial Airways, KLM, Lufthansa, Air France, SABENA, and Qantas, are often cited as the world's oldest or founding airlines, we should not forget that the Russians proceeded apace with airliner design in the 1920s.

Of massive latent commercial significance, across the Atlantic, there lay a grand array of 1920s American airline companies who would begin to flourish as aviation took hold across that vast continent. In the heart of the United States, difficult flying conditions and the need to carve out new airways and routes also represented the beginning of a new age and a new industry. The transport of mail provided the subsidy and the impetus to airline growth, as it did in Europe.

Curtiss Condors, Ford Tri-motors, Lockheed Orions and Vegas, and assorted Northrops, Boeings, and a brief flirtation with Fokker high wing wooden-built monoplanes, that were not always resistant to American conditions, populated a fleet mix of expensive diversity. It would take the metal-built Boeing 247 and Douglas DC-2 to change everything for carriers. America also had a nascent flying boat based service, the New York Buenos Aires Airways (NYBRA), which was absorbed into Pan American Grace Airways.

The American airlines, and the airliner builders that served them, advanced their respective arts at a pace that made Imperial Airways look very peculiar indeed.

The fact that by the mid-1930s, the American Lockheed Super 14 Electra would be the pride of British Airways super-fast European service from London Heston Aerodrome, and would be latterly used to fly Prime Minister Neville Chamberlin to Germany, proves the point that national pride is one thing, but the economics and ability of a superb machine soon outweigh any such patriotic preferences. The confused and perhaps complacent British aerial 1920s mindset, cast from a band of small start-up Edwardian era air carriers, had resulted in strategy as policy and national will for 'air' that was unfocused and spread too widely across too many themes and ideas. Leadership had been missing.

We ought not to forget that despite historical perceptions, long before American dominance, the British were beaten into powered flight, beaten across the Channel, and that the first proper powered take-off, flight and landing in Britain by a British pilot, was on 1 December 1908, when J.T. Moore Brabazon used a French aircraft in the form a Voisin machine, built by Eugene Gabriel Voisin at Issy les Moulineux Paris. Although Samuel Cody has claim of flight from a few weeks earlier.

The French were also expanding their airlines, and with competitors in mind, Lord Weir's British Government committee recommended direct State assistance towards the building of British aerial transport services. But for pioneers like Air Transport and Travel Ltd, founded by Holt Thomas, it all came too late, and this airline was closed down and absorbed into Daimler Airways.

Airmail

Early services carried more mail than passengers, and even in 1950, delivering the State-operated Royal Mail by air, accounted for up to twenty per cent of payload on some BOAC services, especially to Africa and Asia. What of Plesman's brilliant KLM, or the French Government supported Air Union of France, or Lufthansa? The British, as so often happened, took their time while their direct European competition raced ahead – in the case of KLM – literally.

British domestic aviation was surprisingly strong in the 1920s and 1930s with routes to remote Scottish islands, the Midlands and the North, providing a fast alternative to the railways. Services to Blackpool and East Anglia were commonplace, if weather-dependent. So concerned were the railways that they invested in small airlines or set up their own 'air' departments. As an example, the Great Western Railway (GWR) set up a GWR air service from Plymouth to Bristol and Cardiff, operating three days a week in the 1930s – with a call made to the windy top of Haldon Hill outside Exeter in case anyone wanted to access the local ports. Imperial operated the service for the GWR.

Despite such fascinating moments, several of the British independent airlines would be absorbed into the new national carrier of Imperial Airways, including the lead players of Sir Frederick Handley Page's own Handley Page Transport Limited with its three HP W8B machines (Handley Page Transport carried over 3,000 passengers in 1922); the Instone Air Line Limited (former coal exporters and shipping line operators) and its single converted, Vickers Vimy Commercial, and four de Havilland DH 34's. Daimler Airways brought three de Havilland DH 34's to the mix and the British Marine Air Navigation Company added two Supermarine Sea Eagle amphibian flying boats. These airlines built British domestic route networks and services to Paris and other European cities. Services to Scotland and the Channel Islands were also started, only to be somewhat neglected by the later amalgamation of airlines that became the great instrument that was Imperial Airways.

Imperial was to inherit 1,760 miles of cross-Channel European routes, the operations were based not at Heathrow, but at Croydon Airport, which had opened on 25 March 1920. The first scheduled overseas service of Imperial did not start until 26 April 1924, when a daily London-Paris service was opened with a DH 34. The British independents that had been formed into Imperial had made a big success of developing European routes, but Imperial (with government edict) seemed to want to focus on overseas long-haul mail and elite passenger services, perhaps at the expense of previous European and domestic achievements by the small band of British airlines that now lay within Imperial's umbrella. Dutch, French and German airlines would soon punish Imperial's complacency in Europe.

However, in 1925, out in central and east Africa, Sir Alan Cobham was undertaking 'The Empire Air League Imperial Airways Survey', with the specific remit to assess the issue of aerial mail and transport services. The idea of landplanes across the bush, and for flying boats taking off and alighting upon African lakes, came from this survey. The first contract for such services went to The North Sea Aerial and General Transport Company Ltd, who received the rights from the Colonial Office to operate from Khartoum to Kisumu on Lake Victoria. Sir Samuel Hoare undertook an African inspection tour and soon considered that Cobham's own airline interests, in the form of the Cobham-Blackburn Airline, might operate local east African services for Imperial, but Imperial soon acquired the small concern and launched its own African affair that linked Cairo to Cape Town. So began Imperial in Africa.[3]

An Imperial Air

From 1924, Imperial Air Transport that was officially formed as Imperial Airways gained its first chairman, the business tycoon Sir Eric Campbell Geddes. Geddes was formerly General Manager of the North Eastern Railway and also ex-Inspector General of Military Transport in France in the First World War. He ran Dunlop, and fellow Dunlop luminaries Sir Hardiman Lever and the expert accountant Lt Col Sir George Beharrell, DSO, (another ex-railway expert) were streamed into running Imperial. In fact Dunlop supplied offices, solicitors, and other resources to Imperial. Given that the government had little interest in 'air' matters, we can be grateful that a force as large as Geddes was present to push all the right buttons. He had railway and Ministerial experience as Minister of Transport in 1917–1918 and transferred his skills well. The same could be said of Sir Sefton Brancker as Director of Civil Aviation. It should be recalled that at this time the Air Minister did not sit in Cabinet. Britain was not then truly 'air-minded', and it appears that the strategic aerial lessons of the First World War had not penetrated the minds of government and civil servants in their ivory towers in London.

A Colonel Frank Searl, who had expertly run the London bus service and achieved high utilisation of equipment, then to run B.S.A. Daimler Airways, was appointed Imperial's first Managing Director. But even with such expertise, Imperial constituted a diverse and expensive fleet of British aircraft procured from a range of sources. Merger with British Airways in 1935 would only confuse the mix further. Lower training, operating and maintenance costs from standardised fleet procurement did not enter the mindset – but using British equipment did.

The first new airline type commissioned for Imperial Airways was the Handley Page W8F, which was ordered on the 3 November 1924. In the first year of operation, Imperial flew 853,042 miles, carried 11,395 passengers and 212,380 letters, a quite astounding figure given the old aircraft types, their maintenance issues, and the mix-and-match nature of the inherited operations.

Any observer who resents the description of Imperial's early days as being within a torpor, needs to recall that the British did, in 1932, only have thirty-one registered airline transport pilots and the same number of actual in-service airliners. By comparison, the 'foreigners' on the European continent saw 135 French airline transport pilots flying 269 aircraft, the Germans had 160 airline pilots flying a 177-strong fleet on a route network whose total mileage exceeded the British and French airlines network mileage combined. The unanswered question was why?

In latter years, the great corporate-political torpor continued, much to the frustration of the aviation experts who operationally managed and staffed BOAC, many of who had started their careers at Imperial Airways and its antecedents.

Luckily, back in 1920s Britain, a few key players *had* realised that action to promote a British airline industry was needed, not least in the face of subsidised Dutch, French, and German rival carriers. With support from Prime Minister Stanley Baldwin, the independent British civil air services were amalgamated, regulated, and then State-financed into a more cohesive British airline service. So it was that Sir Samuel Hoare, as Air Minister in 1922, drove the process through. It was not easy; the mindset of government and nation was maritime – not of the air. His Majesty's Treasury was not really interested and it would take Sir Herbert Hambling of Barclays Bank (Deputy Chairman) to drive the process – it is said with direct encouragement from then Prime Minister Andrew Bonar Law. Law was soon out of office, so it was Stanley Baldwin who was the man to approve the State, tax-payer funded subsidy of one million pounds over a ten year period for the new 'air' line. The Hambling Committee had framed and driven the process and it would lead to an entity named 'Imperial Airways'. The name was suggested by George Woods Humphrey and replaced the original suggestion of 'British Aircraft Transportation Service', which was seen to be vulnerable to the pejorative acronym of 'BATS'.[4]

Imperial's dominant position led to airliners being created for Imperial and its route demands. So was born the British practice of designing airliners to the peculiar needs of the dominant, State controlled, national carrier – a characteristic that would touch the VC10 itself decades later. Back in the 1920s, the two key airliners that emerged from the process were tri-motors of 1926, the Armstrong Whitworth Argosy, of which seven were constructed (their engines proved troublesome), and the de Havilland DH 66 Hercules. The emergent Qantas would take four DH 66s and Imperial operated seven. The DH 66 was the first airliner to be designed with excess power and a durable, reinforced, steel (not wood) airframe. A cockpit canopy to convert the open-cockpit was later designed and retro-fitted to the Imperial machines. The Handley Page HP 42 and Short Brothers flying boats were to follow. Elsewhere in the world, airliner design was much further ahead, and Imperial was, despite British impressions, not alone in conquering the skies.

In 1924, Imperial became the main airline and employer of British civil pilots. The first sixteen pilots were gathered together, and soon others of experience would come to the airline. These men truly were the pioneers of British airline building and without them Imperial, BOAC, and the subsequent story would never have happened. Some of them started flying biplanes for Imperial and ended their careers flying VC10s for BOAC – surely something remarkable in terms of experience and achievement.

Imperial Heroes

Imperial and BOAC pilot O.P. Jones would achieve great fame – eventually commanding BOAC four-engined flying boats and VC10 airliners, and flying Prime Ministers and VIPs. Many of his Imperial colleagues would finish their careers as BOAC, Comet, Britannia, 707, and VC10 pilots. Dudley Travers, a former cavalryman of the First World War, went into the Royal Flying Corps and then to Imperial Airways, arriving with a DFC and Croix de Guerre no less. Millions of flying miles later, he was a legend as a flying boat commander, he would also become an Imperial 'Master of the Air' – one of only five men so ennobled – in doing so he would make the East Africa flying boat route his own before retiring from BOAC in the 1960s.

Jack Kelly Rogers was another of Imperial's illustrious adventurer pilots and commanded the BOAC Boeing flying boat that brought Winston Churchill across the Atlantic in wartime. It was Kelly Rogers who attended Imperial's crashed flying boat, *Corsair,* on the Dungu River in Africa in 1939–1940, where he further cemented his reputation as man of action and certainty.

Men like Jones, Kelly Rogers, Travers, Wilcockson and others, epitomised the great era of aeronautical advancement. Without them and their travails, BOAC and its VC10 would never have happened. We might also recall that without the behind the scenes diplomacy of HRH Queen Elizabeth II and her husband, Africa and the Commonwealth would have imploded long before BOAC and its VC10s dominated those tropical skies. Africa, always the cauldron of politics and good and bad deeds, framed Imperial, its successor BOAC, the Comet, and lastly, the VC10.

From single-engined prop-jobs made of wire, canvas and wood, to sleek-hulled 'Empire' flying boats and then to giant, T-tailed Rolls-Royce powered VC10s straddling the globe, it all seems an incredible achievement, yet one seemingly 'lost' to history beyond the enclave of the aviation enthusiast. We should briefly add the names and deeds of some of the other men who made all this happen. Lead names of the Imperial years included: Rhinhold F. Caspareuthus, Gordon P. Olley, Athelstan S.M. Rendall, Gordon Store, Rex Oxley Taylor, Arthur S. Wilcockson, C.F. Wolley Dod, and Alan B.H. Youell.

Captain C. Nigel Pelly was another example of the derring-do at Imperial and BOAC. He had worked for Hillman Airways and then Imperial, before becoming a BOAC man. Perry piloted Lockheed Electras, Canadair Argonauts and Britannias. Of note, Pelly flew Prime Minister Neville Chamberlain to meet Adolf Hitler in 1938 for peace talks. Pelly was one of the wartime BOAC Mosquito pilots operating the clandestine, unarmed Mosquito service to Sweden from Leuchars in Scotland. This was the 'ball-bearing' airline that collected vital Swedish ball-bearings for British industry and which also carried VIPs, returning airmen and spies, in and out of Sweden in the bomb bay of the BOAC Mosquitos. Their aircraft only had one defence against marauding Luftwaffe night fighters – speed. Seven BOAC Mosquito pilots would die in this service, including Captain Gilbert Rae.[5]

Ronald Ballantine of Imperial Airways & BOAC: Commander of the Air

Ronald George Ballantine, who ended his career as a VC10 captain, was born at Plymouth on 2 August 1913, and as a young man learned to fly privately. By the time he was twenty-one he had obtained his commercial flying, navigation, and wireless licences, enabling him to join Imperial Airways. Ballantine flew as a second officer in the three-engined, open cockpit, Armstrong Whitworth Argosy on the Croydon-Brussels-Cologne route, then moved on to the Handle Page HP 42 biplane airliner.

Ballantine next flew on the Imperial Airways routes to Africa and Asia before being appointed to his first command. Transferring to Imperial's eastern hubs, he was based in Hong Kong, flying the de Havilland DH 86. During this period he carried out an aerial survey of the route to Bangkok via Hanoi, across the unknown territories of Siam and Indo-China, and he established a 16-hour record for the Rangoon-Calcutta return journey. Although Ballantine had joined the RAF Volunteer Reserve (RAFVR) in 1939, he was retained to fly for BOAC. He flew in the evacuation of France before being posted to Egypt, where he flew in support of operations in the Western Desert. In one incident, when supplying fuel to the besieged garrison at Tobruk, Ballantine successfully landed his Lockheed Hudson after the two preceding aircraft had been destroyed by enemy fire, only for the undercarriage to collapse as his machine hit a shell hole and was wrecked. Ballantine spent the night in a trench and he managed to escape just before Tobruk fell.

Ballantine flew regularly on the London-Cairo route, staging through Lisbon, Lagos and Khartoum. Among his passengers during this period were General de Gaulle and General Patton, it was also where he first met Ernest K. Gann. After he had been seconded as Chief Pilot to the newly formed Hong Kong Airways, Ballantine returned with his wife Cherry to England in 1949 to fly BOAC's new Rolls-Royce Merlin-powered Canadair Argonaut airliners.

On 6 February 1952, he flew the new Queen Elizabeth home from Africa following the death of her father, King George VI. Ballantine soon converted to the Bristol Britannia, before transferring to the Comet IV fleet under the command of Tom Stoney. In 1963 he converted to the Vickers VC10 – going on to be a senior fleet captain. When he retired in 1966, he had amassed 21,400 hours flying time during a career in which he had flown an estimated five million miles. Ballantine then went to Singapore as Director of Flight Operations for the Comet-equipped company Malaysia-Singapore Airlines, which subsequently became Singapore Airlines.

Ronald Ballantine retired to his home in the 'Berkshire BOAC belt', an hour's drive from Heathrow. There, this tall gentleman and true commander of the air, retired to his garden and his earlier passion for art and colour. Ballantine was friends with the author Ernest K. Gann and featured in one of Gann's books. Ronald Ballantine was a pioneer aviator typical of his breed, encapsulating all that was best of his era and his genre.

As a child, the author visited a Lagos-bound BOAC VC10 flight deck and met Captain Ballantine. Nearly three decades later the author bumped into an upright, tall gentlemen at a village flower and jumble sale and got talking about BOAC with the stranger, who turned out to be the man he had last met when he was a boy taken to see a VC10 commander in a cockpit high over the Sahara desert – it was Ballantine.

Beyond the posh people in the cabin and their social issues, men like Ronald Ballantine were the founding core of British civil airline operations, they *were* Imperial and BOAC.

C Class Celebrity

The brave Australians would beat the Americans and the British across the world's greatest oceanic aerial challenge. On 31 May 1928, Charles Kingsford-Smith and his crew of Ulm, Lyon, and Warner, flew from Oakland California to Brisbane, arriving in Australia on 9 June. They did it using one of Dutchman Anthony H.G. Fokker's own F.VII tri-motors, the *Southern Cross*. It would be another three years before Charles Lindbergh would attempt the Pacific (by a northern route).

Charles Kingsford-Smith ('Smithy') and Charles Ulm then rubbed British noses in it by 'rescuing' an Imperial Airways attempt to run a mail flight through to Australia in April–May 1931. The Imperial machine, the Hercules Class *City of Cairo*, crashed at Koepang during an emergency landing due to headwinds. The Imperial pilots, R. Mollard and H.W.C. Alger, managed to save the mail and pass it on to an Imperial-chartered Kingsford-Smith crew who had crossed the Timor Sea from Darwin in the famous *Southern Cross*. The mail was saved and delivered onwards to Brisbane. Imperial's Mollard, who had hitched a lift with Kingsford-Smith, was told to purchase an aircraft in Australia for the return Australia-Great Britain mail attempt. He did so, but the return mail was actually flown all the way back up the line to Imperial's main station at Akyab in Burma by Kingsford-Smith under charter to Imperial Airways. Unsurprisingly, the flight from there to Croydon was performed by an Imperial machine and crew.

In May 1934, the official British Royal Mail charter and pennant was handed to Imperial Airways by the Postmaster General, Sir Kingsley Wood, at the consent of the King (George V). Carriage of mail at an agreed tariff, and by 1937 on an un-surcharged 'Air Mail' basis, would now underpin Imperial. So was born, under the management of Imperial's Company Secretary (not a stenographic title) S.A. Dismore, the 'Empire Air Mail Scheme' to transport mail across the British colonies at a cheap and fixed rate. George Woods Humphrey, who had entered the 1920s airline business with Frederick Handley Page and then Daimler Airways, was by now a significant figure for Imperial as General Manager.

However, it took from 1933 to 1937 for the government to enact the mail legislation, it being approved by the House of Commons on 20 December 1934, but did not achieve in-service reality for another three years. Yet there was a significant unintended outcome – aircraft with more cargo (as mail) capacity were required and they would be heavier and, as the runways to serve such machines did not exist in Africa or Asia, there was only one answer – flying boats. So at Imperial's needs, were born the range of small to medium size 1920s and 1930s flying boats that built Imperial's wider network. Within ten years, giant C Class flying boats would, in every sense, imperially dominate the airways.

Imperial Airways, locked into a British psyche of lumbering biplanes and early flying boats delivering a slow but reliable service, came late to the game, and ultimately responded to American alloy-bodied, monocoque, monoplane airliner developments with two 1930s monoplane airliners.

The first was the Armstrong Whitworth AW15 Atalanta of 1932. It was built of a combined wood and alloy tube construction, and was Imperial's first 'hot and high' airliner-to-order, in that it had a large high-lift wing (with lower wing-loading), and four powerful Armstrong-Siddeley 'Serval' engines rated at 340bhp each – derived from the wonderfully named 'Double Mongoose' engine. The cantilever-wing was high-mounted to allow ground clearance and keep the engines away from rough ground and runway debris. Despite a large and cavernous fuselage, only ten passengers could be accommodated – the rest of the space was for the lucrative empire mail and for cargo as they were vital consignments on the Eastern routes where the Atalanta was deployed in Africa and India. Here was Imperial's tropical airliner for difficult runways. Eight were built and set a formula that persisted up to BOAC's VC10 requirements.

Imperial's next machine, a large tropical route landplane, was the belated, 1938 AW27 Ensign, which was a descendant of the Atalanta, but it was underpowered, required modification to American powerplants, and was made in small numbers prior to wartime use. But, prior to that event, a greater success came in the form of the elegant de Havilland DH 91 Albatross – alas built of wood, and yet highly aerodynamically efficient, but taking over five years to come to fruition in 1937, by which time any market other than a British one, had long since been secured by the DC-3.

Despite such moments, Imperial remained trapped into a peculiar torpor. The French also remained in a dinosaur biplane nationalistic mindset. Yet Britain's massive Short's built C Class flying boats, introduced in 1936, *were* a great success and created a stately golden era for Imperial and the British. The C Class engendered unheard of affection for an airliner and they were loved by crews and passengers alike. In Africa, the C Class (and the three G Class) became beloved legends, even in the remote bush areas, and upon their withdrawal in 1946 many tears were shed. The VC10 would be the next airliner to achieve such endearment and status in Africa – and beyond.

Imperial's 1930s fleet equipment mix was an expensive melange of landplanes and flying boats that ranged from giant flying boats to variously named, or classed, Scyllas, Ensigns, Hannibals, Heracles, Atalantas, Frobishers, and to Boulton and Paul P71As named *Britomart* and *Boadicea*, a fleet of twelve-seat DH 86 machines tagged the Diana Class, and two Avro 652 six-seaters. It looked like a free-for-all and would only be exceeded in the bizarre by the post-war British use of Junkers JU 52 airliners!

Over at KLM and Qantas, much more rational and cost-effective fleets were being built.

First Class Travellers

Imperial's landplane passenger services were slow and stylish. The arrival of the big flying boats only speeded things up a touch. Existing standards of railway inspired Pullman-style luxury were retained (Imperial's early directors were of course, ex-railway managers).

The new Shorts Company built C Class flying boats with deep fuselages carrying not just people, but mail, tonnes of mail, and with grand cabins, became true icons of a grand era. These machines could fly from rivers, lakes and sea ports where a one or two mile take-off run presented fewer problems than a landplanes bush take-off. It was from these circumstances that Imperial procured its giant flying boats and wrote a new chapter in the history of aviation. So were born the Imperial Airways Short S23 C Class Empire flying boats at a 1935 cost of £50,000 each, and their Poole, and then Southampton bases – latterly with the S26 flying boat, which was a larger and longer range version that itself led to the two even larger S33 examples that went straight into BOAC wartime service in 1940. Through the C Class Imperial, of which it ordered twenty-eight, and of which the first example, *Canopus,* flew on 3 July 1936 and entered service in October 1936, created the world's largest carrier of mail and freight. So too did Imperial offer the world's most luxurious airline travel in the world. At one stage, the giant flying boats only had room for six passengers instead of sixteen, so great was the weight of the mail – which took precedence. So a new era, and a new industry, was also born upon Imperial's C Class wings.

By 1938, Imperial was operating five services a week from England to India, of which three continued to Australia (a ten-day total journey), and had eighteen Africa services a week operating through the hubs at Alexandria, Cairo and Khartoum. Imperial, self-appointed preacher of its own rectitude, called itself;

'The greatest air service in the world', which was probably true in one context, but it was definitely not the fastest.

Be it on a landplane or a seaplane, luncheon was eaten from tables laid with linen and napkins; wine coolers abounded, as did single malt whisky. The menus include the serving of 'Cornish' chicken in the skies over the middle of rancid African jungles. Roast woodcock was served, as was gingered melon and 'Toast Imperial'. Château-bottled fine wines were dispensed by an all-male waiting staff of deferential stewards. The first stewards were used by Imperial in 1927 on the Armstrong Whitworth Argosy services to Paris. Early cabin services were picnic offerings, but by the advent of the HP 42/43, and then the C Class, a true First Class offering was created. The horrendous thought of females as servants in the air had not at that time been even considered in the days of the Raj. The realities of a female Concorde pilot, or female cabin service directors, were it seems, not just decades away, but things from another world, one far too dreadful to contemplate old boy ...

Change was slow to dawn upon the rarefied airs of Imperial's impeccable progress. It was all an anachronism, even in its own day, but it worked, and Englishmen were proud of their airline; but was Imperial actually an extension of national psyche and pride as they looked down upon those less superior than themselves? Thus did Imperial meet the expectations of its passengers as the, 'Englishmen of their Empire'. Such realities framed the British, Imperial and its attitudes: Imperial flew the flag for King, country, and the elite of society. Workers, tradespeople, shopkeepers, and administrators – the white under-class of the Empire did *not* fly Imperial – instead they travelled out to their colonial postings by sea, on some very old ships. The class system pervaded everything.

An extreme view? Not at all, for it was reality. Poor people, and even middle-class people, simply did not travel by air at this time, unless of course they were servants of the airline itself.

Flying the Furrow

Whatever its failings, Imperial had talented and brilliant pilots, station managers and staff, who could think laterally, improvise and solve problems if forced down in the bush. A few Imperial pilots may have been arrogant or egotistical, but most were cleverer than that. Imperial created the world's first true multi-armed intercontinental network, and it threw money at establishing aerial routes to serve the British Empire. It was Imperial who built runways, airports, hotels and en-route facilities in the most hostile of environments in Africa and Asia. There was even an Imperial-built hotel for night-stopping flying boat passengers constructed beside Lake Naivasha. At Khartoum, Juba, Mwanza, Victoria Falls, Bulawayo,

Kano, Lagos, and across Africa, Imperial spent millions of pounds carving new airports and facilities from barren ground. At Juba, in the southern Sudan, the Imperial passenger could turn ninety degrees and head west across the seething forests and stunning landscapes of central Africa to track towards Lagos (latterly, from there one could depart for Belem in Brazil by Boeing Clipper), before trotting along the so-called 'Gold Coast' to Bathurst.

In the deserts of what was then Arabia and the Sudd of East Africa remote yet complete airports, with full facilities and passenger bedrooms, were built. At Sharjah, Imperial created a new aerodrome in the desert, and that outstation became today's international airport. At Wadi Halfa, Malakal, Kisumu, remote outposts of Imperial were created to serve the original five-day service to Durban, and the aerial branch line via Victoria Falls and Bulawayo to alight upon the Val at Johannesburg. Imperial 'rest-houses' were built in Tanganyika and at Lumbo at Mozambique's main port. Traverses of the Upper Nile, and detours to zoom the C-Class over Murchison Falls were the very stuff of Imperial legend in Africa.[6]

Perhaps the most spectacular undertaking in terms of engineering and resolve was the ploughing of a furrow across the deserts of what was then called 'Persia' to cross Iraq and link British interest in Egypt and Palestine to Baghdad. At first, building a railway line was considered, but this was dismissed as too expensive. After the RAF had carried out ground and aerial surveys across the region of British mandated territories from June 1921, the idea of actually ploughing a marker track across the desert was conceived. By late 1923, low-flying pilots could follow the furrow, which even had marker 'arrows' ploughed to assist direction finding, and emergency landing strips and fuel stores. After Director of Civil Aviation Sefton Brancker's 1924–1925 aerial survey expedition to 'prove' the route from Europe to India (Brancker was assisted and piloted by Alan Cobham), the route was commercialised in 1925. This was largely due to the combined efforts of two 'air' enthusiasts, the new Air Minister (the Leftist Labourite Lord Thomson) and the urgings of Sir Samuel Hoare (a Conservative in that year's new government), Imperial's machines would make use of the furrow on the new airmail run to India and for years to come as its low flying passenger craft traversed the desert to the east. In 1926, following Imperial's own route and out station building, carried out by Charles Wolley-Dod, the new government-subsidised route was opened to Baghdad, by 1931, Delhi was reached.

Soon, equipped with radios, Imperial's new airliners, themselves ploughing along at under 2,000ft, could at least deviate from the furrow's track, but it remained an excellent emergency resource. VC10s would later fly high over this route, the furrow unseen 30,000ft below. But they would still be traversing Africa, and emblazoned with the Union Jack and a Speedbird logo handed down across the decades of imperialism.

From these wonderful route-building days came BOAC's inherited network, its requirement for 'hot and high' capable airliners and today's mass travel that means a person can leave the bush or outback in the morning, go to an airport and arrive on the other side of the world as quickly as twelve hours later.

The key early routes laid down by the 'chosen instrument' of Imperial Airways and handed to BOAC followed distinct courses. The UK–Africa journey of nearly 8,000 miles took ten and half days and several night-stops en route. By the time the C-Class had got it all sorted, it was a five and half day run. Cairo was a major Imperial crossroads and the port of Alexandria provided a similar base for flying boat services. From Egypt the route turned south to East Africa and South Africa, or south-west via Khartoum to skirt the Sahara to alight at Kano, then Lagos, Nigeria, and onwards to Accra and Takoradi. In this region West African Airways (WAA), as an Imperial Airways local arm, replaced the Liverpool-based Elder-Dempster shipping line as the colonial transport arm. From there local services were extended along the west coast. Central African Airways (CAA) linked up with the routes of that part of Africa.

Alternatively, the turn of the route was to the east at Cairo and onwards to the Gulf, then to India, and soon, on to Singapore and Australia. This first stage of Imperial's core service to the Orient was the strategic Egypt–India route surveyed by Sir Alan Cobham in 1925. The first through-service from England to India was opened in 1934, and India was brought within one week's travel from England. Australia lay beyond. The Imperial route from Cairo led to Karachi, Calcutta, Rangoon, Singapore, and in later years across Java, the treacherous Timor Sea, and then to Brisbane (1934), and soon onward to Rose Bay Sydney in 1936 (where local flying boats still operate and the old maintenance ramp is still visible) – in thirteen days covering just under 13,000 miles. Onward services by flying boats of Tasman Empire Airways Services to New Zealand soon followed.

For Imperial, from Singapore to Brisbane and Sydney – in association with Qantas as 'Qantas Empire Airways' – the record was impressive, but the flight times and overall journey times were not, especially in comparison to those of KLM, which provided Imperial with its main competition on the route to India and beyond, and soon surpassed Imperial's European ambitions in route network terms.

In the 1980s, BOAC's successor, British Airways, would employ a pilot who, upon his retirement, was the last British man with a valid large four-engined flying boat licence and experience that went back to wartime days. His name was Ken Emmott and it was Emmott who flew the Hulton-owned Short Sunderland flying boat *Islander* away from England in the 1990s, thus finally severing the last link with the age of Imperial Airways.[7]

Koninklijke Luchtvaart Maatschappij NV – KLM's Dutch Brilliance with British Links

Founded on 7 October 1919, with a royal charter to assist it, KLM was, by 1920, running proper 'airline' standard services from Amsterdam to London, Hamburg and Copenhagen. The early KLM services featured British pilots. In fact KLM's early days were an Anglo-Dutch amalgam of aircraft and crews from Croydon Aerodrome, with the first scheduled flight being a DH 16 G-EALU from Croydon on 17 May 1920. KLM's early flights were performed by DH 9 and DH 16 aircraft owned by Aircraft Transport and Travel (AT&T). The wonderfully named Captain Spry-Leverton ran KLM's London office from 1921 to 1953. In 1939, Winston Churchill and his family flew to the Netherlands on KLM.

Within four years KLM was sending monoplane Fokker F VIIs on flights to Batavia in the Dutch East Indies (now Jakarta, Indonesia) – 9,522 statute miles and a fifty-five day route proving journey time. By 1929, KLM had created a weekly scheduled service of seven days duration to Batavia. Just a handful of years later, this KLM service would take five days as an express service using the latest Douglas equipment. KLM operated the world's first intercontinental long-haul flight in June 1927 as a charter for the American businessman, Van Lear Black. 'The KLM', as it was known, would race eastwards in Fokkers and Douglas machines to establish the world's first true, scheduled, long-haul service. Within five more years, KLM's European route network served twelve major European cities and would soon despatch the Douglas DC-2 and DC-3 to the Far East with utter reliability on a several-times-a week, scheduled basis. By October 1937, KLM was running a thrice weekly DC-3 departure from Amsterdam to Batavia with regularity and safety as a vital link to its Dutch colony in Asia, and also offering connections to Asia and Australia. Soon, KLM would not even need the State subsidy with which its early operations were underwritten – even by 1938 KLM's Netherland's Government funding was just 4.5 per cent of expenditure.

KLM's founder, Albert Plesman, was a genius, an entrepreneur visionary, a driving force of a character who seized opportunities and, despite his long standing customer relationship with Anthony H.G. Fokker, thought nothing of racing to Los Angeles to secure early delivery of the new DC-2 – which would lead to the KLM DC-3 division. From such beginnings, from such energy, grew the legend of KLM. Imperial Airways managed to get its achingly slow, long haul landplane-seaplane-train-boat route to Karachi (and then Delhi) in the early 1930s, whereas KLM, by using dedicated, high-speed DC-2s (and then its DC-3s), carried on to Calcutta, Rangoon, Bangkok, Palembang and then to Batavia, Surabaya and Denpasar, just a short but risky over-ocean hop from Australia, and all without the need for constant changes, train and boat connections. KLM's DC-2s and then

DC-3s flew at 10,000–12,000ft cruising altitudes, where cooler airs made life in the cabin bearable, Imperial's biplane winged dinosaurs flew at 500ft to 2,000ft in the stinking airs of the tropics and life in the cabin was difficult, and made even more so by the dress code for the colonial men of status – ties, suits and hats.

Indeed, KLM was Imperial's true competition, and as late as March 1938, when Britain's Lord Gowrie, as Governor-General of Australia, flew home to London, he travelled by KLM on a tour of the then Dutch East Indies and then rode the KLM express DC-3 service from Batavia to Amsterdam, then connecting for London – eschewing Imperial's flying boats.

Imperial had countered the KLM express service with a sedate but stylish flying boat service to Singapore as part of an eleven day flight from London to Brisbane and Rose Bay Sydney via Darwin. But en route, KLM and its KNILM East Indies subsidiary, worked with Imperial in a rare act of international airline friendship.[8]

ENGLAND-SOUTH AFRICA SERVICES

ENGLAND, EGYPT, ANGLO-EGYPTIAN SUDAN, BRITISH AND PORTUGUESE EAST AFRICA, UNION OF SOUTH AFRICA operated throughout by Imperial flying-boats

Southbound ENGLAND - EGYPT - SOUTH AFRICA					Northbo
Beginning Tuesday 18 April 1939					Beginning 7 from KISUM
Miles from South- ampton	PORTS OF CALL Junctions and Termini shown in CAPITALS (See Notes on the right)	Local Stan- dard Time	Green- wich Mean Time	Days of Services	Miles from Durban
				Every	
	LONDON (Waterloo) ......dep. Southampton England ...... arr.	19 30 21 28	18 30 20 28	Tues. Thur.‡ Fri. ★	286 DU Lou
624 1005 1325 1704	SOUTHAMPTON ......dep. Marseilles France ......dep. Rome Italy ......dep. Brindisi Italy......dep. Athens Greece ...... arr.	05 30 10 40 13 45 16 30 20 20	04 30 09 40 12 45 15 30 18 20	Wed. Fri. Sat.	803 BE 1316 Mo Mo 1666 Lin 1887 Dai
2291 2403 2992	Athens......dep. ALEXANDRIA Egypt ......dep. Cairo Egypt......dep. Wadi Halfa Anglo-Egyptian Sudan ... arr.	05 00 10 00 11 25 15 35	03 00 08 00 09 25 13 35	Thur. Sat. Sun.	2081 Mo 2519 KI: Kis
3441 3867 4200 4536 4682	Wadi Halfa ......dep. KHARTOUM Anglo-Egyptian Sudan ...dep. Malakal Anglo-Egyptian Sudan......dep. Juba Anglo-Egyptian Sudan ......dep. Port Bell (Kampala) Uganda......dep. KISUMU Kenya Colony ...... arr.	04 45 08 15 11 40 14 30 18 05 19 20	02 45 06 15 09 40 12 30 15 20 16 35	Fri. Sun.‡ Mon.	2665 Por 3001 Jub 3334 Ma 3760 KH Kh 4209 Wa
5135 5329 5550 5900	Kisumu ......dep. Mombasa Kenya Colony ......dep. Dar-es-Salaam Tanganyika Territory.....dep. Lindi Tanganyika Territory......dep. Mozambique Portuguese East Africa .. arr.	06 00 09 50 11 55 14 10 16 10	03 15 07 05 09 10 11 25 14 10	Sat. Tues.	4798 Cai 4910 AL Ale 5497 Ath 5876 Bri
6413 6930 7216†	Mozambique ......dep. BEIRA Portuguese East Africa......dep. Lourenço Marques Portuguese E. Africa dep. DURBAN Natal ...... arr.	05 30 10 05 14 25 16 35	03 30 08 05 12 25 14 35	Sun. Wed.	6196 Roi 6577 Ma Ma 7201 SO LO

Imperial's Africa Service Timetable.

Plesman's airline in 1938 could get you 12,500 miles in sixty-three hours in safety and comfort; this speaks volumes for the man and his company. By 27 June 1938, KLM was flying Lockheed Super Electras to Batavia, and then on the Qantas route to Cloncurry, Longreach, Brisbane and Sydney; total flight time from Croydon to Sydney via Amsterdam was six days.

KLM almost won the 1934 MacRobertson air race from London, England to Melbourne, Australia. Instead, a tiny, single-seat British de Havilland 'Comet' racer triumphed. But behind this headline, second place was taken by a proper big airliner – a KLM DC-2 no less. The DC-2, *Uiver* (Stork), astonished the world with its second place, and a first place by handicap class amid a flight time of seventy-one hours twenty-eight minutes at the hands of Captain K.D. Parmentier. So an airliner had competed against a racing machine and proved a massive point about American design and Dutch operational expertise – British was no longer best by default. In 1946, KLM would become the first airline in the world to operate a post-war flight from Europe to New York with a DC-4, operating a twice-weekly service via Glasgow, on the Atlantic, northerly route. In 1954, KLM then became the first airline in the world to operate the L-1049C Super Constellation – beating BOAC again. KLM and the Dutch had been underestimated. KLM never looked back and as it now approaches its 100th birthday, it remains the elder statesman of the air – alongside Qantas.

Imperial's Dutch rival – 'the KLM' – was simply brilliant at what it did.

'Speedbird' – Defining a Brand

Imperial's machines had been labelled with the 'Speedbird' legend, which had been created in 1932 by the designer Theyre Lee-Elliot as a corporate logo for

C Class alights.

Imperial Airways. This 'winged' illustrative device, with its upwards tilted 'nose' or 'beak', was an emotive, yet strong piece if imagery that not only captured the era, but endured across the following four decades as a corporate logo. Created at the height of the Art Deco years and the great era of poster art, typeface and logo design developments, the 'Speedbird' design represented an evocation of flight in a blend of bird-like design and industrial strength, yet of minimalist style. Lee-Elliot's design may have been influenced by the earlier, pre-1920s avant-garde works of Edward McKnight Kauffer.

The Speedbird emblem was plastered all over Imperial's marketing and upon the noses of its aircraft. BOAC adopted not just the emblem, but a 'Speedbird' call-sign for its flights and even today, British Airways pilots use 'Speedbird' as their identifier. The emblem itself was slightly altered for the 1960s, with a larger 'wing' and sharper nose or 'beak'. BOAC's famous blue and gold livery made the most of Imperial's logo. Lee-Elliot's emblem lasted into the 1980s as part of the British Airways livery, but was then superseded by a stylised derivation of a 'Speedwing' that had a tenuous visual link to the original emblem and its design.[9]

With the arrival of Shorts C Class flying boats and Speedbird-branded DH Albatross machines as the Frobisher Class, Imperial's late-1930s routes and service offering was extensive, reliable and frequent, and had become a true servant of the Empire and the men and women of it.

Whatever its British attitudes and wings of elegant Empire aura, Imperial Airways was a major airline and a major national instrument. The Imperial C Class flying boat operations were the best and most successful in the history of the flying boat – even if there were thirty-three stops en route from England to Australia in 1938! From its behaviours and beliefs came BOAC – then cast into a fast changing world. Much that was good and bad, was passed down from Imperial to BOAC.

Chapter 4

A Great Corporation:
BOAC and the Politics of Power

There was a curious paradox at play in the tale of BOAC and its VC10 story. On the one hand BOAC dictated what they needed and wanted, and yet when presented with their desire, criticised it publicly, only then to launch the chosen instrument with a massive global advertising and PR campaign across fifty countries (including Times Square in New York) the likes of which airline customers and passengers alike, had not previously seen.

In the early 1960s, BOAC had even commissioned the writing of its own corporate history and employed a respected figure to research and frame the BOAC story. *Speedbird the Complete Story of BOAC* was brilliantly written by Robin Higham and constituted the most thorough and forensic telling of the events that shaped BOAC – albeit mostly from BOAC's viewpoint.[1] Yet it was not ever published as intended, and it took the author twenty-six years to see the book in print by other means. This was because successive BOAC leaders vetoed or delayed its publication. Such were the political issues, legacies and personalities that had created the story. It seems incredible that a corporate body – albeit a nationalised one, then privatised, should apparently suppress the telling of its own story. But as we now know, there were things best veneered over in case the wretched public found out.

Before all that happened, shifting sands were at play – as ever in the political and corporate world.

The British Overseas Airways Corporation, originally correctly shortened as B.O.A.C., but latterly framed as BOAC (yet seemingly never, Boac, unlike QANTAS becoming termed as Qantas), was, like most official corporations, a melange of issues and agendas. On the positive side there was vision, strength and employee 'family' pride in working for a great national entity. On the negative side there were management hierarchies, egos, vested interests and agendas, there was also a confusing mixture of outcomes of corporate decisions made by committees and their compromises of thinking and behaviour. BOAC's early board all had to face the issue of interference from the State and its Civil Service political puppets. All of which meant, that by 1958, BOAC was like a car designed and funded by a committee – a disjointed amalgam of legacies and ideas that was going to need help, or it might fail to proceed.

Proof positive of this actuality, was the aircraft fleet mix operated by the company and the greatly multiplied costs inherent within such equipment and its operation. BOAC then compounded the problem by ordering the 707 and the VC10 amid a fleet of Comet 4s; turbine-powered, but propeller-driven Bristol Britannias; piston-powered Douglas DC-7Cs, Handley Page Hermes and remnants of other 'stop-gap' machines. BOAC's ageing fleet of Lockheed Constellation, Douglas DC7 and Boeing 377 Stratocruiser equipment, that were often four-engined upon departure and three-engined upon arrival, amid their massive associated operating costs, would slowly be withdrawn as their operating advances were undermined by progress in design and the demands of new airways across the world. Yet, in even in 1955, the prop-versus-jet quandary had *still* not been resolved by BOAC's managing board.

Post-war BOAC retained large flying boat operations until 1950 – even as it was entering the Comet 1 jet age. Indeed, BOAC spent money on new flying boats – the Solent Class – and on a base and Terminal at Southampton, where, on 31 March 1948, the Sandringham Class flying boat, G-AJMZ *Perth*, alighted with twenty-one passengers on a service from Iwakuni, Japan. This was a significant long-haul achievement that few airlines could match. BOAC was rightly proud of its post-war continuation of the large flying boat service, but in just a few years, the large flying boat would be forgotten by the world's airlines and by BOAC itself, despite some British minds insisting that spending the money developing the Saunders Roe SR 33 'Princess' was a viable 1950s strategy.

BOAC purchased three Boeing 314 Clipper flying boats from Pan American Airways, these were not part of the wartime lease-lend mechanism and BOAC purchased them for cash. These giant Boeings, as the first Seattle company machines procured by the airline, had to be serviced back in America at Baltimore after every few flights on the West African service. It was an expensive and risky undertaking, but highly successful.

A joint Imperial Airways and 'Qantas Empire Airways' (QEA) – as a Qantas corporate subset designed to service the link the two ends of the UK-Australia route from hubs at Singapore and Brisbane – was founded in 1934 with Imperial and Qantas owning 50/50 shares in the venture.

At Rose Bay in Sydney, the Imperial/QEA services would terminate the flying boat route from London. QEA (Brisbane) S23 C Class flying boats would operate a reliable shuttle service for nearly four years prior to the outbreak of war, and continue through wartime events until the late 1940s. Rose Bay would see QEA lose two C Class machines in crashes in two months, in October and November

1944, when the S23, VH–ABB *Coolangatta,* crashed on 11 October and S33, VH–ACD, which was lost on 18 November. Rose Bay was not a happy little cove that month.

The real roots of BOAC's long-haul network surely stem from the Imperial Airways HP 42/43 and Shorts S23 C Class flying boat operations. From those wonderful days when routes were carved out of soil and sky to Africa, Asia, and beyond, came the BOAC network that Constellations, Comets and then VC10s would ply. There, the die for our modern services was cast. Today, few travellers realise that the 'everyday' airline services were carved out by pioneers in the toughest flying conditions.

From as early as 1940, BOAC inherited the old Imperial Airways legacy of being an airline and a national instrument of policy, prestige and delivery of colonial mail and rule, under a government framed 'State' remit, this meant that BOAC was a beast with several personalities and perhaps even with disorders. In 1943, BOAC's second chairman was The Hon. Clive Pearson, who wrote to the Air Minister Sir Archibald Sinclair to try and define exactly what was BOAC's real remit? Was it to create its own airline service, or was it to follow specific government edicts? BOAC after all, could not take private, commercial decisions, yet as a paradox, was not a *direct* instrument of what, at the time, was called 'Service of the Crown'. Would the Air Ministry be a thorn in BOAC's side or a back room supporter? *Who* really was in charge?

In 1943, BOAC also had to operate had-in-hand with the new RAF Transport Command and ignore opportunities to build up its own experience as an actual airline – in the knowledge that the American airlines were working to frame all possible opportunities as soon as the war ended. In America, civil aviation dominated military transport aviation. Whereas in Britain, the RAF dominated what had been Imperial's civil operations as they became wartime BOAC affairs. In March 1943, such was the confusion over BOAC's operating remit that its chairman and its three senior directors all resigned. A new board was announced which included two interesting appointments, one being the head of the retail grocers, Marks and Spencer, the other being the leader of the National Union of Railwaymen. However, a viscount of the realm, Viscount Knollys, was appointed as BOAC's new chairman. It was a strange selection for the non-airline and air-minded people; the focus was on finance and set themes, and perhaps not on making the most of the hard won wartime operational experience that BOAC had already accrued. Inside BOAC were men (and women) who had rare airline operating experience on a global route network, yet these employees were now to be commanded by a group of figures emanating from the hierarchical British class and social structures stemming from a pre-war era. There was little operational airline experience at the top of the new board and senior management – although one member had helped run the wartime ATA ferry pilots organisation – but that person was a woman! Something of a shock to the all-male 'old guard'.

Such were the issues facing BOAC and its structure.

But there were men of huge experience within BOAC, who, as they rose through the ranks, guided the day-to-day operations of the airline's vast network. Men like Ross Stainton, who began his career with Imperial Airways in 1933 as a lowly trainee station officer in Africa. He ended it as a senior BOAC figure and, as 'Sir' Ross, having proudly turned BOAC's operations and cabin services into the highest class Blue-Riband product, even more so on the Super VC10 services which were recognised as the highest quality offering in the market at the time. Once again the VC10 would be touched by the hand of Imperial. Another BOAC luminary who emerged from early days at Imperial Airways was Campbell Orde. Such men were steeped in 'air' experience. Whatever the prejudices of the Imperial or British attitude, there were men amongst its ranks who performed amazing, sometimes incredible feats, and led lives of service and utter professionalism. Further names of men like O.P. Jones, J. Kelly Rogers, G.H. Easton and many more abound.

In 1945, the government created a new Air Minister in the form of Major General Ernest Lord Swinton, who then created the Swinton Plan for BOAC's post-war operations. As part of this, BOAC would lose some of the routes that it had built up in wartime. These routes would be handed over to new start-up airlines.

BOAC was a nationalised mechanism that began its true peacetime life in 1946 – as a result of decisions taken in 1939 when the services of Imperial Airways were absorbed into the war machine. By 1945, BOAC emerged from its early wartime years rich in experience, but cash-poor, and operating a bizarre and expensive fleet mix with a huge costs base. BOAC had seven types of seaplane or flying boat, and ten types of landplane. Most of these machines, except the American DC-3, were uneconomical to operate. Other airlines were also securing proper, economically effective airliners. BOAC would have to abandon flying boats and cobbled-up converted airframes and get hold of some 'proper' airliners surely?[2]

BOAC needed a strategic, defined, and informed policy as an airline business. But such policy was a long time coming.

In 1946, the new Civil Air Transport Act under a new Labour Government and a new Air Minister, Lord Winster (who had succeeded Lord Swinton), created the nationalised airline transport structure. BOAC soon received a British Government grant of just over nine million pounds – a staggering sum given that Britain was bankrupt after six years of war. By 1951–1952, BOAC's State funding had declined to £1.5million. BOAC moved towards commercial solvency and did not, for some years, need to take up its grants. But the truth was that BOAC was a symbol of sovereignty and power in a waning world of British influence and a declining Empire. By 1959, BOAC employed 20,000+ and had a route network approaching 100,000 miles serving six continents with hundreds of daily departures. Soon, with the VC10, BOAC would offer an unbroken, BOAC operated round-the-world service.

In 1946, the brilliant Air Marshal Sir Wilfrid Freeman framed the domestic and intra-European British airline that was itself a corporation – British European Airways Corporation, known as BEA. Lord Douglas of Kirtleside was BEA's first chairman. He had been co-pilot on the Handley Page Transport Ltd 'airline' flight of 2 September 1919, he had also held British commercial pilots licence No.4. In 1940 he contributed to the plan of the Second World War.

There were many links between the two corporations post-1946, yet Caribbean and South American services from Britain were originally given to British Latin American Airlines Ltd, which changed its name to British South American Airways (BSAA). BSAA, with its unfortunate fleet of unlucky Lancastrians and Tudor airliners, was an airline soon to be subsumed into the great power that was BOAC itself. But it would be 1958 before BOAC resumed a direct link from London to South America – an often forgotten part of the BOAC and VC10 stories.

BOAC, like London Heathrow Airport itself, was a state-within-a-state and strong leadership was required. Even at its start, its fleet was old, mixed, hopelessly uneconomic and largely inefficient. In 1948 BOAC had forty-seven overseas bases or stations, and operated ten types of landplane and seven types of seaplane, each with their own training, maintenance, crew, and route costs.

A Question of Class

Post-1945, the old elitist days of First Class only travel would be swept aside. 'Tourist' or Second Class travel at high speed on long routes would become the great demand – and those within British aviation and the 'White Paper' that framed BOAC's remit, predicted such.

As an instrument of British national will, by government edict, BOAC had to use the national exchequer to fund its operations – irrespective of profit or loss. Interest, fees, airframe amortisation, fuel, fleet, crew and staff costs presented an accounting nightmare within the multi-layered behemoth of BOAC. Workforce and management were also both mired in previously established behavioural psychologies. Change and change management would come to BOAC at the expense of time and money. BOAC was founded with finance that was a State loan and indeed, it had paid that loan back by late 1955. But from 1956 the costs of fleet re-equipment, the delays of the Comet disasters and postponed introduction of the Britannia, the costs of interim measures, all allied to other mounting global operating costs, meant, that by 1957, BOAC needed money. This arrived in the form of government-sanctioned monies that were at the behest of a minister – who may or may not have any knowledge of business or airline transport affairs, especially if he was a lowly MP elevated to a position of temporary ministerial power. BOAC was a Treasury funded machine, or if your politics were different, a monster of a corporation.

Yet unlike many other major world airlines, who were members of bodies such as the International Civil Aviation Organisation (ICAO) or the International Airline Transport Association (IATA), BOAC had a government appointed management team led from a ministerial and governmental edict at Ministry of Transport (latterly Ministry of Aviation) behest, and handed down to a board – the leadership or Chairmanship of which was appointed by government itself. Then came another managing director and a subset of directors beneath that station. BOAC was, in 1939, Britain's first nationalised major industrial concern (long before the railways) and despite later claims in Parliament that the running of such industries on a day-to-day basis could not be subject to interventions from MPs of the House of Commons, the truth was that the management of the airline, the accounting procedures and the strategic decisions of the airline, were influenced by, and often set by, government itself.

In 1949, faced with the need to work with the overseas airlines of newly independent or emerging nations (through which Imperial's and thus BOAC's route had run pre-war), an act of Parliament to create BOAC Associated Companies Ltd, was passed. This allowed BOAC to work with, and invest in, smaller foreign airlines – creating the forerunner of partner deals and code share agreements, but above all, creating local 'feeder' services and smoothing traffic rights along the routes of the tit-for-tat global airline agreements mechanism. From the Caribbean to Africa and Asia, BOAC took shares in local regional airlines, some of which would make huge losses.

It was Sir Miles Thomas, DFC, who helmed BOAC from 1949 to 1956. He tried to clarify the working or operating behaviours and the accounting practices of this strange many-headed corporation. Tough new accountants were brought in under a lead figure, a 'Comptroller' – Basil Smallpiece (latterly to be knighted). Smallpiece would, in later years, actually run BOAC as managing director. Thomas was behind the idea of a re-engined BOAC Comet 5 specification – re-engined with Rolls-Royce Conways, but a new engine would not change Comet's small cabin (Comet 5 did not appear). Despite this, Thomas, as with much of BOAC and much of the industry, still favoured the future as propeller based – with the Britannia proponent. The brilliant Sir Peter Masefield, being a mid-1950s figurehead of that large turbo-prop 'club', stated to the media: 'We believe in turbo-props.' Yet as the paint was still fresh on the Britannia 312, he would try to promote the A.E.

Russell design team's Bristol 200 short-medium-range tri-jet design against the de Havilland proposal which would become the Trident. Further comments in the debate suggested that airlines and airliner manufacturers were going with the jets as a result of necessity rather than desire.

Jet costs still frightened accountants.

In the summer of 1958, even the Americans were still debating the turboprop or jet conundrum and Lockheed's newest iteration of the Electra line was poised. For the 1958 Albert Plesman lecture, the Douglas Company's Engineering Vice-President, Arthur E. Raymond, categorically suggested that there was a future for a short-haul prop-liner and a future for the longer ranged jetliner.[3] Each delivered its own benefits in kind in its own operating circumstances – so claimed Raymond.

Perhaps it was the combined failure of the Comet 1 and the brilliant success of the Viscount, which created the temporary in-passing fetish for the turboprop, notably the four-engined turboprop. The sliding graph of operating costs versus speed, and the economies of soon-to-arrive 'high-bypass' turbofans, would surely render all but the smaller, twin-turboprop feeder liner redundant. However, in 1958, it was Britannias, Vanguards and 400mph+ Electras one minute, and yet 707s, DC-8s and Tridents the next. The onward march of the urgent turbojet and then the turbofan would eclipse the millions of pounds and dollars sunk into turboprop sales pitches.

Had five years been wasted?

Then came the French and their jet Caravelle. The British, however, perhaps stung by the loss of the V1000, paused before taking up the VC10. Into the gap leapt the Americans. All this and more forced Douglas to create a Boeing 707 lookalike competitor and then forced the British and BOAC to demand a machine to perform firstly a different task, and then a similar transatlantic task. The VC10 and then the Super VC10 would have to answer *both* demands. No other airliner has ever had to bridge two operational arenas and be tasked with succeeding in both, yet criticised by the airline that demanded such abilities.

BOAC, from 1939 to 1958, expanded massively. In 1938 Imperial had carried 68,000 passengers, in 1958 its successor, BOAC, carried 480,000. Change was massive in its scale and soon, so was BOAC and the number of airliners it required.

BOAC Buys British

Would BOAC support British industry and its workers by ordering British airliners? It might, but political requirements and marginal seats in key constituencies were hardly the stuff of an airline – unless that airline was taxpayer-funded and ordered about by a political animal of ministerial rank. Such considerations would affect the fate of the Vickers VC7 airliner variant. And what if a new British Government decided to stop funding the development of the RAF's new jet transport future – the V1000 itself? Where would that leave parallel BOAC interest in the VC7 derivative? This was the political and corporate mix post-1951, just as George Edwards (not then a 'Sir') and the team at Vickers were designing the V1000 and VC7 future far beyond the Comet 4's capabilities and far beyond any, as yet unseen rival.

There remained the fact that the big problem for the British aircraft manufacturing companies was the very small home market for their aircraft designs. Any British machine had to have overseas customer appeal, yet within the BOAC and BEA State-sponsored design dictates that focused on British needs, an inherent self-limiting factor was obvious for the British family of airframe makers. Greater numbers than the home airline market could support were required to ensure a profitable production run. The Vickers Viscount leapfrogged the problem and achieved global success, the V1000 and VC7 could have done the same thing.

The structural policy problems were not solely BOAC's fault – the airline was a British Government and Civil Service edict; yet BOAC had in part, had a hand in creating that very landscape and then went on to criticise the airframe it had not only requested, but dictated operating performance requirements for – the VC10 itself.

Meetings between Vickers, BOAC and the British Government took place at this time. Messrs Thomas, Straight and Smallpiece appeared for BOAC; Vickers 'pork-pie' hatted Edwards made his mark. Promises of increased thrust and payload range from the developed Rolls-Royce Conways, as improvements to the VC7 variant of the V1000, were all very well, but BOAC's Smallpiece dealt in the now, and the now was that the VC7 was not what BOAC wanted on transatlantic routes, and only existed on paper. But surely that did not mean that BOAC would put up with new, but small capacity Comet 4s with their range issues, or face the 1960s armed with the Bristol Britannia and its straight, unswept-wings and whirling props, however quiet it was? And were not Boeing promising to enter the jet age with a new large airliner? But, that airliner would be unable to service BOAC's vital cash flow earning African and Asian routes due to its runway performance issues.

Confusion and contradiction reigned – again. The deployment of strategic irrationality seemed too obvious for words.

Then came yet another British general election and with it came a new wave of non-aviation-minded government men and another new minister. The Comet disasters at BOAC, the delays in securing the Comet 4 and the Britannia's engine problems, all piled up alongside the Suez crisis, European uncertainties, and the looming end-of-Empire in Africa and the British dominions. Quietly, the commercial relevance of the aerial links between London, New York, Washington

D.C., Chicago, and the US West Coast, were also lining up as soon to be vital operational and financial issues for BOAC. Competition on long-haul routes from Pan American, KLM, Air France, and the new Lufthansa, was also building.

Sir Miles Thomas resigned from the heavy burden of running BOAC in 1956 – perhaps worn down by the political chicanery required in running a nationalised industry as an airline and being regularly upset from strategic policy decisions and their execution by a revolving door of ministers. There had been five Ministers of Civil Aviation, all of them in the House of Lords from 1945 to 1948 and there were four new Ministers of Transport, all of them in the House of Commons, in six years up to 1958. BOAC itself – up to 1958 – had seven chairmen from its on-paper inception in 1940. Harold Hartley had experience of 'air' via his time at the emerging start-up BEA, d'Erlanger had 'air' experience too, and soon Air Commodore Whitney Straight, MC, would bring military and civilian expertise to the arena as BOAC Managing Director in 1947–1949 and subsequently as chairman in 1949–1951 and executive vice-chairman to 1957. Intriguingly, Straight, an ex-RAF pilot and assistant to the Duke of Kent, was not as 'British' as he appeared – being American-born of 'society' parentage but becoming a naturalised Briton. He was, however, a cousin of C.V. Whitney – a former chairman of Pan American Airways! Was this where BOAC's 'preference' for American airframes stemmed from? Over the next few years, Labour and Conservative Governments would come and go; so too would BOAC leaders and Ministers of Aviation and Ministers of Supply.

In the days of the Imperial to BOAC construction – circa 1938 – Lord Reith had advised freedom from national duties for the new airline – if better aircraft were available from foreign manufacturers, BOAC should be allowed to purchase them. This attitude, of course, conflicted with government decreed edicts about Imperial/BOAC as a national 'instrument'. But British leadership in the 'air' arena should not, said Reith, be solely tied to commercial operations that were self-supporting.[4]

In April 1956, Basil Smallpiece found himself working for a new BOAC Chairman – Gerard d'Erlanger, a man with vital wartime operational aviation experience running the Air Transport Auxiliary (ATA) – yet he would be a part-time chieftain. The board would appear together for just one or two days per month. The board was responsible to the minister and the minister responsible to Parliament. It was not a forensic strategic plan. We can see that structurally BOAC was just like Imperial and like the colonial mindset, British leaders may well have been slow moving and, we have to suggest, slow to adapt and slow to seize opportunity. As such it was little different from many inward-looking management and corporate mechanisms and structures once they have grown large and of superior, self-entitled self-view. The privately funded Vickers of course, under Sir George Edwards, suffered from no such provincial thinking – Viscount, Valiant, and V1000/VC7 proved that.

As BOAC persevered with the Comet 4 on transatlantic routes it was never designed for (a fact so often either hidden or obscured in the narrative then and now), Boeing were rushing into a wider future. British national pride was, however, understandable as BOAC's Captain M. Majendie launched the airline's first scheduled Comet 1 service into the air from London Heathrow in 1952, and the same pride would pertain when the Comet 4 beat the 707 across the Atlantic over five long and difficult years later, but pride had gone before a fall once before and might do so again. The Comet versus 707 transatlantic air race was more about PR puff than actual operating performance and costs. BOAC was 'flying the flag' and inconvenient truths could be veiled by pomp and circumstance.

For the 1950s, BOAC was structured into several internal, route operations divisions as:

(a)   Western routes: USA, Canada, Caribbean, South American
(b)   Eastern routes: Australia, India/Asia, Far East
(c)   Southern routes: West, East, South Africa

The MRE, or 'Medium-range Empire', routes defined the structure and the Far East routings were 'Dragon Routes'.

Until the advent of a cheaper second cabin concept that came into international airline agreement in late 1952, airline cabins were mainly configured to a luxury standard with a 60 inch seat pitch, and for BOAC, specially designed sleeper seats pivoted down into an almost flat recliner. In fact it was American domestic developments that led to the new, no-frills, cheaper 'Coach' standard brand of airline travel. These new cheaper tickets opened up the floodgates to mass US domestic air travel and transatlantic airlines soon realised that they could make more money by putting more seats into their aircraft, and by cutting out the lavish cabin service standards of food and amenities. However, even in the new 'Tourist Class', seat pitch was 36–40 inches – down from 60 inches, yet with plenty of room to stretch out and sleep. It looked a good deal for the new customer base and allowed many more people the opportunity to travel, but in reality it was a closed shop rigged marketing ploy created and agreed by the members of the international airline community via their airline 'club'.

BOAC converted several of its Lockheed Constellations to carry sixty-eight passengers on Tourist Class oceanic runs and the ticket cost of a return flight from London to New York in the new cabin was 'just' £173, which was a massive reduction on the previous cost of £254. Meal services remained of quality and toilets spacious. BOAC even provided complimentary perfume and eau de toilet on board. In hot tropical zones, the smell in the cabin was now more eau de Elizabeth Arden, rather than the eau de armpit of Imperial's sweltering days.

BOAC's revenue shot up once it was able to fit more seats into existing cabins and the seat per mile cost improved. With some ticket prices halving, this – in 1952 – was the gateway to the age of mass travel, however, this was more Second Class, and not yet the true 'Economy Class' that was agreed by the international airlines in 1958 with even cheaper fares and its close-coupled seats of 33–34 inches pitch – which would soon become the industry standard beyond the curtains of the deluxe environment of First Class. Business Class (today's Second Class) had not yet been thought of and would not manifest for decades. But even by the 1960s, the cost of an Economy Class ticket on a BOAC VC10 or 707 service was often more than the annual wage of a working man. It would not be until the 1970s that true mass transit travel, available to all, would become a wide-bodied airliner reality.

At many BOAC stops an ex-Imperial Airways station existed, and when BOAC was born, the only thing that changed was the name on the signage. By 1947–1948, BOAC had a fiscal deficit of a staggering £8million. BOAC, mired in the processes of government, Civil Service and board, lacked KLM-like dynamism, only slowly moving towards rationalisation of its fleet mix and operating practices.

Fast forward to the late-1950s and chaos still seemed to rule in terms of aircraft types and aircraft requirements. In 1953, the true Tourist Class had been agreed as a new revenue earning concept by the international airlines and the services came into being in the summer of that year. BOAC were seating up to seventy passengers in Tourist Class cabins in 749 Constellations and soon its stop-gap fleet of tired DC-7Cs. A new era of travel for the people, not the elite, opened up.

At BOAC the Comet 1s had come and then gone – grounded upon the wings of disaster – the sleek and sound Bristol Britannia had been ordered, but was greatly delayed in its long-haul variant by engine icing issues; second-hand giant Douglas DC-7Cs were quickly procured. BOAC had previously found the US dollars to purchase its own fleet of Boeing Stratocruisers (for which some US airlines received subsidy for operating, due its 'issues'), so furthering the BOAC-Boeing relationship that had started with the BOAC Clipper flying boats at Baltimore.

Boeing 377 Stratocruisers soon plied BOAC Atlantic Blue-Riband routes (yet latterly to be so unwisely sent to work on BOAC African services). Some BOAC Stratocruisers were all First Class 'Monarch' seating only (often all-male), and carried less than forty passengers, other BOAC Stratocruisers launched the new 'Coronet' Tourist Class services to America and had a higher seat-count of up to sixty. Yet the Stratocruisers were afflicted with engine, airframe and aerodynamic issues and became a bit of a blot on Boeing's high-quality reputation; Pan Am suffered four Stratocruiser losses and other operators had incidents.

Across the BOAC global network, huge numbers of spare engines had to be placed to serve the intensive (and expensive) maintenance needs of such large, piston-powered fleets as led by the temperamental Stratocruiser and piston-hungry 'Connies'.

There were also the military-derived airframes that were the Handley Page Hermes and Canadair Argonauts, in fact, a plethora of types in the BOAC stable. The 1950s fleet mix was almost as confusing and expensive as Imperial's had been in 1938. Where was the consistency of strategy, vision, policy and execution for the airline, or those that managed it? In the structure of the corporation's dictated existence from varying and opposing political parties and policies, we might see the root of some of its problems.

British Government Ministers of Transport/Air 1940–1964

1945:	Lord Swinton	1956–1959:	Watkinson
1946–1949:	Lord Winster	1959–1960:	Sandys
1949–1951:	Rees-Williams	1960–1963:	Thorneycroft
1951–1953:	Maclay	1963–1964:	Amery
1953–1954:	Lennox Boyd	1964:	Jenkins
1954–1956:	Boyd-Carpenter		

BOAC's management leadership was appointed by the State:

BOAC Chairmen/CEO/Managing Directors 1940–1964

1941–1943:	Clive Pearson	1949–1956:	Sir Miles Thomas
1943:	Sir Harold Howitt	1956–1961:	Sir Gerard d'Erlanger
1944–1945	Lord Knollys	1961–1964:	Sir Matthew Slattery
1946:	Sir Harold Hartley	1964:	Sir Giles Guthrie
1947–1949:	Whitney Straight		

Note:

1943:	Walter Runciman, as Imperial/BOAC Chairman and Director General Civil Aviation BOAC
1946:	Air Commodore A. Critchley, Director General BOAC
1951–1956:	Sir Basil Smallpiece, Financial Comptroller/Deputy CEO Whitney Straight, Executive Vice Chairman to 1957
1956–1964:	Sir Basil Smallpiece, Managing Director BOAC
1964:	sees Sir Giles Guthrie, appointed to run BOAC

BOAC-BEA Merger in 1954?

In 1974, BOAC merged with BEA to form the 'new' British Airways. Yet the first suggestion of a BOAC-BEA merger had been made as early as 1954 by Sir Miles Thomas. This idea would have solved the problem of BOAC's long haul routes not being integrated into a British domestic and European network. Surely BOAC and BEA could feed each other with passenger traffic. An agreement – not one for merger, but for connecting services – was reached, and BOAC moved its Zurich base to Rome in exchange for ceding rights to BEA in other locations.

When BOAC Chairman Sir Miles Thomas resigned in March 1956, the airline was making a profit, yet still framed by annual tax-payer funded State grants. BOAC was no longer costing the tax payer £8,000,000 a year, but it remained far from cost-effective. The problems with the delays to the consequent BOAC fleet and crew costs created a deficit of £2,700,000 in 1957.[5] Wisely, Thomas had got out before trouble set back in. Yet BOAC was only narrowly failing to reach its sixty-five per cent profitable load factor requirements, but its fleet and operating costs were abnormally diverse and high by any standards and a huge contrast to KLM's lower cost-base. Then came the costs of restarting Comet operations with the revised Comet 4.

Comet 4 Contradiction

History, as it is written, records that the de Havilland Comet design was beyond compare as a world beating revolution as the world's first jet airliner, one that was stymied, not by design problems, but by unexpected structural issues that manifested as the Comet 1 disasters. History also records that after the investigations, Comet 4 entered service with BOAC, beat the Boeing 707 across the Atlantic into commercial service (surely a hollow victory) and went on to an illustrious career as the shining light of British airliner brilliance.

Underneath the nationalistic pride of the Comet 4 there were, however, often conveniently unmentioned issues with the design and operation of it. We should not forget that BOAC divested itself of its entire Comet 4 fleet very quickly indeed – when the airframes were still young. The question was why? The answer was, things had moved quickly on.

Over at KLM, the dynamic Albert Plesman was not so sure that the Comet was so vital to survival, and on this occasion, held back from fleet procurement. Plesman thought the Comet 1's max-range payload and small cabin was of a serious economic and operational issue, and he noted the untested nature of the Comet technology. Fate would provide clarity, and KLM quite happily waited to enter the jet age with the DC-8 nearly a decade later.

In an interview with the author, Group Captain J.C. Cunningham, DSO and two Bars, DFC and Bar, CBE, the great wartime night-fighter and de Havilland test pilot, discussed such issues that he felt, 'the luxury of hindsight' could latterly be used to illustrate.[6] Cunningham would never have criticised de Havilland's or the Comet in public, nor 'reacted' to questioning of the legend, but as a pilot and man of intellect, he knew full well that Comet was flawed, and the issue of its wing slats being removed at prototype stage and the later issues and accidents with the Comet's take-off technique, obscured an aerodynamic truth. Comet's narrow cabin and limited capacity also proved that it was an insular and perhaps incomplete design.

To Cunningham's defence of Comet, Albert Plesman, KLM Royal Dutch Airline's founder and leader, might have argued that the Comet's capacity issues were obvious early on, even in 1957, and were the very reasons why KLM – as one of the world's leading airlines at that time, was prepared to let its competitors rush into Comet orders – had *not* ordered the Comet, thus leaving the prop-driven KLM fleet behind its jet-powered competitors for years, yet with minimal apparent detriment to its popularity or resulting finances.

The brilliant John Cunningham knew what he was about and was correct that the Comet 4 was a fine machine, but even he had difficulty side-stepping the issues and specifically the BOAC- related issues; despite the fact that the Comet had nearly double the thrust-to-weight ratio of an early 707, this was achieved by the Comet being smaller and lighter and thus constrained in its size and range. The Comet 1 disasters and ensuing delays pitched the Comet 4, notably in BOAC guise, into the new 1960s battle of the bigger transatlantic jets. Yet there remained the original early 1950s issues of the Comet's very small, narrow cabin and resultant limited passenger and mail/cargo carrying abilities. Comet 4 still had, despite fuselage extension, limited two-class passenger accommodation. BOAC Comet 4s were rarely configured for the maximum eighty passengers possible and early machines were configured for just fifty-two passengers. Latterly, other major airliner operators struggled to get ninety seats crammed into the longer-bodied 4C variant. In BOAC Comet 4 operations, notably on African and Asian routes, these factors would manifest on a regular basis via overbooking, off-loading, lack of availability, and reduced income due to an inability to carry people and freight. BOAC said it made a profit on the Comet 4's seat per mile and revenue-per-tonne costs, but many observers were sceptical.

On Empire route services, notably the prestige run to Johannesburg, via Nairobi, BOAC Comet 4s were configured to have an over-wing cabin zone curtained off, behind which, large mail and freight cages resided. It is anecdotally recorded that on occasion, faced with stranded passengers unable to get a seat on a fully booked Comet 4 service out of Nairobi, BOAC staff removed such freight holds, borrowed three rows of seats from the East African Airways Comet 4 hangar, and bolted them in on a temporary basis! More commonly, Comet 4 could not offer freight consigners the capacity they required for ever-increasing traffic.[7]

John Cunningham correctly noted that the Comet had been given the runway performance to, 'get up and off', as he stated it, from tropical airports. Cunningham had been to Seattle and flown the 707 prototype 367-80, and praised its general flying characteristics, but correctly identified the issues of lack of power and such effect on likely tropical runway performance, and the concerns over asymmetric handling with the wing-pylon mounted engines. But the Boeing was bigger, stronger, and crucially, the cabin was wider and longer than the Comet 4's, and more able to be developed to add passenger and cargo capacity: a 707 could earn more money with four engines than a Comet 4 ever could.

After Comet 1 and its losses, the revised long-range Comet 3 was viable, but BOAC wanted more, so begat the even more delayed Comet 4, which provided service not just for BOAC, but, via the BEA 4B and the 4C variants, several other overseas airlines.

It is said by many, even aviation experts, that in their Caravelle, it was the French who pioneered the idea of mounting a jet engine on a stub or pylon off the back of fuselage, but that is in error – because it was the Germans in 1944, with the FW 283 athodyd research airframe, who first designed such a jet engine layout and mounting configuration.

Whatever the provenance, perhaps BEA really ought to have purchased early Caravelles, or got de Havilland to licence build them (de Havilland's were already supplying the Caravelle's nose section under contract, and Rolls-Royce supplied the engines) and many airline accountants and engineers said so, but the thought of BEA buying an exotic foreign machine was simply too much for the British management minds on BEA's board and within government. Or what about saving five years (on the Trident gestation) and creating a British licence built Caravelle, or even a three-engined Caravelle variant? Would this not have solved many problems very quickly and above all very cheaply? All that de Havilland's would have to have done is brace a central engine into the rear air stairs void, plug in an S-duct fin-based orifice and an exhaust, and the competition (notably the Vickers Vanjet) would have been beaten overnight by an already flying proven airframe tweaked for the 1960s.

The idea had legs and was indeed suggested in 1958 by famed aviation commentator Stanley H. Evans, but it was all far beyond BOAC, BEA, and British minds. Meanwhile, the low-wing loading slippery Caravelle even sold to United Airlines in America and became the defining short-medium-haul tool for many airlines. Latterly, the Caravelle morphed into a JT8D-9 fan jet powered final iteration of Europe's best selling 1960s twin-jet, in total selling 282 airframes.

If the latter, aft-fan engined TWA Caravelle order had progressed, the superb French airliner's undoubted place in history might have been even more significant.

Caravelle could not be procured for BOAC. British airliners were preferred – until it came to ordering the Boeing 707 fleet, but at least that was not French! Such were the attitudes displayed. A little known fact is that the Australians at Trans-Australia Airlines (TAA) got very close to ordering Caravelles for domestic and regional services and it is reputed that only political pressure stopped them doing it – and rival Qantas had decided on prop-driven American Lockheed Electra's for regional use.

But, in 1955, on its first-flight, had the rear-engined, low-sweep angle (20º) winged Caravelle set certain British minds thinking? Could the Caravelle concept be rethought? Time would tell. Vickers of course, had, prior to the Caravelle, previously been researching a rear-engined, twin-engined, jet airliner since 1951 and had mounted a small jet engine off the back of Wellington in 1947.

Meanwhile, even the Russians were announcing twin-jet and tri-jet short to medium-range airliners in the forms of the Tu-134 and Tu-154 series respectively. Both were T-tailed (with tall empennages and large horizontal/elevator surfaces to try and reduce the deep stall risks), they were swept-winged and had good payload-to-range figures, only in wing aerodynamics (with a distinct lack of leading edge devices being apparent) and of poor engine economy, did they lag behind. Such machines provided years of excellent service to the Soviet Union and its satellites.

Some commentators insisted that the Comet 4B/C could, and should, have sold by the 'hundreds', but such a view ignores the constraints of the Comet's cabin economics. By the time the Comet 4C was in full production for other airlines, BOAC had, having insisted that it could rely on Comet 4 to fend off rival airlines and their 707s and DC-8s, suddenly moved on to 707s and then VC10s and sidestepped becoming a major Comet 4C operator. Time and tide had waited for no man, not even de Havilland's oh-so-elegant Comet 4.

BEA had also used a high-density five-across Tourist Class layout in the their Comets – seating ninety-nine passengers and really excelling on routes to Cyprus, Rome and Madrid, despite the fuel-thirsty four-engined Rolls-Royce Avon configuration – even if a Caravelle could have done the same thing on two Avon engines! But that was French and it seems, beyond consideration. If only the Vickers Vanjet two, or three-engined airframe had existed.

Runway Power

Of significance to later events, even at this stage of 1950s design, a pattern was evident: British jet airliners had more power and better runway performance than their American counterparts, and less payload capacity. BOAC's decision to try and use their Comet 4s on the North Atlantic run smacked of confusion – the Comet 4 was not designed for such a route, despite subsequent impressions created by the modified historical narrative. The Comet 4 long-haul runs to Hong Kong or Johannesburg made much more sense, except that the loads accommodated were so small. And did not BOAC now prefer propeller-driven machines like the Britannia anyway?

The dear old Comet, Britain's bright, shiny hope had little hope of competing against Boeing's specifically designed intercontinental machine. It was into this overall toxic fiscal mix that the procurement of the VC10 was about to become another BOAC issue.

The 1950s British Government, via Transport Minister Watkinson, had tried to impose a civil servant upon BOAC's daily management, a Sir George Cribbet, as chief executive. Basil Smallpiece refused to accept such a move and heated debate ensued across the BOAC board. A compromise power structure was devised, yet it was a one that left the civil servant with a great deal of power and the ability to act as d' Erlanger's deputy.

Basil Smallpiece found himself elevated into a new role as BOAC managing director.

Flight magazine's opinion on 27 April 1956, was that the new BOAC management structure now had aviation experience and could work well. But then came the thorny question of BOACs new fleet for the 1960s – be it American or British built? Or American-built with British engines? And what of the now mooted British supersonic project that over-enthusiastic airline people inside and outside the factories and boardrooms said would be in service by 1965? Some sages of the airline business knew better and said so. None other than BEA's Chief Engineer and board member Beverley Shenstone – soon to be a President of the Royal Aeronautical Society (RAeS) stated (to much criticism) that the British supersonic project would take ten, not five years, to materialise and would not enter service until 1975 – and he was proven to be correct. Shenstone (creator of the Spitfire's unique forward-swept twin-axis elliptical wing shape) would latterly be appointed a board director of BOAC and was not alone in his late 1950s argument that the national carrier needed to decide quickly and clearly just which aircraft it was going to support. The whole prop-versus-jet-supersonic argument was a mess, and a point of vacillation. Decisions, far reaching decisions, were needed. Shenstone, a 'foreigner' remember (he was Canadian), yet a friend of Edwards, said so in *Flight* and the national newspapers, to much criticism from 'the establishment'. As so often, he was correct of course, which really got up other peoples' noses.

The corporate water was as clear as mud.

And what about building Boeing 707s in Britain under licence with Rolls-Royce engines? Would that be a good political idea that might override engineering or operational requirements? It *was* actually mooted, but sidestepped.

A Created Confusion?

Comets, Britannias, and confusion reigned. But hang on, said BOAC as a State-sponsored government-influenced, nationalised mechanism; we better have a big four-engined jet! There then came a moment of decidedly poignant irony when, faced with a reality that it would be five years before BOAC could procure a suitable long-range British-designed jet airliner, the government asked Vickers if it could resurrect the V1000/VC7 project! Transport Minister Harold Watkinson had no political choice but to ask Vickers about the chances for a reborn V1000 as a VC7.

Edwards told Watkinson that the V1000 jigs had been destroyed and that the whole thing was finished and done with.

For its 707 order (an on-paper aeroplane), BOAC had spent millions in dollars as a net outflow from the UK Exchequer at a time of vital UK foreign currency and export sales demand. BOAC had fifteen 707s on order by early 1957 – at nearly £50 million. No more foreign currency spending was to be allowed. BOAC's next procurement would *have* to be British. A new airline transport world was being born. Unlike Imperial, BOAC would now have to act with haste, if such a thing was conceivable. The options were the proposed Handley Page HP 97, as a direct derivative of the Handley Page Victor bomber, over which there were design concerns about its T-tail; and the de Havilland development of the Comet 4 with larger wing, and possibly, Conway engines, as a DH118, or a de Havilland DH121 as a civil airframe; or the Vickers Vanjet – as part of the two, three and four-engined jet airframe development family from which a suitable machine could be selected. It was from the Vanjet studies that the VC10 eventually arrived as a design.

Government gave the nod to develop the new BOAC-operated and defined, British designed and built, four-engined jet airliner – a machine for Southern hemisphere routes, *not*, we should note, principally as a lean, transatlantic cruiser for the New York or Los Angeles express runs. Basil Smallpiece was of an opposing mindset and thought that the creation of a British iteration of a 707-type idea was preferable, but he was involuntarily removed from the process due to ill health. Go-ahead was given from the government to Vickers to proceed – not with an immediate firm order, but with a commitment to the machine, and there was also the likely RAF Transport Command order to help. Intriguingly, the Vickers factory lay in Minister Watkinson's constituency of Woking, Surrey, which may or may not have been of advantage.

BOAC looked at Vickers' ideas for the Vanjet and told the government that one of the proposed Vanjet-derived designs would be 'economically appropriate' for the routes they required it for. This was a phrase well worth remembering, as it proves that BOAC knew full well where Vickers were going in design terms, and thus that the subsequent VC10 design concept and highly engineered build quality should not have been a surprise to BOAC in design and operating costs terms.

Numbers Games

Thus, with firm orders from BOAC, the VC10 story was about to begin, but even the act of ordering was beset by BOAC confusion. Were, as BOAC claimed, thirty-five VC10s 'ordered' in January 1958 (with an option for twenty more), with Vickers apparently insisting on such numbers? It seems not.

We rely on Vickers own records, and the report by Vickers' Dr Norman Barfield[8] into the affair, to disprove such erroneous myth. Barfield was clear that Vickers man Edwards had stated that there was 'not' a positive stand to demand an order for thirty-five VC10s, and that this was a discussion number that reflected (and indeed was indicative of) BOAC's own claims that even with its 707 and VC10s as ordered, BOAC had stated that it would not have enough aircraft! So how could 'thirty-five' be a Vickers ploy, as opposed to a defining and to be argued-over number by BOAC. If it said it needed many more airliners, how could BOAC then prevaricate over pre-existing VC10 orders as it did? Vickers contends that there was no 'ultimatum' to BOAC and that increases in 1960s passenger and freight numbers, as predicted in BOAC's own official traffic analysis plan (after a dip in 1959 across BOAC and BEA), led to BOAC's suggestion not just of needing twenty-seven more airframes, but also of finding a way of meeting increasing freight demands – hence the non-passenger VC10 pure-freighter variant that Vickers designed, and the cargo-door equipped VC10 passenger/freight 'combi' – as latterly delivered to EAA and BUA. By 1961, having claimed it had been forced into ordering the VC10; BOAC suddenly upped its VC10 order book and hinted at a larger version!

The paradoxes and internal inconsistencies in BOAC's claims and positions can only provide the observer with evidence of BOAC's allegedly confused and dysfunctional mindset at the time. Internal inconsistencies presented by a party always reveal truths, or otherwise, as found within its behavioural action and subsequent analysis thereof. True, BOAC had the impossible job of balancing the issues of what government had decreed to it, and of rationalising and executing those demands, but BOAC was part of that process and had its own internal strategic contradictions within a mechanism that seemed to come straight out of a management book on how not to do it. It seems that strategic irrationality was deliberately created across the set. Looked at from today, it all seems incredible.

For external opinion on the machinations of BOAC, we can refer to the observations of former aircraft designer and 1950s aviation writer Stanley H. Evans, whose public and private views about BOAC's strategy were scathing. Evans stated: 'I have nothing but abysmal contempt for the technical ignorance of the cohorts who have brought BOAC to such a sorry pass with its deplorable melange of aircraft types. I firmly believe the whole managerial structure of BOAC is archaic in this technological age.'[9]

Derek Wood, the well-known aviation writer, who would go on to write the brilliant, *Project Cancelled*, also stated that the cancellation of the V1000 represented the main cause to result in the effect of the death of the prospects for British airliner manufacturing and sales in the 1960s.[10]

Such BOAC machinations would come back to haunt the VC10 in the mid-1960s. But back at the turn of the decade that such a wonderful piece of industrial design as the VC10 should emanate from so much trouble was a rare highlight. A true 'Speedbird' would soon grace the skies. It would come from England's leafy county of Surrey, yet be born of the true grit of a Tyneside engineering ethos going back decades into the industrial revolution.

Prior to the Second World War, a young engineer named Rex Pierson had joined Vickers – long before his rise to rank as chief designer; post-1945, there would come the genius of George Edwards and his talented team, who would, in less than two decades, produce a broad range of the finest civil and military airframes ever to stem from one manufacturer. Pierson kept Vickers close to the RAF and it paid dividends. Edwards would do likewise. Barnes Wallis was part of Vickers, so too was Supermarine and its Spitfire and post-war jet fighters. From Viscount to Valiant, from the V1000 to the VC10 and to Concorde, Vickers had the glittering future of British aviation in its hands. Yet others – men of less vision – would destroy that golden opportunity as they clung to the U-bend of political and corporate existence beyond the gates of Weybridge. Somehow, the VC10, and then Concorde, would transcend such games of smoke and mirrors. Vickers *would* ascend.

Chapter 5

Vanjet: Design for the Future –
Valiant to VC Series

The long and convoluted Imperial Airways and BOAC narrative formed the roots of the foundation of the VC10 story. But the true plot of the VC10 airframe was shaped in a scenario that is best framed by one word: Vanjet.

The Vickers Vanjet studies were a 1950s series of on-paper jet airliner designs that drew upon the Viscount's brilliance in order to frame a jet future. The process was complicated, but actually took place in just five years. Vickers had tried a jet-powered iteration of their Viscount as early as 1949 when it mounted a Rolls-Royce 'Tay' turbojet in a pod under each (existing) wing of a Viscount airframe. That idea came after Vickers had pondered if two or even four smaller 'Nene' jet engines could be fitted to their Viking airframe on underwing pylons. Prior to that – in late 1945 – the Nene-powered Avro Lancastrian was not quite the first true jet 'airliner' in that it had two of its four piston-powered engines replaced with jets, but never entered service other than giving joyrides. Six jet-converted Lancastrians were built and flown, and they latterly flight tested the Rolls-Royce Avon. But the jet Lancastrian was not a production machine.

Therefore, it can be argued that the Vickers-Armstrongs Nene-powered Viking, allotted the Ministry code of VX 856, soon to be registered G-AJPH, was, upon its first flight on 8 April 1948, Britain's first true jet-powered airliner, even if it was a converted piston-powered wartime airframe.

The Nene Viking was ordered by the Ministry of Supply and took a Vickers Viking airframe and used its great strength to provide a mount for two early Rolls-Royce Nene turbojets, each of 5000lbs/2269Kg thrust. Newly sculpted jet-engine pods were grafted onto the existing wings with minimal local structural changes being required – notably thicker gauge metal skinning to the wings and an added metal skinning to the elevators. A new four-wheel main undercarriage design retracted up into the engine pod (besides the jet pipe), with two short undercarriage 'stub' legs per side. On 25 July 1948, the Nene Viking flew twenty-four passengers from London Heathrow to Paris Villacoublay in 35min 7sec – less than half the normal flight time for a propeller-driven Viking.

From this successful research airframe came Vickers next iteration of the jet future of the airliner; for, by fitting two of the 6,250lb/2,835Kg rated Tay engines – a developed version of the Nene – to an early model Viscount V630 airframe (redundant after Rolls-Rolls managed to uprate the Dart turboprop used by the Viscount and thus permitting an airframe stretch), something that was a major learning step was built. Again the Ministry of Supply was behind the project and the Tay-powered Viscount was designated as a V663. Like the Nene Viking, the Tay Viscount (first flight 15 March 1950) used a twin-stub leg, twin-wheel undercarriage, under each main wing, retracting beside the jet pipe. The Viscount's superb aerodynamic design and strength meant that again, no significant structural upgrades were required for the jet conversion, despite the increased speeds and stresses. Of great note, the slippery Tay Viscount seemed to be faster than the prototype DH Comet 1 – both airframes being flown at the 1950 Farnborough Air Show. The Tay Viscount was used as a research machine, principally for developing a Bolton Paul design for a powered control system that was to be deployed in the Vickers Type 660 bomber – the Valiant. The Tay Viscount was then used to test-fly the world's first electronic flight control signalling system. But the key factor was that in the Vickers Tay Viscount, a capable, high-speed airliner-type airframe came to fruition.

Indeed, the Tay Viscount was the most manoeuvrable, fastest-climbing of the early 1950s jet-converted research airframes. Given that it was based on the 1946 design origins of the Viscount, this speaks volumes for the talents and strengths of the Viscount product. Such strengths would manifest in the Vanjet studies that became the VC10. And a quick look at the 1960s Boeing 737 design, specifically at the engine wing-pod design, reveals that the Tay Viscount was an eerie precursor of the little Boeing's form. But something new, a new shape was now required.

Rear Engines and Clean Wings?

Why rear-mounted engines? Surely the lowest drag was to be achieved by burying the engines in the wing roots, as had been suggested by the Comet, the V1000, and would be seen on the Vulcan, Valiant and Victor? But the wing root location also gave rise to complex, but solvable structural issues, cabin noise and potential risks from fire, and fuel tank proximity in the event of engine explosion or crash landing – or so said arguing theorists in each camp!

So design fashion soon favoured the 'podding' of engines – either slung under the wing off pylons, or on a short pylon-stub wing at the rear of the fuselage, a la Caravelle. Vickers decided to pursue the rear-mounted engine pylon-stub wing configuration. The reason for this were the significant adverse drag rises and losses in wing lift coefficient that hanging the engines off the main wing in underslung pylons gave rise to. Engine pods and their pylons disrupted airflow over the leading edge and created 'plumes' of displaced and disturbed airflow around and over the local area. Any leading edge devices would have their function interrupted by the pylons, and trailing edge flaps would need to have gaps in their area to allow for jet exhaust from the podded engines. Above all, an unnecessary rise in drag, and a drop in 'span lift distribution' efficiency were the vital demerits of the under-wing pylon/pod configuration. Engines on the wing also directed thrust, vibration, noise and distress onto the rear fuselage skin and windows – all of which could be felt and heard in the cabin. 'Buried' engines, as in the Comet and Valiant, were not immune from such effects either.

But American designers insisted that engines slung off the wings were much safer in a crash than rear-mounted engines and fuel lines. But were they correct? Would big, underwing-mounted jet engines, placed so close to the wing, really decide to conveniently 'break off' cleanly in a fire or ground impact, and get their hot and dangerous parts away from the airframe? This was what American designers believed, but they were proved on occasion to be incorrect; big, hot and heavy jet engines hanging off the wings were likely to smash into the wings and rupture the main fuel tanks in those wings, or spray hot turbine parts onto the wing tanks – resulting in a fire and structural failures of the wings towards the wing root. In many examples, including the BOAC Boeing 707 fire at Heathrow in 1969, the British Airtours 737 in 1987 at Manchester, and the British Airways Boeing 767 fire at Las Vegas in 2015, the exploding wing-mounted engines created the subsequent fuel tank-fed fires and airframe damage. So the claim that wing-mounted engines were safer in a fire, or a crash landing, was proven in most circumstances to be a myth. And surely, a correctly designed rear-mounted engine in a reinforced rear 'cradle' was much stronger and such engines might not break through the fuselage or snap off. Only in the circumstance of in-flight fire and engine separation could such wing-mounted engines be deemed to be 'safer' – provided they did not rupture and ignite the wing fuel tanks as they burned or fell off!

Some designers argued that, just as with closely-paired wing root mounted engines, any paired or closely aligned rear engines could have adverse effects upon the neighbouring engine in the event of turbine blade breakage or main turbine compressor burst. Surely, adequate armour plating and firewall design could lower the risks of such possibilities? And at least they were not inches from a main fuel tank.

Nevertheless, a wing/engine design configuration debate raged in the 1950s. Paradoxically to the argument, while the 707 and DC-8 might have wing-pylon mounted engines, the 727 and the DC-9, from the same manufacturers, and their previous pylon preferred certainties, did not.

Boeing had deployed German research findings into swept-wings and pylon or podded engine layouts into the B-47 bomber, which featured the first major iteration of a 35° swept-wing airframe powered by underwing podded engines. It looked like a huge success, but the drag-rise from the pods and the lift-loss penalties were considerable for the B-47, with Boeing wind tunnel data indicating notable losses in span lift distribution. The loss of span lift distribution efficiency was said to result in a denuded efficiency figure and the engine pods created eighteen per cent of the entire airframe's total parasitic drag figure.[1] And surely speed and range would be compromised by such drag rise and lift loss as seen with underwing podded engines? There were also in-service structural issues with the wing. If Boeing was going to repeat the configuration for the 707, a little learning would have to be applied. Indeed, Boeing had to devote large amounts of resources to fine tuning the 707s engine pylon design; for the DC-8, Douglas had to take several bites at the design apple, with major design modifications being made during series production to solve drag issues stemming directly from the wing aerofoil and pylon and pod design combinations.

Vickers decided that the aerodynamic losses associated with wing-pylon mounted engines, particularly in terms of lift coefficient, were far too serious for an airliner design for which the key need was extra lift to deal with difficult runway environments. To that end, Edwards was initially said to be very keen on retaining

VICKERS VANJET

Vanjet Studies.

the Valiant and V1000 style wing root engine layout with its exceptionally beneficial aerodynamic advantages, but a clean sheet and a new design solution was to prevail. Such were the factors and choices as to how and why Vickers eschewed the 707 and DC-8 style of engine-mounted engines, abandoned the wing root engine layout, and pursued the VC10s expertly designed 'clean wing' configuration. Such expert design work would have much lower drag than wing-mounted pylon-pod engine 'barnacles', and also deliver noise reduction in the cabin.

The demanding VC10 specification lift-coefficient needs drove the decision to put the engines at the back and left the wing to deliver as much lift as could be generated.

Teutonic Design Ideas

As previously stated, the first known suggestion of an externally rear-mounted jet engine (on stub wing/pylon) came from Hans Multhopp's 1944 design studies in Germany for the Focke-Wulf FW283 athodyd-powered jet airframe; however, that machine was not built, but its designer was seized and taken to London in May 1945, spent time at the RAE Farnborough was then to be gifted to American aviation under Operation Paperclip. Multhopp was the creator of the T-tail, swept-winged fighters, rear-mounted jet engines, and 'lifting-body' research. At Farnborough, Multhopp, and colleague Martin Winter, designed a swept-winged interceptor which the subsequent EE. Lightning very closely resembled.[2]

The Dornier concern had devised fuselage and wing-mounted jet engine pylons and pods in 1943, and as with Multhopp's works, such ideas were not wasted by the Allies.

However, we can, beside the DH Comet 1, evidence Vickers 1940s studies into jet airline design as the origins of British jet airliner success and rear-mounted engines. Perhaps, somewhat aping Multhopp's 1944 FW 283 athodyd design, with its rear engines on fuselage mounted pylons, Vickers had designed a rear-engined jet airframe in the form of a pilotless remotely-controlled bomber project entitled SP.2 in 1951. Of note, the company had earlier mounted a small jet engine on a stub pylon from the rear fuselage of a Wellington bomber in 1947. Proof positive then that, from immediate post-war days, Vickers were thinking of a wider future and rear-mounted engines. The completion, in late 1949, of the Tay Viscount underlines the point, because from thoughts of the Tay Viscount came Vickers design proposals for more advanced jet airliners – rear-engined ones.

The Vickers Commercial, or 'VC' series, saw the Vickers Wellington-based Viking airliner cited as the VC1, the Viscount as the VC2 and a VC3 stemming from a developed Varsity proposal which was not made. In 1946 came the Vickers Commercial VC4 – a study into a potential transatlantic civil jet airframe – which although never made, put down some early research findings. In 1951 came the VC5 as a projected long-range passenger variant of the Valiant V-bomber and in 1952 came a suggested BEA medium-range version as the VC6; neither being proceeded with. The legacy of these designs manifested in a V1000-based VC7 derivative, which died in 1956 with the V1000 project.

Due to the impending Douglas DC-8 and DC-9 numerical branding, Vickers sidestepped these numbers and its next actually produced 'VC' would be the VC10; somewhat confusingly a design that stemmed from the 'Vanjet' studies which had to some extent mirrored the VC2 origins – the Viscount. Of interest, a reverse-engineered, scaled-down VC10 known as the VC11 as a proposed medium-haul Vanjet reiteration, was mooted in 1959–1960, which was in effect Vickers last project (stillborn) prior to BAC amalgamation in 1960.

Little known is that Vickers had, in 1952, devised an idea for a small or 'little' twin-jet of fifty to seventy seats potential, for a specific and difficult airline requirement – that of short, regional, or inter-State flights in Australia by domestic airlines. It was a step on from the jet-powered Viscount and its potential was later mirrored in the success of the similar Fokker F28 airliner – notably in Australia.

A 'Little Jet' from Down Under

As in Africa, Australia had difficult operating runway requirements (hot temperatures and short tarmac strips) and large payload capacity needs. Could a high-lift wing, twin-jet be cheaply built and sold to the Australians for around £500,000 per machine? Vickers design team called this idea the 'Little Jet', and in it lies a wider context that mirrored themes within the 'Vanjet', for the 'Little Jet' needed a clean, thin-section wing for better runway performance in the outback heat and for high-speed short sector timings, and that meant rear-mounted engines and perhaps a T-tail. Was this the gateway to subsequent thoughts? The likely increase in jet turbine size and front-fan compressor design was soon realised to be the death-knell of the wing-root buried jet engine. New turbofans would be large and have fan blades rotating in their inlet airflow 'mouths' and rear compressor, and even 'aft fan' sections. There would only be three places that they could be mounted on an airframe – above or below the main wing on pylons, or hung off the tail. These were the combined factors that led to Vickers studying the rear-engined jet. The Caravelle was being designed at the same time (1953–1955), but it relied on a big wing area and low-wing loading for its lift coefficient – not on a panoply of leading edge and trailing edge lift devices. Neither was it T-tailed; it was, however, uniquely, rear-engined.

The Vickers Vanguard was BEA's new short/medium-range tool, designed and delivered as requested, and yet now BEA was touting around the British aircraft manufacturers for a similarly sized regional jet it had eschewed when it requested the Vanguard in the first place! Engineering men inside BEA – such as Beverley Shenstone – were powerless to stop what became the Trident's re-scaled downsize, the only option being to resign, which would be a high price to pay. So the development of a smaller British twin-jet or tri-jet of fifty to seventy seats was fraught with layer upon layer of unintended consequences. Bizarrely, Trans-Canada Airlines (TCA), forerunner to Air Canada, made the most of its 'winterised' special edition Vickers Vanguards and the 139-seat stretched Vanguard II model with a weight of 141,000lbs. BEA ordered six such airframes – labelled as Type 951s, but TCA even operated its near 2,000miles range Vanguards on long-haul Canadian routes. We might wonder in hindsight if BOAC could not have persuaded Vickers to create a long-haul extra-fuel tankage Vanguard for a BOAC long-range Vanguard serving London-Rome-Cairo-Nairobi-Salisbury-Johannesburg by 1959, as a Britannia alternative.

Hunting, de Havilland, Bristol and Handley Page, were all creating proposals for a small, fifty to seventy seat jet airliner with the potential to be stretched to a medium-range 100 seater. Naturally Vickers, having supplied BEA's Vanguards, wanted the business. So Vickers began to think about just such an airliner – one not so dissimilar from recent 'Little Jet' ideas, and which would become the two-engined and three-engined variable task Vanjets before the BOAC requirement would dominate, and Vickers would leave the regional or intra-European twin and tri-jet of BEA formula for others to frame. Curiously, in 1959, a VC11, as a down-scaled post-VC10, would be a strange, reverse-engineered suggestion for the BEA regional jet, but it was abandoned as Vickers went for the BOAC long-haul order and amalgamation of the industry saw other projects given preference in the wheeling and dealing that created the British Aircraft Corporation in 1960.

Advanced Projects Office

From Vickers SP2 and 'Little Jet' sketches, circa 1952–1953, came plans for such a jet airliner with a swept tail, and from that, in early 1955, came sketches for having the axial-flow jet engines (Rolls-Royce Avons) mounted at the rear – in the fashion of the pioneering Caravelle that would arrive from Sud Aviation in Toulouse in 1955. From these plans came an idea that the twin-engined version might serve BEA, and a three-engined version (the third being a centrally mounted, fin-intake S-duct configuration) to serve BOAC – although in the end the tri-jet would become a BEA context and the BOAC suggested airframe be given four engines. The early sketches (see below) form the basis of the futuristic Vickers Advanced Projects Office civil jet thinking. Soon, a Viscount-base was discarded, and the larger fuselage of the new Vanguard substituted as the base unit. Here arrived, in 1954–1956, the true 'Vanjet' studies.

In a drawing dated 11 June 1956, a Viscount fuselage was extended by 40ft, mated to a Vanguard wing and carried four Rolls-Royce Verdon engines. A Mk1A version carried 'slipper' wing-mounted fuel tanks. Next came versions using the Vanguard fuselage, and by Drawing Number 79924, a swept-wing of Valiant provenance had been added to the design. At one stage the thought of using the main wing from the Supermarine Scimitar was mooted (Supermarine being a Vickers subset). But a more advanced and more expensive version was mooted in Drawing Number 79925 when a completely new 35° swept-wing was envisaged. Before long, early-model 'Conway' turbofan engines were suggested, deleting the axial-flow Avon and adding a significant performance boost and the possibility of more than seventy-five seats in the cabin allied to the medium-range payload formula. By this time, swept main wing and swept vertical and horizontal tail surfaces were set. Some iterations had mid-mounted tailplanes as in the forthcoming Caravelle, one had a T-tail and another had the tailplane mounted rather vulnerably underneath the rear engines. Cabins were seen as four-abreast, and a unique combined four/five abreast stepped configuration as ever-increasing capacity options. Rear airstairs were also suggested, and the twin and tri-jet Vanjet concepts had the air of real, tangible success.[3]

More Australian and Canadian Suggestions?

As the two and three-engined variants firmed up in the Vickers drawing office in 1956, the company had talks with not just BOAC and BEA, but also with existing Viscount customers such as Trans-Canada Airlines (TCA) and with Trans-Australia Airlines (TAA). Of significance, Canada's TCA was a Vickers customer and talked closely with the Vickers design team when 'winterising' Viscounts and Vanguards for Canadian operations, as well as suggesting new ideas. TCA had been instrumental in selling the Viscount in America. Canada also had its own manufacturing subset, Vickers Canada Ltd, as well as Avro (A.V. Roe) Canada. On the other side of the globe, Australia's TAA had previously approached Vickers with an idea for a 'super' Viscount – a machine with a longer fuselage mounted on a Viscount wing. (The Vickers Vanguard and the Lockheed Electra both might qualify as super-Viscount themes.) Such a machine would add payload on difficult Australian domestic routes. Without realising it, TCA's ideas, and then TAA and its Jim Dailey, who proposed ideas to Vickers, had in fact presaged the Vanguard and a developed Viscount/Vanguard concept – maybe even one with jets.

BEA's chief engineer, the influential Canadian, Beverley Shenstone (whom had been very well known to Vickers after they had offered him their top design post in 1946, had been close to the Viscount and Vanguard designs, and up to 1946, had worked at the top of Canadian aviation and in Canada's Government), was also closely involved in these design lineage steps. Developing the Vanguard was in hand – but giving it jets came a bit later. New thoughts were required.

Of interest, an article in *New Scientist,* on 9 April 1959, categorically cited BEA's chief engineer, Beverley Shenstone, as providing design guidance to the use of the T-tail configuration in the DH Trident and the Vickers VC10. Shenstone believed in tail-mounted engines and the consequent T-tail design and persuaded de Havilland to accept it, and Vickers to look at the concept's advantages. His private correspondence with Stanley Evans and others in the industry at the time, further evidences that Shenstone was a major influence behind the scenes towards the T-tail configuration gaining ground for the Trident and the Vanjet/VC10. He had, of course, been very close to Edwards and his team during the Viscount development. So Shenstone appears to be a VC10 sub-influence, but we might suggest that George Edwards (initially favouring wing root-buried engines) was getting there anyway without Shenstone's missionary work!

Australia's Mr Dailey also told Vickers that TAA would be considering Douglas DC-8s in order to 'keep up', which must surely have flagged up a warning at Weybridge, as well as reminding everyone about the potential of the V1000 project.[4] Did it not prove that 'Little Jet' had had potential – as its progeny, the Vanjet might?

Other major airlines were in conversation with Vickers about its Vanguard as jet derivatives. The whole 'Vanjet' project was beginning to take on a viable commercial potential. On 25 June 1956, Vickers' Mr Lambert replied to an enquiry (by telex no less) from old Canadian friends at TCA and their Mr Glenn, who had enquired about the weight penalties of increasing the fuel capacity of the Vanjet to 55,000lbs. Vickers reply was that the 'penalty' would be 600lbs; was the Vanjet truly beginning to look viable?

Typical Vickers over-engineering was seen in many of the Vanjet design studies, this included a T-tail with not just a 'bullet' fairing at the fin-top, but also a ventral 'plate'. Designers use one or the other as an aerodynamic device to tune airflow at the top of a tail fin, but both was overkill, surely?

After intensive maintenance attention to the Viscount's wing spar – regular 'filleting' had had to be carried out to keep ahead of potential trouble – Vickers had moved towards a multi-spar wing ethos; as seen in the Vanjet and resultant VC10.

Thousands of man-hours went into Vickers specifications for its jet airliner. Range, max payload, airfield details, runway performances, climb rates, fuel flows, flap angles, lift-coefficients, wing loadings, and the original 'clean' wing studies all began here. Money was saved by the suggested use of Vanguard cockpit windows and frames (VC10s would reuse the two main Vanguard windscreen panel designs), and the use of Valiant toolings in the wings and fuselage wherever possible. For some months, the basis of Vanjet ideas used the Vanguard's 'double-bubble' fuselage as a direct transfer of costs and paid-for tooling. This was latterly abandoned for a completely new fuselage structure, but costs went up and you could not lay responsibility for this on anything but Vickers own process and decisions.

A lot of work went into designing a safe 'cradle' rear engine mounting system for the two and three-engined Vanjets. Thus included designing strong, transverse engine mounting beams across the rear fuselage (they were to be drop-forged alloy) and adding triangulating bracing struts to locate the engines and their thrust actions upon their mountings. Bracing in the third, ducted central engine, and feeding it from a fin-intake S-duct, provided a major challenge. Boeing and de Havilland would soon be studying the same issues for their tri-jets respectively. Vickers Vanjet research works were privately funded and a great deal hung on the outcome – jobs and lives.

The 'Jet-Viscount Scheme' had, by this time, become the 'Jet Vanguard Scheme' and then the 'Vanjet'. The VC nomenclature was then added to the title and the studies became 'Vanjet VC10'.

Up to fifteen 'Mks' of the Vanjet series were speculated in drawings and separate specifications files. A typical seventy-five seat, 1,000nm range was the baseline for the twin-jet idea and 100-seat 1,500nm or even 2,000nm options with three-engines (using an S-duct in the fin leading down to a rear fuselage mounted engine), were all on the books in the Vickers drawing office. Indeed, Vanjet Mk15 had proposed three rear-mounted Conways, a wing of 18,000sqft, a 2,500nm range from 45,500 gallons of fuel, and a payload of 21,000lbs. Here, within these Vanjet specifications, lay airliners of DC-9 and Boeing 727 potential, years before those machines came

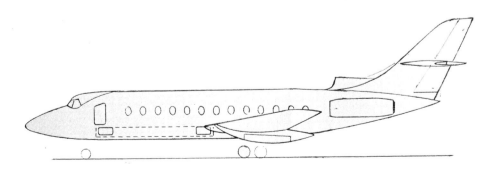

Viscount to Vanjet.

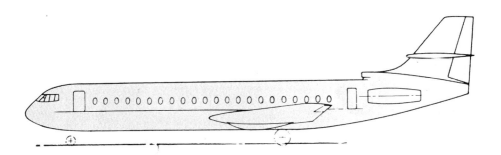

Vanguard to Vanjet.

to fruition. There was even a forward fuselage, upward opening cargo door option for a 'combi' variant drawn up in 1954.

Vickers drew up several Vanjets with two and three class passenger cabins and high density configurations at six-abreast, but with a 39inch seat pitch, not the 33inch pitch now seen across the airline standard. Fuel tankage was flexible too, the twin-jet short-range version of Vanjet might offer 1,700 miles with wing tanks only, but add three engines and a fuselage ventral tank and a 2,000, or even a 3,000 miles capable airframe resulted.

Vanjet VC10 Mk II: Drawing Series Number 79926 – Birth of the true VC10?

A medium-range three-engine Vanjet was considered – a sort of narrow-bodied DC10 of its day perhaps? Of often ignored significance is that the very first Vickers label of VC10 was applied to the three-engined, T-tailed, Vanjet study as defined 'Vickers Commercial 10' specification drawing. But it was not pursued in this form (see illustration). This Vanjet iteration was to be cited as Vanjet VC10 Mk II/III/IV and in drawing number 79926/sheet 3 we see a Vanjet proposal of three engines, a clean wing and total fuel capacity of 80,5000lbs or 10,450 imperial gallons as 8,450 in the wing tanks and 2,000 in the centre fuselage tank. It was in Vanjet drawing 79926 proposal that up to 108 passengers could be accommodated at a still very comfortable Economy Class seat pitch of 36 inches, that the real steps to a 100-plus seat cabin were defined.

Intriguingly, these Vanjet studies – firstly using Valiant wing and then a new, more swept-wing – all featured Dieter Kuchemann's streamwise wing tip design – deleted from the final VC10 prototype drawings and then re-added to the first actual production series. The design drawings of the final four-engined version of the Vanjet VC10 Mk4 clearly also depict a curved trailing edge to the engine-stub wing and the beginning of the elegant T-tail and tailplane motifs.

There were over eighty paper studies for the Vanjets, all consuming not just time and resources, but Vickers own money. Rolls-Royce Avon-29 engines would give way to early Conway 10s, two and three-engined airframes would become the four-engined Vanjet. Wing sweep would go from 30° to 32.5° and the more obvious reuse of Vanguard and Valiant parts bin components would be reduced to create new, dedicated, Vanjet/VC10 parts and toolings. From here came the shape, the style, and the details of the true VC10 as we knew it. Vickers absorbed the costs and the time it took to create the new standard of airframe.

By 14 April 1954, the idea for offering a Vanjet in two-engined and in three-engined variants, with all the economies of design and build, yet providing the operating flexibility of the varying engine number, framed the true potential of the Vanjets in the world airliner market. With V1000/VC7 on the go at Weybridge at the same time, these must have been heady days – perhaps reflected by the following official statement made in a Vanjet document at the time by Vickers:

'Technically there can be no doubt that Weybridge must be capable of designing the Mk4 and the Mk5. If we do not, who else in this country can do it better, or, who do we combine with to become a success. Failing this, once more the Americans get the last laugh'.[5]

But Vanjet as a three-engined machine was going nowhere because of the actions of one customer – the main potential customer – BOAC, again! What killed the three-engined Vanjet, and thus its two-engined variant? The answer was BOAC's insistence that it would not fly the Atlantic on three engines – ever.

How different this was from the ensuing tri-jet and 'big-twin' jet airliners that have subsequently plied the oceans for decades. Back then BOAC was clear – four engines were demanded.

Vickers had had a simple answer to that – fit four engines to the existing design for Vanjet!

So was born the very genesis of the final Vanjet VC10 as a four-engined airliner. Here was the original, smaller, non-oceanic, VC10 concept that was the precursor to the production item. In a document proposed on 14 April 1957, the Vickers design team conjectured upon the Vanjet 'VC' series and their potential global markets, for here were two related airframes – not the originally proposed two and three-engined designs, but now the separate three-engined and four-engined airframes that would be of performance and economic appeal across the world's airline routes, not just tailored so closely to one British airline and its operating requirements as to become commercially and operationally unviable upon the global stage – as the Trident was to befall as a fate.

Such dual versions of one base airframe as Vickers was now suggesting, could be vitally attractive to BOAC and BEA, and many other airlines all over the world.

Vanjet Specification B8613

In the final Vanjet idea of Specification B8613, it is the four-engined, 245,000lb/ kg airframe with a payload of 34,000lb/kg that was suggested. Here was the first four-engined idea of the previously suggested three-engined 'Vanjet VC10'. Span was 125ft/m, length 160ft/m, height 39ft/m, gross wing area was 2,600ft/m, and a cruising speed of 580mph cited. A cabin pressure differential of 8lb/sq.in would allow a 38,000ft cruise. Wing sweep was still 30° (soon increased to 35°). Critically, the range was a healthy 3,000 miles/km and the payload almost 35,000lbs, which was in most airline accountants minds the critical point for making long-haul money.

The T-tail was high and well swept; the horizontal tail and elevators, large and effective. The leading edge devices were also large and the wing clean. Use of Vanguard cockpit window tooling was latterly discarded except for the two main panels, resulting in the definitive VC10 windscreen and cockpit side window design motifs. The engine nacelle/stub wing design was also highly advanced to near VC10 production status. The use of a Vanguard 'double-bubble' or twin-lobed fuselage had by now been discarded, and the expense of a new circular-section, keel-built, heavily reinforced fuselage approved.

This was the four-engined Vanjet VC10 in its obvious iteration; in weeks it would be a swept-winged four-engined design with a 130-seat cabin. Here was the defining moment of significance; the clean 35° sweep wing had a large leading edge slat of long span, with a greater degree of leading edge angle than ever seen on any airframe at that time, or until Boeing's 727 of a decade later. A military specification version of this four-jet Vanjet was framed. Here was the penultimate step to the mighty V1000 specification VC10 – one step from a production design. All that was needed were time, money, and an increase in airframe size and engine power.

The original twin-engined Vanjet could have predated its later rivals, the BAC 1-11, DC-9, B-737 or F28/100 by years, and taken sales from the Caravelle. The three-engined Vanjet could have scooped up many sales long before the B-727 dominated the world and the quality-built, but ground-hugging Trident had failed. The four-engined Vanjet became the VC10, but not without some delays.

A huge and brilliant future lay on the drawing boards. Vickers airliners were potential global masters of the airline fleet order books, with a common, low cost base (from £500,000, £750,000 and £1,000,000 per airframe respectively) range of related airliners with various engine number options, and all offering structural, operating, and maintenance similarities that could greatly reduce an airline's costs and offer real value for money. A pilot could fly more than one version if the controls and handling were similar enough. The only difference between the airframes would be the numbers of engines fitted and any potential fuselage length/cabin capacity options chosen. Vickers could build the twin-jet with fifty seats, or a slightly stretched version with seventy seats. The tri-jet could seat eighty or 110 depending on seat pitch or fuselage length increase; the four-jet might seat 100–130 dependent on seat configurations chosen. Common cockpit, and common servicing and operating factors across the Vanjets, from twin-jet and tri-jet, would, if they had been built, have been realised long before Boeing or Airbus attempted the same.

So was set the Viscount-Vanjet-VC10 lineage.

The Vickers design department veterans say that it is vital that observers realise that the key to the realisation of the VC10 design was the process from the jet Viscount onwards. To quote one retired Vickers veteran, Dr Norman Barfield, in conversation with the author:

'It was the jet Viscount and the way that it became the Vanjet using Valiant bits that was the origin of the definitive VC10. We got there step-by-step through all that work.'

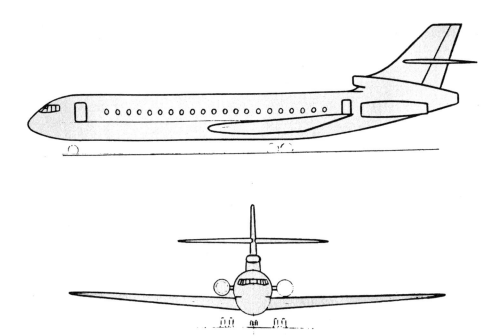

Vanjet Tri-jet.

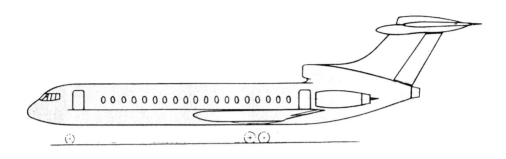

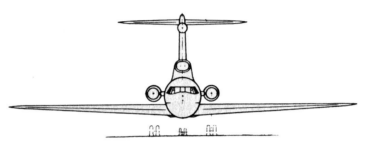

Vanjet T-Tail.

Neither should we forget that BOAC had an early look at Vickers proposals and said that one of them was 'economically viable'.

Intriguingly, hidden in the Vanjet archives (now held at Brooklands Museum) there lies the Vanjet Mk16, which was a medium-range design with two underwing-pylon mounted turbofans and a third (rear) engine buried in an S-duct under the tailfin. As such, this design presaged later 1960s Boeing 727 update studies and BAC Hawker Siddeley airbus type concepts. Remove the third tail-mounted engine and the similar shapes of the Boeing 757 or Airbus A300 twin-engined airliners became obvious. So Vanjet gave us the VC10, but it could also have given us the first 'big-twin' airliner after VC10 was launched. But the Vickers 'big-twin' was not to be.

THE VICKERS DESIGN LINEAGE 1948–1959

VIKING-VISCOUNT-VANJET-VC10

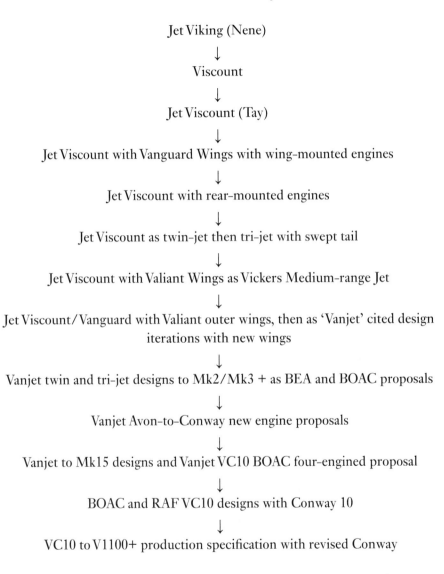

Jet Viking (Nene)
↓
Viscount
↓
Jet Viscount (Tay)
↓
Jet Viscount with Vanguard Wings with wing-mounted engines
↓
Jet Viscount with rear-mounted engines
↓
Jet Viscount as twin-jet then tri-jet with swept tail
↓
Jet Viscount with Valiant Wings as Vickers Medium-range Jet
↓
Jet Viscount/Vanguard with Valiant outer wings, then as 'Vanjet' cited design
iterations with new wings
↓
Vanjet twin and tri-jet designs to Mk2/Mk3 + as BEA and BOAC proposals
↓
Vanjet Avon-to-Conway new engine proposals
↓
Vanjet to Mk15 designs and Vanjet VC10 BOAC four-engined proposal
↓
BOAC and RAF VC10 designs with Conway 10
↓
VC10 to V1100+ production specification with revised Conway

Note*
(a) 1950s, VC3–VC6 and 'Little Jet' studies in parallel
(b) 1953–1956, V1000/VC7 jet transport studies
(c) 1959–1965, VC11 as reverse-engineered scaled down VC10

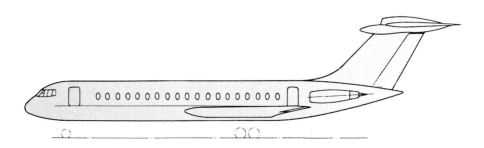

Vanjet Four Engines.

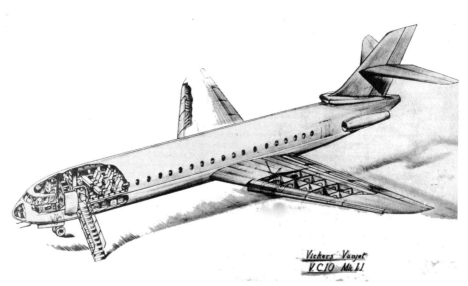

Vanjet VC10.

Chapter 6

Highly Detailed Reality:
VC10 and the Realisation of a Dream

* Warning: Contains Graphic Technical Content

By early 1957, despite the strategic confusion created by the UK Government and BOAC, the State (in all likelihood, blind to its own airline strategy failings) took a decision to allow the funding for BOAC to order a large, four-engined British long-range airliner. BOAC would go on to say that it would have been happy to have a British version of the 707, or even a British, licence-built 707, but that government – BOAC's accounting paymaster – insisted on a British-designed product. BOAC seemingly having conveniently forgotten that the political imperative for such a government decision had stemmed from the issue of BOAC itself ordering nearly 50 million pounds worth of Boeing 707s at a time of shortage of Sterling in the UK Exchequer![1]

The de Havilland DH 118, Handley Page HP 97 (an HP 80 Victor derivative), Bristol 200 and the Vickers Avon powered Vanjet iterations, had come and gone – all on paper. And after the loss of an HP 80 Victor in July 1954 due to its T-tail design – the tail unit came off – Vickers had to prove that their T-tail was truly safe (the HP 80's fin height was shortened for subsequent production). The key point, however, was that only Vanjet had morphed into a design specification that was the essence of the forthcoming airliner – which turned into the VC10 after much deliberation.

By now, despite its previous statements of needing an ever-increasing fleet of jets, BOAC now decided to order just twenty-five VC10 type machines to be deployed principally on the airline's eastern and southern routes medium route empire – the 'hot and high', or 'MRE' network, with its difficult operating environment of high temperatures and (at that time) very short runways and minimal facilities – the old weight, altitude and temperature (WAT) limited, runways and airports of Imperial Airways.

BOAC mooted its transatlantic requirements and early thoughts of a larger or 'Super' type VC10 were discussed. But, if BOAC were to 'swap' orders for the MRE route Standard-type VC10s for Super VC10s (therefore reducing the number of Standard VC10s), then the loser would be Vickers, not BOAC. There seemed, however, to be strange BOAC and government attitude at play, Vickers would have to 'prove' that they could design and deliver the VC10 to very strict BOAC demands, before the airline might offer real and total commitment to the machine as orders. In the background, BOAC had a very large sword to wave over Vickers heads – the 707 and its potential Rolls-Royce Conway powered BOAC-specific variant. The ability to carry a 35,000lb payload over a minimum 2,500 mile range at Mach .82 to Mach .88, and to have full, high temperature operating ability from un-lengthened runways, were the key demands. And out on the tropical eastern routes, a regular 35kt headwind would also have to be dealt with. Oh, and can you make it viable for the North Atlantic winter conditions to New York, Boston and Toronto as well, suggested BOAC.

The BOAC problem was to carry a good payload of 25,000lbs/40,000lbs for 2,500 miles from a hot temperature and/or high altitude runway, and reach the destination against headwinds and tropical weather – without offloading fuel, passengers, or cargo, and avoiding an unplanned refuelling stop.

The key issue of the VC10's advantage over the 707 and DC-8 was its lesser take-off requirement for runway distance and carrying much more payload. That advantage was reduced by the longer runways soon built. But when looking at runway distances cited, we must remember that these often include not just the amount of runway needed to 'rotate' ('Vr') or 'unstick' the aircraft into the air, but the extra runway distance also required to include the ability to stop from a high-speed rejected take-off (for example, at 100kts+ due to engine failure). Such runway length requirements were set by British and American authorities. For example, a VC10 at typical passenger load, might actually lift off the ground in 4,000 – 5,500ft, but the (additional) required stopping distance might be another 2,000ft – thus giving a total runway requirement for lift off and a high speed 'abort' as a safe operation of 7,000ft. Rival Boeing and Douglas machines might need 10,000 – 11,500ft total runway distance requirements according to official figures.

The VC10's first flight take-offs were in under 2,500ft (2,150ft!) actual distance to 'unstick' lift-off from the especially extended Brooklands 3,800 – 4,500ft runway that featured a high-speed taxiway bend. After departing, the newly manufactured VC10s and Super VC10s would land at nearby Wisely, at the Vickers test base. The in-service take-off weight for a Standard VC10 was up to 312,000lbs and for the Super VC10, 335,000lbs, but because the Wisely runway length of 6,000ft was insufficient for safe operation to the abandoned take-off runway length required at full load, a limited maximum take-off weight was applied, this being 260,000lbs. This still allowed test flights with a duration of over six hours. The first-flight from Wisley with a decent payload saw G–ARTA 'unstick' and fly in under 4,500ft and the landing of G–ARTA on the Wisely 6,000ft runway, saw G–ARTA stopped

3,600ft from the runway's far end after a ground run of just 2,550ft.[2] The brakes and tyres might have been a touch warm!

BOAC's demanding routes required actual take-off distance to rotation ('Vr') and safe lift-off climb ('V2') that varied with aircraft weight and local temperatures. As some 'runway distance required' figures meant that combined total safe take-off and emergency stopping distances, so some statistics also refer to a take-off distance to achieve a 35ft 'screen' height for obstacle clearance. But whatever the vagaries of the statistics quoted, the facts were clear, the VC10 – wait for it – took off in a shorter distance, at about a 25% slower speed, and did so with a full or almost-full max-range payload, all prior to climbing quickly and steeply to gain safety height. A VC10 required at least 2,000ft less runway than a (weight/payload limited) 707, but in really testing African 'hot and high' conditions, the 707 might need much more extra runway length than that with a load 10–20 tonnes below its maximum allowable normal take-off weight. Such airfields saw temperatures of 85° – 90°F/30° – 35°C or more, and altitude elevations of up to and over 5,000ft, and minimum runway lengths of 6000–8000ft. Until runway extensions were made, many of these runways were unusable by a 707 or DC-8 carrying any viable long-range load, or they would be unable to take-off at all.

Typical, 'Difficult' BOAC 'Hot and High' Airfields and Route Sectors 1962

Cited at the then dated runway lengths and the international standards (BCAR) runway temperature plus extra 15° Centigrade and with a/c payload fuel reserves at sixty minutes.

- Colombo to Cairo at 3,550 miles from 6,000ft runway
- Lagos to Kano 481 miles from 7,600ft runway and Kano to London at 2,750 miles from 8,610ft runway
- Kuala Lumpur to Calcutta at 1,610 miles from 6,000ft runway
- Mexico City to New York 2,080 miles from 13,500 runway at 7,350ft elevation
- Nairobi to Johannesburg from 8,000ft runway at 5,327ft elevation
- Salisbury to Nairobi from 6,000ft runway at 5000ft elevation
- Singapore to Karachi at 2,959 miles from 8,000ft runway
- Singapore to Sydney at 4,050 miles from 8,000ft runway
- Addis Abba (7,320ft elevation) to Nairobi from 6,000ft runway

To meet its demands, BOAC issued the toughest and most unfair large airliner specification ever issued to a manufacturer. The VC10 would have to lift a payload of 38,000–40,000lbs from a demanding tropical runway and have 2,500 miles range and be able to beat a 35kt headwind. Nevertheless, Basil Smallpiece and the newly Knighted Sir George Edwards signed the BOAC VC10 contract on 14 January 1958.

As we know, in hindsight, various claims about who said what and who demanded what in terms of orders have been made. BOAC ordered thirty-five Standard V1000 VC10s and Vickers reacted with a price of £1.5 million per airframe, with £1.75 million per airframe cited for the potential Super VC10. Thirty-five VC10s was, in 1958, likely to be more than BOAC then thought it wanted, yet did not BOAC very quickly say that such a number, even allied to its 707 orders, would not be enough for its 1960s predicted traffic growth plan? By the time the contract was signed, Vickers and its team got on with the job – using pre-existing Vanjet, Valiant and Vanguard experience to good engineering and fiscal effect. Between 1958 and 1960 there began 'movement' in the BOAC fleet requirements and the airline's VC10 standpoint. Here began the 'swap-shop' between Standard and Super VC10 orders.

The VC10 contract was rewritten in 1960 and curtailed the Standard model order to fifteen and asked for thirty of the Supers. By 1961 the contract had changed to just ten Supers and thirteen Standards. Yet the next contract would be twelve Standards and seventeen Supers. BOAC seemed to be able to 'play' the order book at will. And Vickers had to bite on the medicine.

At great cost, Vickers built two vast new assembly factory 'halls' at Brooklands to cope with the VC10's size, notably the fin height, but early fabrication of the airframe took place at the Brooklands Assembly Line Hangar 'W1' (now a housing estate). The 'Wing Shop' was adjacent to this main 'W1' hangar. With the VC10 parts in jigs and frames, the main fuselage body structure was mated together minus the tail fin and wings and engines. Then the airframes were taken on special wheeled trailers or cradles over to the so-called 'Cathedral' large assembly 'shop' or hall – where all the final assembly was carried out by fitting the fin (road-freighted in from the Hurn factory), rudder, tailplane, engines and undercarriages.

As the design process proceeded, fiscal and time savings could be made by Vickers by using its prior experience (notably of Vanjet), but greater expense in time and money would be required from Vickers own purse as the design development and BOAC operating requirements were firmed up with the airline supplying its actual airfield operating figures for tough locations like Nairobi, Karachi, Lusaka and Salisbury.

Max-payload for the VC10 would be 39,769lbs/18,039kgs in BOAC specification. Super VC10 would lift 50,406lbs/22,860kgs as a type 1151 for BOAC (the East African passenger/cargo Super VC10 would lift 60,231lbs/27,360kgs). The payload range would approach 4,700 miles+.

The original Vanjet-Vanguard costing basis using existing jigs and toolings, but this would have to be leapfrogged as the design developed and we have to state that this was Vickers own affair and not BOAC's responsibility. But this was how the design process evolved to meet the airline's requirements. By discarding earlier designs as evolving Vanjet proposals, the VC10, like the V1000/VC7, had become a true long-haul machine. In the Viscount, Vanguard and Valiant, Vickers had pioneered new ideas and new techniques, notably in structural terms and in 'fail-safe' and double 'fail-safe' structural load and stress pathway design to reduce airframe fatigue from flight, ground, and pressurisation loadings.

So VC10 offered not just 'spare' structural load paths, but a double redundancy with extra load paths all designed to take up the load if a principal structural member was damaged and another invoked. This technique ensured that the VC10, which would be subject to some pretty rough conditions on basic tropical runways, would not suffer from structural weakness. We can opine that like the entire industry, Vickers benefited from the structural lessons of the Comet 1 tragedies, however, Vickers had, prior to those tragic events, decided to make a tougher (if heavier) structure and use more reinforcement than de Havilland had. From 1948, the Viscount had used curved elliptical shapes for all fuselage cut-outs such as doors, windows and panels – before, de Havilland's used the riskier, square cornered cut-outs for such items on their new Comet 1. So the men at Weybridge knew their stuff. The VC10 would also bring multiple, protective, fail-safe dual flight-control designs, which would create new standards in this design area. An 'Iron duck' nickname was latterly attached to the ship-like construction of the VC10 – Vickers once being great shipbuilders.

The Team

Sir George Edwards operated a truly integrated team of experts and artisans. Under Edwards, a real team spirit existed at Vickers. The resultant quality of their designs and products were, of course, world-class and world-beating. It is not possible herein to mention every employees name, but between the men of the advanced projects design office, the engineering projects teams, and the vital shop floor workers (or 'associates' as collegiate corporate speak might now call them), we can, for the record, cite vital VC10 project contributors. Any omissions herein are accidental or the result of the author, fifty years down the line, being unable to further research a detailed employee list.

Ernest E. Marshall led the Vickers design function under Sir George Edwards leadership, Basil Stevenson was Assistant Chief Designer. Hugh Hemsley was Assistant Chief Engineer and VC10 project engineering leader, Hugh Tyrer was Vickers Chief Metallurgist. Jack Swanson and Ted Chivers were the Senior

Draughtsmen. Frank Ward, Sammy Walsh, Maurice Wilmer and John Davis were lead contributors in the advanced projects team.

The aerodynamics team, the VC10s 'aero' men under Ken Lawson as Chief Aerodynamicist, saw John Hay as Assistant Chief Aerodynamicist, Mike Salisbury as Assistant Lead Aerodynamicist, Roger Back and Heinz Vogel as aerodynamicists. Dieter Kuchemann was a project contributor via his RAE role.

The engineering team was David McElhinney as Chief Stress Engineer, David James as Chief Structures Engineer, John Davies as Chief Weights Engineer and Jim Richards was Deputy Chief Stressman, while David Findlay was Leader Wing Stress. Albert Kitchenside was a Structural Engineer on the wing stress team. The fuselage Project Manager was Maurice Wilmer and Alec Paterson was fuselage build leader. N.W. Boorer (latterly a BAC chief project engineer) worked on fuselage and pressurisation systems.

The engineering systems team covering the innovative flight controls, and electrical systems men, included: Ted Petty as Chief Project Engineer, Harry Zeffert as Leader Electrical Engineering, Jack Ratcliffe, Colin Jehu, and Gerry Hitch, as Senior Electrical Engineers. Gordon Howells was the Senior Engineer on the flight controls. George Aylesbury was Lead Mechanical Engineer. G.W. Webber was the lead autopilot project Design Engineer. One of the youngest men to work on the VC10 was A.R. Walker, who, aged twenty-two, started his Vickers career as a young engineering apprentice in 1957 and worked on VC10, BAC 1-11, and TSR2 up to 1965.

The VC10 prototype (G-ARTA) build production was overseen by Bill Potter as production manager, Ken Keenan as his assistant, with Wally Chapman, Cyril Redman and Harry Welton as senior foremen at Vickers Weybridge. Ivor Tinker and Ron Storey were two well-known members of the VC10 engineering/manufacturing team that created G-ARTA. Edward Read was chief draughtsman at Vickers Hurn on the tail control surfaces.

The flight-test teams for the VC10 and Super VC10 were: G.R. 'Jock' Bryce, Brian Trubshaw, Bill Cairns, John Cochrane, Eddie McNamara, Doug Howley, Roy Mole, Chris Mullen, Roy Holland, Ian Muir and Peter Diss. Later Super VC10 and RAF development airframe flight crews included R. Radford and P. Baker. Vickers training pilots to BOAC and VC10 customers were D. Hayley-Bell and L. Roberts, with D. Ackery in the flight test department.

The vital VC10 (and Super VC10) ground crews, who also travelled overseas with the flight test and route proving flights, included: Ron Bennett, Eddy Capell, Denis Collier, Joe Lindsey, Ken Norridge, Bill Oldfield, Jack Pulfer, John Randell, Toby Tobias, Maurice Ungless, Denis Wells and Bob Wright.[3]

The above lists are not intended to be definitive and many more unnamed and unrecognised men (and women) contributed to the design and build of the VC10.

Design Issues

The key VC10 design issue was not one just of principal power, but of lift and runway ability as en route airfield flexibility – to which power was not the sole story. Anyone could create a rocket ship with power and it might have very high take-off speeds, require a 10,000ft runway length, and more critically, have very high landing speeds and high wing loadings. And what good was a high Mach number cruising speed if the aircraft behaved like a pig near the ground – with safety implications? So power, or more appropriately, thrust, was not the only asset to be valued.

Lift and lifting ability were the crucial factors and they would come firstly from wing design. Thus were set the VC10s key 'aero' design parameters. Then came the new fail-safe split-systems control design philosophy, the electrical and service systems innovations, and then the structural design ingredients. All of these advanced airframe and systems developments combined to create a 'next-step' in large airliner design and many of the VC10s features and achievements can now be seen in recent Boeing and Airbus airframes. If the 707 was, in design terms, the 'best practice' in 1958, then the VC10 advanced the arts in 1962.

The VC10 needed to be stronger and more fatigue and distress resistant than the Comet or an airliner designed for easier routes. Rough runways in Africa would demand a very tough structure that would resist fatigue. Over fifty-five per cent of the VC10's structure (by weight) was machined from high quality, solid lumps or slabs (billets) of metal. This delivered safe sections of very strong, and large, aircraft parts in the wings, fuselage and inner chassis structure which were of consistent metallurgical quality, and had uninterrupted stress pathways or patterns. A superior, smoother exterior finish (aerodynamically beneficial) was also a benefit of the expensive machining process for the alloys used: the VC10s skin – 'smoothness criteria' – was the best in the world and better than that to be found on a 707 or DC-8. And with a reduced panel and parts count, construction was easier and torsional rigidity higher – with fewer joints to flex or fail or corrode.

The main wing skins were machined from single bits of metal 35ft long– much stronger than a multiple panel skin. The VC10's main wing had only seven main panels – ensuring great consistency of strength. Upper wing surfaces were made of a zinc-rich alloy (DTD 5050) and the lower surfaces of an aluminium copper alloy (ST24). The three-part wing structure was therefore very strong indeed, and so too was the central wing box that carried many loadings. Wing-skin milling was overseen by Harry Welton – senior foreman.

From a corrosion resistance standpoint, the VC10 used the best moisture reduction and corrosion inhibition systems ever seen on a civil airliner (arguably never bettered to date) and proved their worth in protecting the VC10s structure in the humid conditions of its main operating arenas. This also made the VC10 less likely to defect and repair than its rival. Any airliner constantly being heated, wetted, and then deep frozen at high cruise level, needed real and effective anti-corrosion treatment – like a Swedish car for example. The VC10 was painted inside and out – 'all over' – and with all hidden cavities treated where required and several layers of corrosion inhibition paints applied throughout the structure. It was, in a sense, rustproofed. These coatings added weight – but they reduced corrosion, and the needs and costs for regular replacement of corroded parts. The 707 did not feature such advanced corrosion protection techniques – so saving build costs and weight – thus creating more likelihood of renovation and replacement costs after purchase to be borne by the customer airline.

The proof was in the pudding, and it was proved early on when BOAC sold the three early VC10 airframes that had spent a decade in the corrosive humid skies of Africa. These machines were actually sold to Boeing, who in 1976 chopped them up in-situ at London Heathrow Airport – an act of deliberate commercial vandalism according to some observers. Ripped apart with their hidden, inner cavities and secrets exposed for the first time since construction, no structural corrosion was found at all and no 'fatigue distress' discovered; noteworthy corrosion would have been normal and expected in any airliner, especially a tropical route operating machine. But the early VC10s were nearly 'as new' under their slightly soiled skins and yellow anti-corrosion paint.

Of course, later in the VC10 and Super VC10 life, after decades of service and years of adverse storage prior to conversion to RAF tankers, some corrosion and fatigue was encountered in structural components – twenty or thirty years into airframe life in a fifty year story.

Supersonic Valiant and the T-Tail Origins of the VC10

Of singular significance was the decision to employ a T-tail configuration – and not just any boring, short, stubby T-tail, but a grand, elegantly swept piece of design with an outrageously stylish sculpted bullet firing atop the fin.

The advantages of the (Multhopp-created) T-tail included better (increasing) control authority than a low-set tail at high incidence angles, a beneficial 'end-plate' effect upon fin drag, and helpful effects in critical Mach numbers with a better ability to balance increased main-wing chord. The high fin also removed the tailplanes from the issues of engine exhaust flow plumes and engine pod flow, and compressibility and interference effects in rear-mounted engine configurations. Only the spectre of the 'deep-stall' or 'super-stall', with its potential for loss of elevator authority and resulting 'locked in' irrecoverable total airframe stall, haunted the T-tail as a design philosophy. Most manufacturers relied on a control stick-pusher to avoid a too nose-high attitude, the VC10 had one by legislative order, but its T-tail was unique in avoiding the worst aspects of the T-tail stall behaviours and characteristics due to its sweep and height, allied to massive elevators that were properly powered. There was never a VC10 deep-stall accident, unlike other airframes.

Many assume that the T-tail stemmed from the need for the 'clean' unencumbered wing design, and that this choice was made during the Vanjet studies. However, as early as 1952 – before the Caravelle's swept, rear-engined shape – Vickers were drawing up a T-tailed, elegantly swept, Valiant derivative. This was the supersonic variant of the Valiant – to a proposed Ministry specification and first drawn in January 1952 with discussion of an informal nature with the RAF's senior air staff. A highly swept main wing, and further swept tailplane, worked to keep the critical Mach numbers in tune at supersonic speeds. Interestingly, Vickers proposed that this Mach 1.38 capable airframe should be Rolls-Royce Conway powered (using existing Valiant ducting, but revised, aft-spar engine mountings). Of particular note, it was in this Valiant Mk2 supersonic design that we see the first use by the Vickers design team of a tall, elegant, swept, T-tailed fin, and of real design interest, highly swept, curved shaped tailplanes atop the empennage.[4] We can see

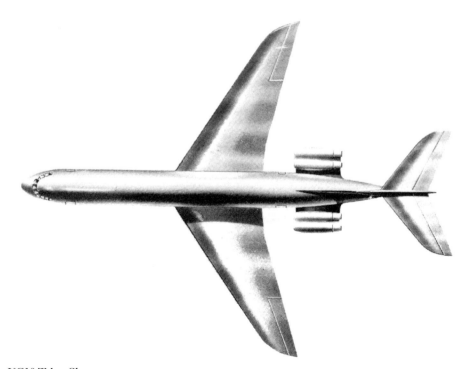

VC10 Takes Shape.

clear origins of the fin and tailplane designs of the later VC10 in this 1952 design by Ken Lawson and colleagues.

Who 'designed' the VC10? The above mentioned men all designed or engineered the VC10, and it is very hard to ascribe to one person the actual shape, or for want of a better word, 'styling'. The Valiant and Vanjet works heavily influenced the shape or style of the VC10, and Ken Lawson's aerodynamics input had an effect on the shapes chosen – notably that fin. But there is a riddle in the tale, because we know that it was Sir George himself who actually sat down and made rough sketches of the aircraft's configuration and basic shape. He might not have fully formed the final touches or the exact form of that 'sculpted' iconic tail, but the reality is that Edwards drew the initial design sketches, by hand at home with a pencil.[5]

'Aero' Issues and Wing Design

Vickers had, via the Vanjet studies, decided on the 'clean' wing, with nothing hanging off it. Rear engines ensured an efficient, 'clean wing' airflow. Yet paradoxically, this aerodynamic advantage removed a structural advantage – known as 'wing bending relief' upon the wing structure from the engines – when the weight of an engine(s) hanging below the wing, offers an opposing force (downwards) to the created 'lift' force that is trying to bend the wing upwards. Engines under the wing – in opposing bending moment – therefore offer a benefit to the wing structure, as less wing reinforcement and strength (incurring weight in the wing) is required to counteract the lift force upon the wing structure. With no such engines on the wing, the 'clean' wing has to be stiffer, stronger, and heavier. This is one of the reasons that the VC10 is more expensive to operate than a 707, because the VC10's wing structure is slightly heavier for the same number of passengers accommodated, with figures of 25.7% of Maximum Take-Off Weight (MTOW) as opposed to the 707-320s 24.6%. It may not seem much, but it had a cost in terms of fuel consumption.

For the VC10, the wing loading was intended to be a low 80lbs/ft^2/394.4kg/m^2, but the penalty of the heavily reinforced VC10 structure saw that figure heading towards 99lbs/ft^2. The Super VC10 had a minimum wing loading of 80.08 lbs/ft^2/394.5kg/m^2, but a maximum weight wing loading of over 101lbs/ft^2 and a max take-off weight wing loading of a not inconsiderable 114.3lb/ft^2/558.1kg/m^2. This was not dissimilar to the wing loadings of the big Boeing and Douglas jet variants, but was ameliorated by the VC10/Super VC10 high lift devices, lower aerodynamic drag and extra thrust. The VC10's wing area was initially set at 2,800ft^2/264.8m^2.

The Tay Viscount (630) of 1950, following on from the Nene Viking this was the true precursor of Vickers jet airframe design and development. From here stemmed the Vanjet and VC10. (*Photo: Vickers/BAC*)

The lost future: V1000 (VC7), 85% complete and just months from a world-market dominating position yet killed off by external players, thus handing global advantage to Boeing and Douglas respectively. (*Photo: Vickers/BAC*)

This Saunders Roe V1000 hydro-dynamic development test model shows off the airliner's advanced design and lines that look far more futuristic than found in desktop models and plan drawings. A nose gear hydroplane was suggested to reduce the 'diving' effect in a ditching. (*Photo: Vickers/BAC*)

V1000's cockpit window and nose design show clear hints of later VC10 motifs. (*Photo: Vickers/BAC*)

Vickers Managing Director Sir George Edwards (left) and BOAC's Sir Basil Smallpiece sign-up for the demanding 'Empire' route specification airliner in January 1958. Vickers top man, Air Commodore Tuttle is out of shot. (*Photo: Vickers/BAC*)

Vickers Advanced Projects Office at Weybridge (Brooklands) with leader Ernest Marshall flanked by John Davis (left), Maurice Wilmer, Sammy Walsh (both to right), 'Jock' Swanson to rear. This is where the genius of Vickers design was born. (*Photo: Vickers/BAC*)

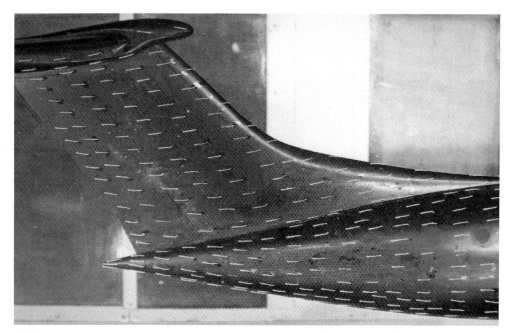

VC10 aerodynamics development – tuft testing the crucial T-tail airflow. Hours of work went into lessening the deep-stall potential. The elegant swan-like bullet fin-top fairing also resulted. (*Photo: Vickers/BAC*)

VC10's reinforced nose structure – this is the flight deck. Note the closely spaced ribs, and thick support structure around the apertures. Truly built like a Vickers battleship! (*Photo: Vickers/BAC*)

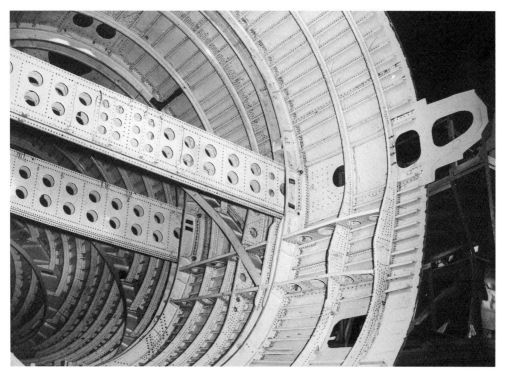

Rear fuselage details: note engine cross beams, (to which the 'spectacle' engine bearer supports were mounted), tail fin hoops, extra cleats, thickened gauges and over-engineered strength. (*Photo: Vickers/BAC*)

Flightdeck: VC10's command post was much roomier than the 707's tight confines. Seat ingress and exit was outside the seats, not beside the centre console as in 707. Deep windows improved the view. (*Photo: Vickers/BAC*)

Super VC10 shows off the T-tail and design features. Note extended stub wing pylon for the engines and 'beaver tail' exhaust fairings. The true height of the fin compared to other T-tailers is obvious. (*Photo: Vickers/BAC*)

The early pre-delivery BOAC livery seen on G-ARVB as test-airframe – without the production series inboard wing fence that Bryce and Trubshaw insisted upon to cure spanwise flow issues at low speeds. (*Photo: Vickers/BAC*)

The Royal Air Force was VC10's other main operator. This stunning shot of a C.Mk1 in action photographed from another VC10 shows off the airframe in-flight in period style. (*Photo: S. Ludlow*)

Going up: G-ARVM, the last Standard-model BOAC VC10 blasts out of Vickers Weybridge site (Brooklands) in 2,150ft to 'Vrotate'. The livery would soon change again. (*Photo: Vickers/BAC*)

The Super VC10 during build in Weybridge site's 'Cathederal' main construction hall; Vickers employed over 7,000 people. Note the rare, soon-to-be revised early BOAC livery. (*Photo: Vickers/BAC*)

East African Airways Super VC10 5X-UVA in all its glory – with the cargo door open. First Class was ahead of the cargo hold and Economy Class aft. A walkway through the cargo had to be kept clear, despite that caveat, this added 'combi' feature was highly attractive to airlines.

BOAC's Captain Peter Cane at the controls of G-ARTA as VC10 development pilot during 1963–1964. Cane was in the right hand seat when Brian Trubshaw had trouble on an early test flight. A BOAC VC10 holds the world record for the fastest time taken for a subsonic airliner to have crossed the Atlantic, in a time of five hours and one minute; a record that stands to this day. The second fastest time recorded also belongs to the VC10, at five hours and fifteen minutes! (*Photo: Vickers/BAC*)

BOAC became British Airways in 1974 and the Super VC10 gained the new livery in full. It lacked the style of the Speedbird design but retained the quintessential emblem on the upper forward fuselage. BA's last SVC10 commercial service was on 29 March 1981. (*Photo: Vickers/BAC*)

Mr Laker's hard-worked British United Airways VC10 with the revised wingtips and the forward fuselage cargo door. (*Photo: Vickers/BAC*)

British Caledonian VC10s had a lion rampant on the fin. BCAL served South America and Africa with its VC10s prior to deploying 707s. (*Photo: Vickers/BAC*)

East African Airways truly "Super" SVC10s looked even longer in the striped livery. This is the ill-fated 5X-UVA that was lost at Addis Ababa in a take-off accident that was not the fault of the pilot nor the aircraft. (*Photo: Vickers/BAC*)

RAF VC10 CMk1 grabs at the sky after using just 1,950ft of runway to 'Vrotate'. Full power, nose high, and performing like a fighter not an airliner. This was the true VC10 advantage; the 707 and DC-8 simply could not match this feat. (*Photo: L. Cole*)

The T-tail, rear-mounted engines and generous slat and flap on the 'clean wing' design are shown off in the RAF's 'hot-rod' VC10: real elegance. (*Photo: A. Hart*)

The 'face' of the VC10's Vickers design, stemming from Vanguard and Vanjet design studies. A rarely appreciated angle to the fuselage roof structure is captured here as the RAF C.Mk1 poses for the camera just months before the type's demise. (*Photo: L. Cole*)

Fire up the Vickers! Another view of the updated RAF VC10 C.Mk1, reveals the upper and lower fuselage contours, 'chined' nose gear tyre, sleek wing box join, and that T-tail with its elegant 'bullet' fin top fairing; pure VC10 style as the RAF get ready to rev up the Conways. (*Photo: L.Cole*)

Doing the business. An RAF Harrier feeds from an ex-EAA Super VC10 as the Conways hum and the fuel flows. (*Photo: L. Cole*)

In-flight: on-board an RAF VC10 during refuelling exercises; the generous space and view from the flightdeck are evident. (*Photo: L. Cole*)

The greatest tail – ever! The magnificent VC10 tail design from Ken Lawson's aerodynamics team. Note the original, curved shape to the lower rudder's trailing edge – changed to an angled shape for later production airframes. Unlike most other T-tailed airliners, VC10 never suffered from a deep-stall and VC10 had natural nose-down pitch at the stall, but a stick-pusher was still an advisable fitting to avoid trouble in certain flight configurations. (*Photo: Vickers/BAC*)

When the prototype's wing was changed to improve its operating characteristics the wing area increased to 272.4m².

The VC10 had a slightly higher aspect ratio than the 707, being set at 7.5 aspect ratio. It was the VC10's advanced aerofoil and more efficient flaps and slats that improved the slow speed handling and the airfield performance of the VC10 in comparison to other machines such as the 707 and DC-8. This slower, low speed handling was a major safety factor benefit to the VC10.

The sweep of a wing is usually measured at the quarter-chord (width) line and a swept-back wing has a higher critical Mach number than a non-swept-wing. The VC10 wing was to be a 35° sweepback wing, but much debate over a 32.5 ° sweepback took place. The final VC10 wing sweep figure was therefore just slightly below that 35° ideal formula of 1940s German advanced wind tunnel provenance that Boeing (but not Douglas) followed in their jets. The maximum operating Mach number (MMO) for the VC10 was set at 0.886 for 31.000 feet and above. Later built RAF VC10s were cleared to Mach 0.925 speed cruise (and sometimes operated above that figure). The designed maximum speed (MD) is Mach 0.94. Later on in the life of the RAF VC10s (as tanker conversions) the MMO was adjusted to 0.866, putting less stress on the ageing structures that were in their fourth decade.[6]

In terms of overall aerodynamic performance, the VC10 was very smoothly finished in comparison to its two main rivals, had more curvaceous nose window design to the 707, and better sealing than any of its rivals. The general finish of the aircraft was exemplary in terms of reducing localised surface issues and airflow degradations and drag triggers. The lack of a ridged cabin window 'belt line' offered significant smoothness criteria advantages over the rival airframes and much lower aerodynamic noise too. Fokker aped the technique for its F28; a mini Vanjet/VC10 if ever there was one.

Such VC10/Super VC10 overall advantages stemmed from forensic work by the aerodynamics team.

However, it was soon obvious in testing that two drag issues were extant – that of confused airflow around the engine exhausts, and that the wing tip vortex was stronger than was anticipated from the wind tunnel tests. The prototype aircraft seemed to produce more drag than predicted, and in some cases buffet (localised flow separation) was encountered; localised flow reversal under the engine nacelles was even suggested by observed tuft testing in flight. So, in original prototype configuration the VC10 had a small drag related performance issue and quick changes to the design had to be made – at Vickers expense. This was all part of the expected experimentation with such a new design. At prototype stage, such findings and changes are normal, and as such should not be perceived or reported as a VC10 design failure: experimentation, observation, and correction are what prototypes are for! The 707, and notably the DC-8, both underwent wing design modifications (in service), with the DC-8 family requiring a continuing series of 1960s aerodynamic redesigns to wing, pylons and engine pods.

To counter the VC10's small drag problem at the rear of the engine nacelles, the famed 'beaver' tail shaped carvings were added – fine tuning exhaust and local airflow patterns – and then further reshaped for the Super VC10. The VC10 engine nacelles had featured a 'Seddon' airflow step between each of the two engines, this consisted of a number of angled steps that produce vortices and thereby 'fill in' the gap area between the two tail pipes. Photos taken from a Canberra of tufted engine nacelles on VC10 prototype G-ARTA showed that this feature was not working as conceived, and to correct this a number of alterations were made to it. The engine exhaust 'beaver tail' nacelle extensions were implemented as a result of these studies, and were constructed and tested prior to final selection and application as a production tooling. Ron Storey oversaw this part of the VC10's development work. For the Super VC10 design, the engine mount stub wing was widened by 15in to reduce boundary layer airflow interference over the pod junction, and the angle of the engine mountings slightly altered – all as a result of ongoing research improvement and taking into account the longer fuselage and its resultant effects on local airflow near the engines.

An Area-Ruled VC10?

One potentially very expensive drag reduction measure that was considered was an 'area rule' aerodynamic application to the rear fuselage-wing and engine stub-wing interaction. This was recalled by VC10 test and development ground crew engineering technician Maurice Ungless (who had worked on the VC10's fuel systems during G-ARTA's construction) in his VC10 memoirs as published at VC10.net.[7] Ungless described the rarely referenced prototype application to the VC10 of 'area ruling' of the airframe for drag peaks and troughs in cross sectional areas throughout the aircraft's length. Ungless recalled that to combat localised drag flows at the back end, two blister fairings were manufactured in the shape of a 'Sting Ray', in plain view and installed on each side of the fuselage over the two rear cabin doors, between the wing and engine nacelles. Apparently, these 6ft x 4ft panels protruded out from the fuselage to a maximum (depth) of approximately 8 inches, then faired into the fuselage aerodynamically at the edges. They were built and tuft-tested and filmed during flight trials, but it was considered that the drag reduction was small and the benefit was not enough to incorporate what was an expensive modification.

Out on the VC10's wing tips, original squared off tips were exchanged for so-called 'Kuchemann' tips (a seen on Vanjet prototypes). These revised-flow tips featured a large radius curve from the leading edge to a sharp corner at the trailing edge in planform – increasing total wingspan by 6ft. Also, the slat housings were realigned to provide for a slightly different slat position when extended. G-ARTA was flown in a large number of different configurations to find out what would have the most beneficial effect on the VC10's cruise drag. G-ARTA had first flown on 29 June 1962, Chief test pilot G.R. 'Jock' Bryce (who would go on to head BAC's operational sales department) undertook the test flying with E.B. Trubshaw (Second pilot) as handling flight crew and R. Holland (Assistant Flight Test Manager), C. Mullen and I. Muir as official technical observers. Soon, there were fifteen tons of technical equipment and fifty miles of cabling on board the test airframe, and over a year of test flying ensued.

Peak Performance

The VC10 wing aerofoil had a new shape – with a flatter top and more cambered lower profile at the wing root – in direct contrast to the 707's 'old' style top-curved aerofoil. The VC10 had a new design of aerofoil tagged as 'peak', or 'peaky' – because it created a peak in the performance graph of lift pressure and induced drag formula upon the wing – that was designed to be more efficient. This 'peaky pressure' distribution was so new it required development. Some have asked, did it lead to the over optimistic initial performance guarantees to BOAC? Subsequent changes to the aerofoil, notably to the Super VC10 design, indicate that this was less of an 'error' by Vickers, and more of a case of discovery during the design of a new theory upon which the VC10 was the first airliner for which this wing profile was specifically designed. For this, Vickers worked together with the National Physical Laboratory (NPL), the Royal Aircraft Establishment (RAE) and also the Aircraft Research Association (ARA) for over six months, and together they designed a wing with a 'peaky' pressure distribution (chordwise). This was so named as the aerofoil produced a low pressure peak over the leading edge as opposed to the previous theory of a fairly constant low pressure section over a significant portion of the wing's aerofoil chord.

Much of the work on this wing must be credited to H. Pearcy at the NPL and B. Haines (ARA), as they came up with the idea for the peaky wing and developed it for the VC10. The result was a wing that was tuned to be 'super-critical' in that it maintained its flow by not only delaying the conventional flow separation upon the aerofoil's lifting surface, but by moving that point of separation from its usual location on the aerofoil. This allowed localised boundary layer airflow tuning to an unheard of level. A two-dimensional transition between supersonic and subsonic flow without creating a shock wave lay behind their 'peaky' aerofoil's behaviour. Transferring such to real-life three-dimensional reality required much research.

Little credited in the VC10 story was the work of a Dr J. Weber, who via her RAE work with Dieter Kuchemann, provided a complementary theory framing the accurate determination of pressure distribution over a definitive wing section. This provided reverse-engineered knowledge transfer about wing airflow effects as the VC10 was designed – notably using an early analogue super-computer (Pegasus). The super-efficient lift mechanism was tailored to avoid compression drag by deliberately creating an airflow expansion wave (a moving localised airflow layer zone) over the leading edge and providing space for the air to act or move within it. Kuchemann and Weber were both German experts given new lives in Britain post-1945. So there *was* some degree of German advanced knowledge filtered down into the VC10. But we can say that the wing was of Vickers – albeit with some 'borrowed' knowledge – like much of UK and US aerodynamics developments post-1945.

The new aerofoil shape delayed the onset of shock waves which normally degrade the subsonic flow and thereby determine the critical Mach number. Boundary layer work was also relevant to the effect gained. The end result was a wing which was very efficient at the top of its speed range, but also worked well at the low speed end with flaps and slats extended. The VC10s slats only had one position – fully open, as opposed to fully closed.

The new VC10 wing avoided the need for major 'washout' twist, or either negative or positive formula (or both) on the aerofoil – camber alterations were minimal, even so, a lot of fine mathematical work went into blending each zone of effect across the aerofoil and to avoid unwanted local aerodynamic disturbances.[8]

The VC10s large trailing edge flap area of sixty-five per cent was greater than its rivals, and of significance, that flap area was uninterrupted by gaps because no wing-mounted engine exhaust efflux flows existed. The similarly uninterrupted leading edge slats curved out and downwards to a higher degree than any slat before it, and only Boeing's later 727 leading edge matched it. This gave rise to the VC10's 'ground effect' cushion of air upon landing – aiding the famous soft touchdown.

Still with the wing design, over at Teddington in the NPL, and at the RAE – also nearby at Farnborough – experts were consulted and several modifications were tried out. In one of the suggested 'tweaks', two inboard slats on each wing were locked outwards by three degrees and then taped and layered over with liberal amounts of balsa wood, hessian cloth and adhesive – thus filling in the gaps. In this configuration the VC10 prototype, G-ARTA, performed several flights from Boscombe Down with tuft testing and in-flight photography and measurements. The leading edge changes seemed to produce beneficial results, so the aerodynamicists designed a new leading edge which could lower the VC10's cruise drag. The costs of this modification might be very high indeed, as would the required changes to the 'setting' of the wing via a change to the wing torsion box spar junctions. This would have meant building completely new wings and changing a lot of the jigs on the wing production line at vast expense and Sir George told the team to find a cheaper way. The consequent design worked almost as well as the fine-tuned, but structurally expensive predecessor, but which was far easier to manufacture – requiring no changes to the wing incidence setting and torsion box structure. This leading edge was eventually fitted to the 1102 and later models, as well as the Super VC10s.

The only real early design 'battle' in the design office over VC10 wing design was to be the wing's thickness/chord ratio. This parameter could be seen as a challenge between the aerodynamicists and the structural engineers – as the 'aero' men would like the thinnest wing possible while the structures men needed depth for strength. With the custom-designed profile of the VC10, a large part of this fight was over before it started, as the wing design was already fixed by the stringent airfield performance demands. For the 1101 type this ratio was 13% at the root and 9% at the tips. Later in the development process this ratio was changed to 17% at the root when the wing chord was increased on the inboard section.

On the VC10 prototype wing in 1962, photos of this event show a very clean wing with one (almost full-chord length) wing fence at approximately three-quarters span to control the spanwise tip flow which without such fence, would otherwise spread decaying air and lift flow towards the ailerons, rendering them less effective and adversely effecting tip stall issues. The original wing tips were squared, but revised to Kuchemann standard – adding to the total span, and then a new, tall, inboard, wing fence would be added to control spanwise flow near the stall speed and benefit engine intake flow – all at minor cost to the lift coefficient from the minuscule reduction in the wing's upper surface area. The tall inboard fence was insisted upon by the Vickers test pilots and was the subject of some debate. Its main benefits (a the cost of a tiny amount of wing lifting surface area) were to stabilise airflow at low speed near the wing root-to-fuselage area, deliver better airflow to the engine intakes, and very interestingly, provide a major airflow effect resulting in an enhanced nose-down pitch at the stall. The VC10 had to be proven deep-stall safe and risky testing took place – but the wing performance was benign and soon finalised.

Removing the new, tall fence, was found to increase the risks of spanwise flow and (the adverse) nose-up pitch. Along with the engine-stub wing aerodynamic effect in acting like an elevator surface (beneficial downwards pitch), the new wing fence greatly aided the VC10s low speed and stall regime handling. No other rear CG, rear-engined T-tailer exhibited the beneficial, classic nose-down auto-recovery pitch at the stall. Here was another unique VC10 designed-in safety factor. It is worth repeating that no VC10 was ever lost in a deep-stall in testing or commercial service. This cannot be said of the other major T-tail airliner designs. Indeed, even BOAC's British airline associate, BEA, lost a Trident and all its passengers in a deep stall and had close calls on numerous other occasions. A BAC 1-11 also suffered a deep stall tragic loss.

Few people realise that the VC10s stall speed with flaps and slats deployed was below 100kts; an astounding speed for a large four-engined airliner. In fact in airline stall tests, crews would take the VC10 up to the onset of the stick-push (with accompanying klaxon warning) at a remarkable 97kts and then heave the nose down quickly. Beyond the onset of stall, the VC10 had the extra safety-measure of the unique, natural, nose-down pitch behaviour that its design delivered. However, the deep stall was not to be trifled with at low power settings and, if the VC10 got to 19° or 20° nose-up at low speed with flaps and gear dangling, it would need very decisive action to avoid trouble. Any 'pitch-up' would be fatal.

A particular 'aero' design challenge was to create a low drag engine pod and stub wing strut installation that was in tune with the wing airflow behaviour and wake. The strut needed to be thin, and yet strong. The 'stepped' swept strut design fed air to the 'dead' air region and tuned the wake flow off the back of the strut, reducing drag. For the Super VC10 the angle of this strut was further refined with a mild infilled twist applied. Another aspect of the engine mounting cradle and stub wing and fin interface was to tune the vibration levels so that they did not adversely interact with each other and tear the structure apart; as had recently happened with the Lockheed Electra's engine mounting-to-wing design interaction. All these efforts were typical of the perfectionist and forensic engineering that went into the VC10 underneath that glamorous profile.

On the elegant tail fin, it was vital that shock wave formations at the join of fin and tailplane were tuned down to low values, so the maximum thickness section of the tailplane was moved forwards relative to the outboard sections – hence the great sweep angle seen in the design and the swan-like 'bullet' fairing atop the fin.

For the main wing, expensive, and heavy, double slotted flaps were considered, but the simpler and lighter Fowler-type was settled upon, but these were subject to a great deal of lift/drag effect work by the Vickers team. Despite the Fowler type flap requiring as much rearwards extension as possible to be effective, the flaps were made to travel to a set angle or value, yet with as much lift as a higher value chord design: a thicker flap panel profile regained any lift losses from decreased flap angle travel. Flaps at 40° on the VC10 provided excellent approach behaviour.

The achievements of the Ken Lawson led VC10 aerodynamics team should always be credited for this airliner's excellence in aerodynamics and handling.

Test pilot Brian Trubshaw took over the stall test regime flying and carefully explored over 2,000 possible stall profile parameters. He said that the VC10 was a machine that pilots could trust, even if they might sometimes forget that they were not flying a fighter jet – such were the VC10s reserves.[9]

From the 1102 series Standard-model VC10 onwards, a revised wingtip design was also incorporated. This saw a bulbous and slightly drooped shaping to the leading edge and wingtip curve, and improved local lift number and better airflow at the tips (lessening the risks of a wing drop) and allowed a wider safety margin at high altitudes. A VC10 could now cruise at 41,000–43,000ft, near what pilots call 'coffin corner' – the thin air regime where lift and speed margins between flight or stall are very small indeed, sometimes less than ten knots depending on the aircraft's weight at the time. The new slightly lobed wingtip is quite noticeable in photographs of the Ghana Airways and BUA machines. A small vortex fence was added to the under surface of the leading edge, a sharp strip appeared on a portion of leading edge and some reshaping added to aid airflow aided matters for the 1102–1103 series. The Super VC10 did not need these lobed wingtips as its aerofoil had been revised along the span. Of note, the outboard wing fence was deleted and two short, mini-vortex flanges added; on the leading edge only.

The use of a specially designed supercritical aerofoil profile was a huge step in aerodynamics knowledge and use, as at the time, such aerofoil profiles were limited – a theoretical gain not yet proven in flight. The designers of the VC10 were breaking new ground, and during the thousands of hours flown on the prototype and the development airframes, they were learning every day. From this they developed the wing. The BOAC 'early wing' VC10 Type 1101 variants were slightly less economical than their latterly modified brothers, but BOAC had declined to include the various improvements that were suggested – although incorporating the changes would have delayed delivery. The BOAC specification VC10 still managed to fulfil all the promises made with regard to the hot-and-high runway performance that were requested by BOAC – contrary to some erroneous later claims. And the Super VC10's developed supercritical wing theory is now all the rage in advanced wing design.

The VC10 had low aerodynamic drag in all parameters – notably in terms of its self-created lift induced drag coefficient, and in terms of its profile/parasitic drag – the faired-in nose, smooth fuselage contours and skin, smoothed window 'belt line' (or lack thereof), and the removal of wing-pylon and engine pod interactions, creating an advantage, as did the unencumbered 'clean' wing design; all offered significant advantages over the opposition. The highly swept fin and tailplane lowered the Mach numbers and the curved and sculpted bullet fairing atop the fin was an ultimate piece of aerodynamic design.

The advanced aerofoil wing offered major drag reductions and the trailing or wake drag was minimal. Worth citing again as a very noteworthy feature was the natural 'nose-drop' at the stall, a very rare feature indeed for a rear-biased, rear CG, rear-engined T-tail aircraft design. Again, wing design, tail design (tall and highly swept), and the beneficial aerodynamic 'pitching' effect of the engine 'stub' wing combination, all helped created this rare, safety enhancing stall recovery characteristic. Unlike most other rear-engined, T-tailed airliners, the VC10 did not suffer from a nose-up pitch at the worst moment of high incidence and rear-biased CG and centre of lift and pressure, which could all combine to attempt to tip a T-tailer over backwards as it reared up. Auto-ignition would keep the engines turning too.

Control systems

Another lead example of the VC10's second generation design approach was in the nature and action of its electro-mechanical-hydraulic flight and airframe control systems, notably an automatic function.

All the main flying controls were fully powered and there was not the cheaper spring or servo tab mechanical effect used. Lessons about control surface effect and reliability had been learnt by Vickers on the Valiant, V1000 and Vanjet studies, and these were transferred into the VC10 main flight control mechanisms. No manual reversion was required. A split-system double redundancy design was used, so if a component in the system failed, the other system picked up the required mechanism of action. Systems of two halves, each with a separate drive from a separate engine power supply source, ensured great safety and fail-safe action. Each half of the system could operate simultaneously and each could act as an emergency standby to the other. So, system A is operated by engines 1 and 3, while system B (powering the same controls) is run from engines 2 and 4 – so a system, or engine failure does not mean that the aircraft 'loses' any or all of its systems. Each part of each system is driven by separate electro–hydraulic power units. The VC10 had four electrical generation sources, the 707 had three.

A total of eleven identical power units provide cross-referenced dual feed to the whole VC10 control system. If all four engines (and thus their respective separately powered systems) should fail, the VC10 had a drop-down electrical ram air turbine (ELRAT) – a 'windmill' electrical generation device designed by Harry Zeffert (and a rarely specified optional hydraulic system turbine HYRAT) in which an airflow-driven windmill of mini-turbine design can be deployed to power the vital flight control systems. Again, this was a VC10 first and not seen on the 707 and DC-8. The ELRAT saved the Super VC10 on two occasions in service and was not an 'allowable defect' if it was unserviceable – a VC10 and Super VC10 could only be flown if the ELRAT was signed off as functional.

Many of the components on the VC10s new systems designs came from established components already used in military and civil aircraft, so they were reliable from the word go, and not likely to suffer developmental reliability glitches. Some of these components, of electro-hydraulic nature, were shared under joint UK–USA licence agreements.

All the main 'primary' flying controls could be operated normally, or by their 'brother' system, if one part failed – albeit it at a slightly reduced rate of action. By using such a continuously 'live' system or mechanism, the VC10 did not rely on a redundant emergency back-up system that would normally lie dormant for years and itself having inbuilt risk factors for its reliability when rarely needed. Weight was saved by not completely duplicating the entire system, but instead creating a split system. The hydraulic system ran at 3,000psi and required steel and alloy pipes of the highest quality where the fluid, a fire retardant 'Skydrol 500' formula, would run. Special seals had to be developed that would not be degraded by the fluid itself. And you could not put Skydrol in your car's braking system!

The electrics were 200volts DC, driven from four separate engine-driven generators and featuring Westinghouse brushless generators – unaffected by high altitude conditions and temperatures. A Ferranti transformer provided the 28volt output of 150 amperes. Any unlikely 'runaway' control surface could be overruled or countermanded by its split system 'mate'. There were four elevator sections and a three section rudder. All of the VC10 control runs were direct physical linkages of mechanical, rod, lever and cable, with a 'Hobson' artificial feel unit adding a carefully graded hand-to-control yoke 'feel' reflective of surface, and speed related aerodynamic loadings being fed back to the pilot. 'Feel' force was proportional to control surface deflection, speed and height. The system was advanced in that it had an altitude related sensing parameter – taking into account reducing air pressure at height, so no false sensations or information was given to the pilot. The complexity and success of this artificial feel system was not matched for many years in aviation or automotive application.

As well as applying to actual moving flight control surfaces, the spilt-system pervaded the hydraulics, electrics, cabin air system, and other functions, thus providing a very reliable total aircraft operating system. So the VC10 flight controls were accurate, superbly safe and reliable. The Plessey Company were behind much of the VC10s electrical superiority. Aspects of this split-system or double redundancy fail-safe design appeared in the later Boeing 747 electrical system power designs, no doubt aided by the presence of former Vickers/BAC electrical design engineers in new job at Boeing's Renton offices in the 1960s. The VC10's new way of systems being double powered, and having a live back-up to its major mechanical systems was new, and marked it out from its competitors.

In terms of function, more new technical feats were established by the VC10 in addition to the new fail-safe control surface operational design because each (separate) section of the control surfaces was driven or activated by a separate power control unit   signalled by duplex autopilots – each of which 'read' or monitored the other. This meant that flight control had multi-function ability and safety, leading to a combination of automatic control, auto throttle, auto flare and a pilot 'hands off' automatic landing ability with a failure rate so low that it was unique. The VC10 was thus, a pioneer (along with Trident) of reliable, consistent, CAT 1 automatic landing, although the Trident took it to Category IIIA runway visibility level on more often occluded European runways. From 1968, the Super VC10 offered full category, in-service auto-land. Using BAC/Elliot signalling technology and auto-land/auto-coupled approaches became the norm in bad conditions. At that time, only five runways on the BOAC Super VC10 route network offered instrument landing systems (ILS) to match the Super VC10's own in-built capabilities. By the late 1970s the Super VC10 systems were removed – having been less often used than planned, and offering a weight and money saving option by their removal. No issues with the systems lay behind such an economic decision.

For the flight crew, the Vickers engineers also designed a new, quick-reference way of controlling all the new split-systems with what was an early form of flight management system – a diagrammatic systems control panel in an electro-mechanical display and control device depicting the shape of the aircraft, and systems locations therein, and the actual in-flight position of that surface – the 'baby aeroplane' as the Vickers men called it. This was made by Sangamo Weston Ltd.

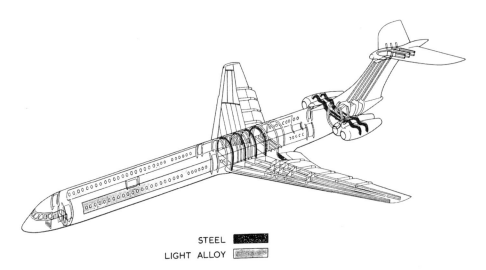

STEEL

LIGHT ALLOY

VC10's Reinforced Structure.

The flight deck was also spacious, well laid out, deeply windowed, and, as even admitted by Boeing 707 pilots, much easier to sit in and manage than their cramped, narrow, control post.

Fuselage and Wing Strength

The VC10 was a monocoque type fuselage structure, but was one that featured extra reinforcements in critical areas. Like a Saab, Volvo, or Mercedes car of the era, the VC10 body was a self-supporting monocoque type, yet one which benefited from over-engineered, extra stiff, localised reinforcements and strengthening to a degree not seen in simpler or cheaper (and lighter) mainstream structures. Of note, the VC10 design was the first time large jet engines had been paired at the rear of an airframe – requiring novel engineering solutions. Overall, throughout the VC10, a multiple load path network was built in – so if a part failed, other elements could absorb the failure and defuse any local fractures or cracks. The central cabin wing box and tail were incredibly strong, cabin and body apertures reinforced – milled from solid panels – and that central keel rail ran forwards to a nose/cockpit section of heavy duty formers, frames, and castings. The door frames were also heavily over-gauged and built up with massive support frames. The more usual practice of multi riveted, multi-welded, multi-panel work was avoided where possible. Huge chunks cut from solid metal alloys, and large machined skins, engendered high torsional rigidity. The wing was multi-spar with four main spar units and a massively strong centre box. This was a wing and hull without compromise. And it paid the price in weight – being several tonnes heavier than the 707 – for the VC10 was built like a proverbial (Vickers) battleship! Such construction saved the day and many lives in service.

Copper rich aluminium alloys and titanium alloys were used – at great expense. Panels were larger than those used by Boeing – so were stiffer and had fewer rivets and joints. The Vickers designers reduced the traditionally deployed numbers of lap joints, splices and seams along the window line – instead, using a machined from solid panel along the entire length of the window belt line. The window line panels were 34ft by 6ft and ¾ in thick. There were fewer crack-raising points and stiffening was integral – not add-on. Diagonally located load support beams, torque boxes, and massive cleating, all created a really strong structure. The additional skin cleats at each frame station would restrict any failure to one frame bay. Channel frames were doubled up with overlapping edges and the fuselage panels were laid transversely over their frames and with circumferential straps over them.

The crucial wing box and centre section, leading back to the very heavily reinforced tail area, was where the VC10s real heavy metal and strength was to be found. All this was new and required much design and testing, but it produced a very strong fuselage with no issues relating to potential pressurisation-cycle induced fatigue, and few of load and impact distress. With its strong spars machined from solid skins and thick skin panels, the elegantly swept and very smooth VC10 wing offered immense strength. All the inspection hatches in the wing had milled from solid frames – another exquisite and expensive engineering solution unique at the time to the VC10. The wing design was strength tested and passed a sixty per cent overload – a figure higher than many airliner wing structures ever achieved, including recent large composite structures– and the VC10 was also subjected to an asymmetric wing deflection test – 7ft on the tip and 6ft the other way at the opposite tip. Even at these loadings, across these tests, the brilliance of the VC10 wing design was proven, no actual test 'failure' in terms of structural (spar) breakage took place, instead, the wing flex and cracking reached a peak loading (at sixty per cent overload) that was deemed as a test limiting 'fail' reading – but not a broken wing – unlike certain other airframes old and current.

Intriguingly, the VC10 had American cabin windows – a product named Oroglas 55 created by the Lenning Chemical Company from a Rhom and Hass (USA) reputedly German-originated process; each window had three sheets of glass and the external pane was larger than its aperture so it self sealed itself into its hole, and added structural strength once glued in place.

The VC10 featured a lightweight, noise absorbing composite floor covering – end grain balsa wood with steel sandwich construction made by the Mallite Company. One VC10 also used a test section composite-type glass fibre reinforced rudder (as 1 of 3 sections), and was the basis of an early Ciba-Geigy composite rudder experiment from which a great deal was learned about such structures. Although it is unlikely that Vickers would have considered using the now deployed, Airbus- type composite fin with its controversial and much debated composite-to-composite and composite-to-metal, asymmetric fin-to-fuselage mounting design that does not use fuselage frames taken up as a chassis bearer into the fin. Issues of composite rudder degradations (notably from hydraulic fluids), rudder failures, composite delaminations and structural failures – allegedly resulting in events such as the Air Transat Airbus 'Havana incident' – reflect the very slow pace of composite fibre design, development and testing mechanisms since the 1960s when a composite fin was tested on the VC10.

Because so much of the VC10 chassis, fuselage, and wings, was made from single pieces of metal, and had much fewer rivets, joints and panels than normal, the resulting structure was very stiff, fatigue-distress resistant, corrosion proof, and had in-built load-paths to carry stresses on more routes in the structure than was normal: A true fail-safe principal.

Low Stress Levels

Key stress levels in the VC10's airframe structure were cited by Vickers at 11,000lbs per square inch compared to 17,000–20,000lbs per square inch in the rival machines. Lower stress meant longer structural life! Cracks in the structure could be lessened and an early estimate of 30,000 flight hours or 10,000 landings (a decade's typical airline usage) before any such cracking might be expected, was soon upped beyond 60,000 hours – testament to the VC10 structure, which was stiff but not brittle.

The fuselage reinforcing hoops were thickened at the point where they intersected the floor – providing extra reinforcement at that crucial junction. In the wing area, massive gauge alloy hoops ran around the cabin and into the wing box. Anti-tear straps and oversized corner fillets all added to a fuselage that was the strongest, most rigid, and most tear resistant yet devised. Around the doors there was further heavy gauge reinforcement. Under the floor, Vickers fitted a 20in wide central keel (another shipbuilding idea!) the entire length of the airframe as a longitudinal torsion box type structure that reinforced the traditional cross beams. Advanced metal extrusion processes were also deployed – the VC10 was solid, but as light as it could be whilst retaining that solidity.

Down at the back, the four giant engines (and their thrust) were held in place by not just massively strong engine mountings beams, but a complex, almost geodetic, 'basket' network of supports, braces, beams and panels that tied the whole tail unit, the engines, and the vertical fin and its loads, into what was probably the strongest piece of airframe structure then seen anywhere.

Designing a structure to hold four Rolls-Royce Conways, absorb their thrust/torque into a safe mounting and letting their effect work, was no easy task. To attach the Conways and their 45+ tonnes of thrust output, safely to an airframe, particularly in closely coupled rear-mounted configuration, was a very considerable engineering challenge. Get it wrong and the engines would either tear themselves away from the airframe, or tear the airframe apart. So, the two main engine beams were very expensive, drop-forged alloy structures, and were the mounting point for the four, 10ft long, external, curved 'spectacle' shaped engine support bearers which had three thrust load-bearing pick-up points for each engine. The downwards acting stress loadings of the four engines upon the engine beams and support frames – notably upon landing – required extensive engineering solutions to ensure long life and safety.

The need to make sure the tall tail fin and its very large horizontal tail surfaces would stay attached and not fail in extremis due to bending and twisting stresses, as well as normal in-flight loadings, was paramount. The fin had vertical spars that grew from deep within the fuselage tail structure and vertical stringers and a very thick skin sheeting all combined to resist twist and failure.

The large tailplane's (bigger than some military jets main wingspans) loads had to be passed down into the fin structure and much local reinforcement was applied. The tailplane was mounted from the its fin-support box via two roller bearings (allowing pivot of incidence setting), with a third mount via the screw-type actuator that connected the fin top to a forward reaching arm on the main fin structure.[10]

Of note, this tailplane incidence screw-jack device featured a safety rod to stop it running away with itself – which could lead to loss of control. A certain other T-tailed airliner did *not* have a screw-jack safety stop and eventually mass fatalities resulted in a screw-jack runaway accident due to alleged maintenance failures. Still in the tail, the steel and alloy support sleeves carried the main loadings to and from the tailplane ribs and castings. The combination of all this Vickers design work saw the VC10 survive three major tailfin overload events and several engine-related incidents in service – whereas other airliners similarly afflicted, have not.

The famous South American turbulence-related incident that befell a VC10, surely proved that this work served its purpose; the tail stayed attached and the aircraft flew home to London – subsequent inspection revealed a failed fin support, but the fail-safe back up structure had carried that failure and its loads.

The tail fin and tailplanes were heated by ducting for anti-icing and used Boulton and Paul built power control units. If one of the four elevators should fail to work, the others could counteract its adverse effects.

A Barnes Wallis Legacy?

Where did Edwards and his team get the VC10's quality of construction ethos from? Where did that hewn from solid, extra-safe structural integrity start? We can cite the Vickers tradition and the effect of Barnes Wallis' obsession with geodetic structures upon Edwards when he worked under Wallis. However difficult Wallis may have allegedly been to work for, his focus on strength, fail-safe design and allied efficiency, can only have manifested in Vickers later, non-geodetic structures. From the Viking, as the company's first airliner, onwards, the all-metal alloy monocoque of Vickers fuselages was reinforced and much stronger than the norm. Just as the geodetic Vickers Wellington had saved lives in wartime RAF service with its multi-load path structure, so too, would the non-geodetic VC10 in airline life. Looking up inside the VC10s tail and rear end, we can see an almost-geodetic network of reinforcing metal work.

The VC10 fin and tailplane – one of the largest structures in the airframe building world at that time, were manufactured at the Bournemouth Hurn plant.

There, a dedicated team of time-served aviation industry artisans constructed this complex structure.

Typical of such men was Edward 'Ted' Read as chief draughtsman on the VC10 tail control surfaces. Read had worked on Horsa gliders in the war, worked for de Havilland on the Vampire and Comet, contributed to building the Airspeed Ambassador, and then spent time in the Vickers design office before moving to the south coast to work for the Vickers Hurn factory.

Edward Read's son, the ex-RAF photographer and industrial film maker, Michael, says: 'My father was so proud to have worked on so many important British aircraft – including the D-Day gliders – but the massive VC10 tail at Hurn was, for him and his co-workers, a major jet age achievement. He would bring the VC10 drawings home and lay them out on mum's pastry table and check and double check everything. Ensuring that the big beautiful tail – which was one of the VC10s' most crucial and complicated components – was correctly built as designed, was a vital contribution to what was then Europe's biggest airframe.'[11]

The VC10's main undercarriage allowed a very soft landing – minimising the shock loading upon the engine bearers and the entire tail structure. The main undercarriage was rearwards swept by 10° and had cranked main beams. The rear of the four main wheels per bogie touched down first and the two-stage shock absorbers took the shock out of the impact forces. A VC10's landings were the smoothest of any airliner and once mastered, flattered the pilot.

Engine development

Rolls-Royce had taken to naming their new jet engines after famous rivers, and their largest jet engine to date, in 1955, was aptly named after the powerful and reliable River Conwy – as 'Conway'. Not only was this engine the largest Rolls-Royce jet design, it was the first viable large turbofan, as opposed to pure turbojet – a big stepping stone in jet engine history. By creating an outer, or surrounding 'bypassed' envelope of unburnt airflow through and from the jet engine, more efficient thrust was created with lower noise levels being delivered by such managed exhaust airflow. A large fan, mounted on the front of the engine, or in an intake with first stage guide fans, could be driven by 'free' energy from the main combustion process and fan, and allow cool flow of airflow around the hot part of the jet mechanism. Some turbofans used an aft-fan, rear mounted and driven, but the front fan was deemed more efficient.

Expanded from experience on the Avon engine, the Conway was a pioneer, the original design of two-spool compressor jet with a larger static vaned front end jet mouth with a revolving turbine that streamed off an amount of intake air and wrapped it over and around the jet core shafts and exhaust flow – as opposed to a distinct large, single 'fan' front mounted entry section turbine later seen as an add-on to the Pratt and Whitney JT3C design. Conway went through numerous iterations from a 9,000lbs thrust device up to its final 22,000lbs rating. The Conway, at an early 13,500lbs thrust, was mooted to be a possible developed Vickers Valiant (to replace Avons) and a V1000 powerplant choice, and then developed CO.10 engines were seen on the early BOAC 707s, but the long gestation period of the Vanjet and VC10 allowed time for the refinements that led to the very powerful VC10-specific Conway 42 and 43 iterations.

Early Conways had 0.3 bypass airstream ratio, then upped to 0.6 and 16,500lbs static measured thrust. This was soon uprated to 18,000lbs, then 20,370lbs, and then to 21,800lbs thrust in the Conway 42 and 43 models respectively. Improvements in Conway thrust came from a larger low-pressure stage and scaled-up stages and components, each by smaller degrees rather than simply bolting on a large intake fan at the front. This avoided excessively higher engine shaft rpm and resultant higher temperatures in the engine's core. Rolls-Royce concentrated on improving the CO.10 and CO.12s' vanes, turbine blades, airflow, and low pressure stages.

The Conway had a fixed intake vane, quite a narrow intake mouth and a slender profile in the engine pod – meaning reduced frontal area and less drag. Intake air is taken in via static guide vanes before hitting the first compressor that had a central core built into a titanium lined duct. Air pressure is more than doubled (x 2.25) before being passed along into the main chamber. There, 38% of that flow is streamed off from the core into the bypass function – the remaining entering the combustor area. At the exhaust end, the bypass air forms a sheath of airflow over the hot exhaust gas flow via re-streaming at near supersonic velocities – hence the noise! The combustor air enters the process at over fifteen times the intake value. Nimonic coated alloy igniter, or flame tubes, ignite the combined air/fuel mixture; the resultant force delivering the thrust to rotors that drive the shaft-driven compressor stages.

Previous Conway experience had revealed areas of high wear in certain valves and nozzles, so for the revised variant engines, hardened coatings, enhanced design and oil system improvements were all implemented. Major CO.12 to CO.42 differences included: larger low pressure turbine, by-pass ratio increased and an increased capacity low pressure turbine. An extra intermediate stage compressor was added to the CO.43 from the CO.42. The CO.43 runs at slightly higher temperatures to the CO.42, but not to a level likely to induce fatigue. The first CO.42 was powered up in June 1960, but it would be 1963 before it was fully tested and certificated. Soon afterwards, the idea of an underwing 'spare' engine carrying pylon for the VC10 was mooted – utilising a lightweight composite bullet-shaped fairing that had minimal effects on airframe trim.

With the VC10's engines mounted from a stub wing from the fuselage, rather than wing pylon, the VC10 Conway application required a new way of mounting components to or from it – using a central mounting 'carrier' beam. Being mounted close to the fuselage airflow meant that special crosswind and localised airflow issues all had to be carefully studied for the VC10's engine intake airflow characteristics and to avoid stalled air causing the engine to 'cough'. The opportunity was taken to expand the 'gap' between the engines and fuselage with an 11in span extension to the Super VC10s engine stub wing mounting design.

Advanced vibration metering was applied to the VC10's Conways with a graphical display at the flight engineer's station – allowing very fine monitoring of any engine vibration issues, be that actual specific-engine vibration, or comparative vibrations levels across all four power units. A second set of throttles were also mounted at the engineer's control desk on the flight deck – again allowing extra vigilance to power settings.

The dangers of turbine or rotor 'burst' in closely paired jet engines was of concern because, in the close-coupled configuration, escaping blades and heavy rotor components could penetrate and damage the adjoining engine or the hull. As with the wing-root mounted engine configuration of the Comet, such paired engines needed careful design to protect each engine and the surrounding area with armour plating (Comet's engines were uncomfortably close to the main fuel tanks). In the VC10's use of paired engines, the powerplants were (unlike in the Comet and the V1000) kept away from the fuselage, fuel tanks and wing structure. For the VC10, a compressor casing capable of containing explosive blade events was designed. The large low pressure fan was wrapped in a flanged steel case and the Stage 4 engine core zone saw a thickened magnesium-rich cladding. Any turbine over speed is countered by an emergency shut-off control that self-actuates in under one second of a turbine burst. Each engine pod is divided into two sections, separated by a fireproof bulkhead, attached to the aforementioned flanged bulkhead. So the 'hot' combustion zone is separated from the cool air zone. Fuel and hydraulic lines are mounted ahead of the bulkhead. The design of the protective barriers between the VC10's paired engines was proven to work on the rare occasion when an engine suffered an explosive failure – fires did not spread, and in most cases, escaping components did not disable the neighbouring engine, nor penetrate the fuselage; and the engine bearers held – although on one occasion bending spectacularly.

Thrust reverse were initially fitted to all four VC10 engines – but reduced to the two outer engines after fin buffet distress from the inboard reversers was discovered. The big benefit of the uprated Conway was that the VC10 entered service with a 'new' engine, but one that had been previously proven in service in its early incarnations. Engine reliability was therefore high from launch.

With a two, as opposed to a three core design, the Conway's engine length and pod could offer aerodynamic advantages over longer and 'fatter' engines.

Conway CO12/540 Details:
Max Thrust at take-off: 20,370lbs/9,240kgs x4
Max Continuous thrust: 16,560lbs
Cruise Thrust: 4,500lbs at 35,000ft with specific fuel consumption of 0.823lbs per hour
Max Pressure Ratio: 15:1
Dry Weight: 5001lbs
Length: 54 in
Engine Diameter: 51 in
Note* Super VC10 and RAF VC10 used Conway 550B (21,825lbs/988kgs) x4. 24,000lbs thrust version not manufactured.

Test Flying and Route Proving

The VC10 and Super VC10 fleet both underwent extensive 'Tropical Trials' flight test development periods on the very routes in African and Asia that they had been designed for. The VC10's first flight in 1962 meant that it had two years of development flying before entering BOAC service, and prior to certification the VC10 flew 4,230 hours of test flying. Somewhat surprisingly, all twelve BOAC VC10s had been manufactured by October 1963 – to the point where several airframes sat new and un-flown as development flying continued with G-ARTA and then the BOAC G-ARVA, G-ARVB and G-ARVF airframes starting the BOAC test period. G-ARVF flew most of the African and Asia route test flying. The Super VC10 followed the VC10 quickly, and first flew on 7 May 1965 – only one month after the standard model entered commercial service, G-ASGA and G-ASGD doing much of the test and route proving flying from spring 1965 onwards.

Of interest, much of the VC10 early 'hot and high' trials were conducted closer to home than might be imagined: rather than flying all the way down to Africa for every such test, Vickers secured use of a high altitude and high temperature runway at the military airfield at Torrejon in Spain. There, on 12 August 1963, the Standard VC10, G-ARVB, left Wisley under the command of Bill Cairns – who performed much of the flight testing of the VC10 in Africa (Peter Baker was co-pilot). G-ARVB flew to Madrid, and then at Torrejon began the harsh testing regime that included heavy landings, go-arounds, and high-speed rejected take-offs likely to cause brake and tyre overheats. Every combination of speed, weight, flap and slat setting, temperature, and engine power, were tried out to frame the performance rule book and flight manuals. Notably, the very high weight, high speed abandoned take-off tests resulted in the brakes overheating and the tyres 'popping' their fuse-plugs as designed in order to avoid explosion by making the tyres deliberately deflate. G-ARVB crawled its way off the Torrejon runway, hobbled by deflating tyres, and much was learnt from such a testing regime.[12]

Clearly, the proximity of the Spanish locations made it quicker and easier to gain experience, but both Johannesburg airport and the Lanseira runway made for actual African operating experience. It was during such testing that the early issues of brake and tyre performance were revealed – leading to modifications and improvements prior to service entry. In cold weather and wet testing, Vickers and Dunlop also noted that a specially flanged or 'chined' nose wheel tyre design could reduce water spray off the undercarriage and reduce the flow of such spray into the engines.

Another interesting aspect of the tropical testing was that the VC10 and Super VC10 test flights followed the old Imperial Airways routes over Africa – actually following the River Nile southwards to Khartoum, prior to entering East African airspace, and then south to Salisbury and Johannesburg. During the Super VC10 test flying, G-ASGB went to South Africa on 8/9 January 1965, and made the first (and only) flight of a Super VC10 non-stop direct from London to Salisbury (now Harare); the destination had been Johannesburg, but adverse winds precluded this. VC10 G-ARVB had been, on 22 October 1963, the first VC10 to follow the length of the Nile non-stop from Cairo to beyond its source – then direct to Johannesburg – the normal BOAC service route for VC10s was from Rome, via Khartoum, Nairobi, Salisbury and then to Johannesburg.

BOAC Team at Vickers

Vickers and the BOAC VC10 development crew flew over 4,000 hours of testing with G-ARTA. BOAC's men, who spent a lot of time at Wisely, included captains, Cane, Gray, Phillips, Rendall and Stoney – all either ex-Imperial or RAF and with Comet 1 and 4 experience. BOAC's top man, Captain Norman Bristow as flight commander, became the 'face' of the BOAC VC10 and Super VC10 flight teams, alongside another Norman – Captain N. Todd. BOAC pilots overseeing earlier VC10 progress were Captains H.J. Field, A.P.W. Cane and R. Knights.

Of significance, Captain Peter Cane had been BOAC's liaison man at de Havilland's during the rebirth of Comet 1 as Comet 4. Cane would conduct the BOAC proving trials for Comet 4 and its new Avon engines, and would then proceed to be BOAC's chief liaison with Vickers during the design and flight proving programme for the VC10. Captain Tom Stoney would travel the same Comet-to-VC10 journey as flight manager, and Captains M. Majendie and J. Nicholls would be the VC10 chief training officers. Captain L. Heron would also be part of the BOAC VC10 development process

Indeed, BOAC kept a wide-ranging team of top men at Brooklands/Wisely as the VC10 was developed and then test flown. J.R. Finnimore was BOAC's VC10 development manager (D. Ashman was in-service engineering manager). J. Romeril was BOAC's Conway engine testing man as head of a power unit development team. Charles Abell was BOAC's chief VC10 engineer. The BOAC VC10 flight crew managers were captains, A.S.M. Rendall (Flight Manager), F.W. Walton (Deputy Flight Manager), and J. Nicholl (Chief Training Captain). G. Sears was Chief Engineering Officer, W. Robinson was Chief Navigating Officer and H. Hughes was the airlines VC10 flight navigation superintendent.

The customer airlines all had resident men at Vickers as the VC10 took shape, their part of the offices was known as 'Airline Alley'. BUA's top man was Captain P.A. Mackenzie, and BUA had its top engineers, W. Townsend and J.R. Sidebotham on hand; EAA had Captain G.W. Mitchell leading the EAA Super VC10 developments.

Vickers Armstrongs – latterly as BAC – advertised the VC10 and Super VC10 in the aviation trade press to potential customers with large full page advertisements that proclaimed the benefits of the 'Clean Wing Jets' and, notably, claimed that the VC10 could be operated between places previously out of bounds to big jet transports. A full page photograph of the VC10 in front of its main 707 rival with the strapline that: 'The passengers will notice the difference' made a point.

It might be assumed that the VC10's 'new' or innovative design work across airframe, aerodynamics, engines, electro-mechanical and other systems, could lead to an untried and untested thoroughbred aircraft of a VC10, being likely to fits of breakdown and unreliability – or with the customer doing the development testing work in the early launch period – as per British Leyland car design of the 1960s and 1970s! But this was most definitely *not* the case. Much of the advanced VC10 ingredients were careful developments of earlier variants or knowledge on Vickers first big jet – the Valiant – and the Vanjet works and, where they were not so extensive, was the high quality Vickers test and development programme, that, when launched into BOAC service, there were very few issues with all this new technology. Only in exploring wing aerodynamics – quite literally at the leading edge of knowledge – did Vickers encounter the need for further modifications. The VC10 had a good entry into service despatch reliability record and only early problems with mechanisms in the brakes and wing flaps and some oil seals (soon solved) were noted. The VC10 was an on time airliner and could, of course, carry its own issue out at remote tropical airfields where, unlike the 707 fleet, the VC10 could not be expected to be able to 'borrow' spares from other operators. If a VC10 was going (rarely) to go 'technical' it would be properly late! Vickers devised a spare engine-carrying pod so that BOAC could ferry an engine to a stranded machine – the pod was under the wing!

The VC10s approach to strength, safety and capability was at the heart of its reliability, appeal and longevity – as well as meeting the route performance demands for which it was designed. Some, notably in BOAC, might say that the VC10 was over-engineered and heavy. We must respond with an underlining of the fact that without its design and build details, the VC10 could not have achieved what it did. Furthermore, no VC10 ever crashed due to structural failure or design defect. No VC10 ever suffered a T-tail deep stall (nor ever needed to deploy, in testing, the back-up anti-stall tail cone-mounted parachute), no VC10 ever encountered a T-tail-runaway screw jack failure leading to the deaths of all on board (another Western, T-tailed airliner did), no VC10 T-tail unit ever fell off (as had an HP Victor T-tail), no VC10 fell out of the sky due to single or double engine failure, and no VC10 ever crashed due to tailplane spar failure. No VC10 ever failed due to corrosion. No VC10 ever crashed due to performance issues at a critical stage of flight, such as engine failure at take-off, or landing, or climb out, or at the go-around. No VC10 ever had to be put down into a field due to uncontained fire, and no VC10 ever stalled after take-off due to icing. Such events *did* occur to other airliners. So the VC10's failsafe design principals were worth it. Can any rival airliner type claim such a record?

And BOAC never lost a VC10 or Super VC10. When operational incidents occurred, the Vickers design saved the day – and lives. In wider airliner service, there was one VC10 and one Super VC10 loss each and neither were due to the fault of the aircraft's design.

What of the aforementioned Andes incident – when, in early 1970, VC10 G-ASIX was hit by very severe mountain wave-air turbulence over the Andes, and thrown violently sideways and experienced a high 'g' bank angle across the sky? Then came a fall downwards, with the VC10's PCU control system unit disabled, the crew performed a masterful recovery with degraded controls (soon reset). Upon landing, the aircraft was cleared for service and flew back to London Gatwick. Only during deep inspection was a crack in a tail-fin support spar component found. The point was, that during the violent incident over the mountains, the VC10's massive and heavy tail, topped by that great tailplane, stayed attached, and although damaged was subsequently found, the other, failsafe principal load paths in the fin even allowed it to fly home across the Atlantic. We can suggest that only Vickers design saved the passengers and crew from a fatal crash that day, and that another aircraft type may have snapped its tail fin – or that a wing-pylon equipped airframe may have lost engines from their pylons as the fuse pins snapped during the violent gyrations. So the VC10 design work saved the day. Thrown uncontrollably sideways across the sky and then dashed earthwards, the VC10 tail fin and tail end, stayed on. It was a very close call – perhaps not stated so at the time, but what better tribute to its designers could one evidence from airline service life.

Through all the advanced design and engineering of the VC10 project, Vickers moved the concept and context of large civil airframe design and manufacture into a new arena – a second generation of airliner design and its operation beyond 'normal' parameters. *This* was the truth of the VC10 story.

*Author's note: Pilot error is not implied nor stated. A culmination of a series events were deemed relevant in both cases.

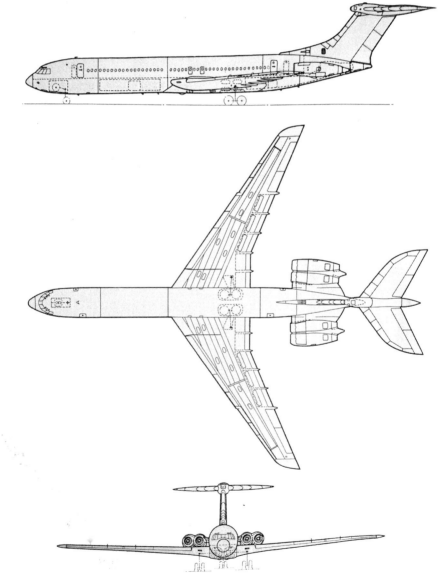

The VC10 as V1151 defined.

Chapter 7

BOAC, Parliament and Planes: Politics, Passengers, Guthrie, and the VC10 affair

In 1963, whatever the fanfares and flag waving of Britain's 'golden era' of aviation, BOAC was in deep trouble, and the taxpayer and their elected representatives were beginning to ask why. Parliament would soon lose patience. Furthermore, the airliners of the claimed era of British brilliance had been somewhat less than that: Only the Viscount had been truly brilliant on a global stage, selling by the hundreds, but Comet had failed and the elegant Britannia seemed to have created a managerial delusion that props, even if turbine-driven, could compete with transatlantic jets. In the late 1950s, BOAC was still relying on a fleet of reconditioned DC-7Cs that simply devoured engines and maintenance costs. Then came nearly £50 million worth of 707 orders.

Initially, in late 1957, BOAC, under the 'air' experience of Sir Gerard d'Erlanger, had enthused about the VC10 and dreams of an all VC10 BOAC fleet were not so far-fetched. By 1958 a £77million contract for thirty-five VC10s, plus twenty options, was reality. But BOAC was soon under new management and an all 707 fleet seemed far more likely. BOAC then vacillated and manoeuvred and it was against this backdrop, and of BOAC's ever-changing orders for the VC10 and Super VC10, that changes took place. The VC10 grew in size and then the real Super VC10 proposal was cut down in scale by BOAC.

Vickers also had cost issues with its original quotes as the VC10 was proving expensive to design and make.

By December 1963, the House of Commons held a debate as 'Order for Second Reading of the Air Corporations Bill' – which was a Parliamentary-led look at the financing and management of British airline corporations in the form of BEA(C) and BOAC itself. This would run on into 1964. Julian Amery as Minister of Aviation, who had replaced Peter Thorneycroft, but himself was soon to be ousted by the general election result, had been taking a close look at BOAC; some feared he might try and get a new man (Giles Guthrie) to do to BOAC what Dr Beeching was to do to British Railways! BOAC at that time was the second largest long-haul airline in the world and haemorrhaging money like jet fuel spewing from a leaking wing tank.

A 'White Paper' on BOAC was to reaffirm that BOAC's obligations were to operate as a commercial concern and that if, or where, any need to operate otherwise than commercially arose – on UK Government instructions, or in response to its advice – that this should be done only with the agreement, or at the instance of the minister, for the government.

Of vital relevance, their existed at this time, the separate 'Corbett Report' into the running of BOAC, which took over ten months to compile and which was estimated by *Flight* magazine to have cost about £40,000 to procure. The Corbett Report observed that during the period 1956–1960 there existed the 'utterly absurd' situation of BOAC having a part-time chairman with a full-time deputy-chairman and a board, the large majority of whose members were once-a-month members/attendees.[1]

Corbett was critical of BOAC's management – in mechanism and structure – which was roundly criticised, and this ultimately led to more musical chairs at BOAC, but it was all done quietly and oh–so politely, with lots of behind-the-scenes niceties to avoid any upset or bad publicity that might annoy the lower orders – the tax payers who funded the affair. Corbett's main attack was made via a very grave charge against BOAC's management, one of weakness over financial control, yet the Corbett Report had neither been given to BOAC, nor acted upon by the government. So the Corbett Report had not been shown to BOAC's Board or other major parties involved – it was being kept away from the headlines. BOAC meanwhile, had, in 1963 alone, racked up a massive £12 million loss. Yet revenue was on the up and over £50million had been handled as transactions. BOAC's load factor in 1963 was 54% – up from below 50%. A beleaguered Sir Matthew Slattery was still running BOAC and its newish fleet of 707s alongside the fast-paced but weak payload capacity of the Comet 4s. With the imminent VC10, BOAC would, by mid-1964, be operating a long-haul fleet of three differing jet types with three sets of costs to service similar routes (the likes of key competitors like KLM, Lufthansa and Qantas, each had just one jet type for their respective long-haul fleets). Slattery, amid BOAC's inherited operational burdens, was caught between a rock and a hard place and most parliamentary observers were kind to him (though not all) as he tried to steer BOAC through a mess that was in some sizeable part, of its own creation under his and his predecessors tenures.

BOAC had been subject to the 1949 Air Corporations Act, which empowered the state, via its minister, to give directions as to the form of the corporation's accounts. BOAC's accounts showed a deficit of £80 million at the end of March 1963, and a total figure of £85 million was likely to accrue. The Air Corporations Bill now asked for an increase of a £100 million deficit on revenue account – to £125 million. This increase was to provide for continuing losses before BOAC could overcome the problems which it faced. The sums were, by 1960s rates, significant to the national exchequer.[2]

Between 1956 and 1962, BOAC introduced five different types of aircraft into service and the cost was staggering – nearly £13 million. BOAC had backed the Britannia in both its versions hoping that it would be delivered in 1954 to 1956, but delays occurred leaving BOAC with a real problem – one that the VC7 could have solved quickly! BOAC's subsequent orders for the 707 seem even more odd when one considers that BOAC's main, money-earning, premier routes were the services to Africa and Asia. Heathrow to New York might have been important, but it was Heathrow to Johannesburg, and Heathrow to Hong Kong via India, that were BOAC's absolutely vital revenue streams. So why order an airliner (the 707) that was not designed to operate effectively on such routes and would take years to be developed into an airframe that could adequately service them once runways had been improved. Only then to have demanded a shot-runway 'hot-rod' as in the VC10!

Once again, BOAC's deliberate actions and contradictions over the VC7 look very strange (if not suspect) indeed and its 707 preference appeared utterly contradictory.

As 1963 turned into 1964, Sir Matthew Slattery and Sir Basil Smallpiece had gone from BOAC. Other board members, most of them titled men, were soon to depart. In their place came a banker – a man of trade and of fiscal experience – named Giles Guthrie, who was soon appointed to place a firmer hand upon BOAC. The BOAC 'club' had been shaken and stirred. Introduction into revenue service of the VC10 was just a few short months away, so too was a change of British Government – likely to reveal more chaos and bargaining over BOAC. The then unasked question was, would BOAC have enough aircraft when the economic and passenger bookings upturn came – which it surely would and did after 1966?

Total VC10 Cancellation? The Guthrie Plan Gains Pace

To illustrate how close the whole VC10 and Super VC10 project came to being cancelled, we know that the British Government and MPs in the House of Commons had openly discussed the costs of compensating Vickers/BAC if the VC10, and more specifically the yet to be born Super VC10 fleet, were to be effectively annihilated by official move. Total cancellation of the entire BOAC VC10/Super VC10 fleet was actually mooted under Guthrie. The fact that Edwards and Vickers had got on with building the VC10 fleet at a very fast rate, meant that by 1964 over half the VC10 fleet had been constructed – real airframes that could not be 'disappeared' without compensating the manufacturer. But the Super VC10 was still in its early build.

MPs on the political Left leapt on the bandwagon and accused the government of not just vacillation, but chaotic management and strategy. The incoming Guthrie may have got close to stopping the Super VC10 in its tracks. What had been an order for thirty-five VC10s had been drastically shrunken, yet with more Super VC10s ordered, but not enough to compensate for the lost Standard model VC10 orders. That order too was curtailed. What had started off as forty-five VC10 orders, had ended up as fifteen VC10s and thirty Super VC10s, only then to be cut down to ten VC10s and thirty Super VC10s. Then came Guthrie and the cancellation of half that Super VC10 order; then all of it. The on-off nature of BOAC's VC10 and Super VC10 orders endured through into Guthrie's final 'chop' to the Super VC10 orders – only seventeen to be built, alongside the twelve Standard VC10s.

An all-Boeing BOAC was at one time a real possibility, but of course, the political fallout over Westminster and Wisely would have been massive. Guthrie may have thought he had the authority to get away with it. Prior to all these shenanigans, the British aviation industry was in the wake of the post-Sandys Report era of mergers, and the creation of the British Aircraft Corporation as BAC after 1960, just as the VC10 was being defined and laid down. Airliners, their design and their orders from the state carriers – BEA's Trident to de Havilland's as part of Hawker Siddeley, and BOAC's VC10 to Vickers, cannot have been irrelevant to decisions taken circa 1959–1961 over BAC.

On 22 November 1963, *The Financial Times* pointed out that if it was the intention that Sir Giles Guthrie should produce a 'Beeching' type plan for BOAC, that this surely would meet with opposition from the Foreign Office, the Defence Ministry, and all those ministries which had an interest in the activities of BOAC – not just as an airline, but, it seems, once again as a national 'instrument'. And as the newspapers said, it would not be possible to estimate such effects, in a simple, profit-and-loss account.

Back in Parliament, the reality of BOAC wanting to spend the astounding sum of $2million (a huge amount in those days) in 1964 on a VC10 advertising campaign saw the comment made in the House during the second reading of the Air Corporations Bill that, 'a two million press advertising campaign has just been launched about the wonders of the VC10, which was constructed to the specification of BOAC and which will be a very fine aircraft.'[3]

In the same debate, Minister Amery told the House of Commons:

'The reason why there is no detailed reference to the VC10 in the White Paper is that no part of the deficit has resulted from the VC10 because it has not yet been introduced into service. It would be quite wrong to accept easily the idea that the VC10 was something pushed down the throat of the corporation. It was not. I think that experience will show that this remarkable aircraft, the quietest aircraft in which I have ever flown, will prove a very great commercial success in a short time from now.'[4]

So the Minister was clear, contrary to BOAC's bleatings, the VC10 had *not* been forced upon BOAC (which had surely been a willing partner), and that *prior* to BOAC's complaints about the cost of operating the VC10s for which it had asked for and influenced so heavily, BOAC was losing a massive amount of money from its operations – which included having the Boeing 707 and the darling of the Empire, de Havilland Comet 4, in its fleet.

The VC10 was, during 1963–1964, plastered all over the national aviation media and the debate. G-ARTA and the early BOAC machines were real – flying in testing. The Super VC10s were being laid down. Surely the VC10 project could not be subjected to a V1000-style last minute termination as yet another 'project cancelled'?

So was set the VC10 prior to, and during its launch era. Then, in 1964, just as the VC10 took flight, came more movement of boardroom chairs at BOAC and more political change in Great Britain's elected government. The ever-changing game of political musical chairs and all its implications upon policy for BOAC continued its sorry course.

But by then there was Guthrie, Sir Giles Guthrie; and the VC10 story took yet another turn. What had been a bit of turbulence, was about to become a hurricane of swirling opinions. Guthrie would openly criticise the VC10's operating economics alongside the cancelled pre-existing Super VC10 order book; order numbers were subjected to the changes – harming the VC10s image before the eyes of world. And as Sir George Edwards opined, if your own national airline was unwilling to buy your product, what did that do for the machine's sales hopes with overseas airlines.[5]

BOAC's prior incumbent, Sir Matthew Slattery, had reputedly wanted to cancel the VC10 fleet in its entirety and create a big BOAC squadron of Boeings, and yet he had to accept the political diktat to support the securing of a British, four-engined, transatlantic airliner of a capacity far bigger than the one BOAC already had to hand in the form of the Comet 4. Slattery was only doing his job in trying to protect BOAC's deeply worrying financial position, but such ignored the other factors that were part of the BOAC story and national function and BOAC's previous commitments to the VC10. Here again was the conflict over what was BOAC's actual role? And where was the money coming from? The fact that BOAC had spent nearly £50 million on its 707 orders and the effects thereof seemed to have been conveniently forgotten by BOAC. As Vickers were creating the VC10, the Amery-plan emerged, and then came Guthrie as yet another man in the hot seat at BOAC tasked with trying to do, or be, more than just one thing – an airline! Then the British Government changed again and Labour, as opposed to Conservative politicians, had their chance to kick the VC10, or support it.

Labour's Roy Jenkins had already kicked the VC10 with his views of ignorant certainty, but the 1963 Minister for Aviation had been the Conservative Julian Amery, and he was clear, BOAC needed a plan to run for profit and he said the VC10 was a great thing. But soon after, the Left and Harold Wilson were in power. The Labour politician and MP John Stonehouse had opinions about British 'air' policy and he too was astounded by BOAC's conduct and attitudes – he became Minister for Aviation and thought the BOAC Board had been of a blinkered and self-serving outlook. BOAC had just cancelled a major tranche of its Super VC10 order and worse was to come. Stonehouse supported the VC10 and its marketing, calling it a 'marvellous' aircraft, yet would always run up against the might and impact of BOAC's and Guthrie's view of the aircraft – which by this time was public knowledge, much to the Americans unalloyed joy. Hidden was the fact that BOAC's VC10 fleet had begun to make money, and by late 1967 the Super VC10 fleet was creating a profit! Stonehouse tried, and failed, to sell VC10s to Middle East Airlines. Edwards had a high opinion of Stonehouse – which helped.[6]

Whatever Stonehouse's emotions and support of the VC10 and its workers,[7] Giles Guthrie had been empowered to run BOAC as an airline business, not a Civil Service instrument of some historical or national fantasy of influence and flag-waving. Apparently, BOAC could now have the freedom to choose what type of airliners it could purchase. Did this give the ex-banker Sir Giles Guthrie, as BOAC's new man, utter freedom to buy and operate whatever airframe he wanted? Of course, by this time, the VC10 was into service and the Super VC10 ready.

Giles Guthrie has received much criticism for his own critical position over the VC10, and yet fairness requires that we respect his job title and the parameters he was instructed to follow, even if they, government and the ruling party, had all changed. But Guthrie's authority and orders were new, revised parameters, new rules for a new BOAC that contradicted existing and cast rules, functions and actual existing VC10 orders – where jobs were at stake – as might be Vickers itself. To usurp pre-existing strategies at vast cost was a position that might be logically argued for by Guthrie, but by then, government and BOAC had long-created a seemingly strategic irrationality that was up and running as an operating policy. After all, the VC10 had been asked for by BOAC and was flying, via Vickers genius, as requested by BOAC; by 1964 and VC10's entry into service, many proverbial chickens had started to come home to roost, and at Brooklands a brood of new VC10s were awaiting their first flight. There they sat, all liveried up in dark blue and white tail stripes with 'Speedbird' emblems and gold coach lines. They would soon be repainted in the new, defining BOAC blue and gold livery with its emotive golden 'Speedbird' on that stunning tail fin, a sight that would become so very evocative and so very famous.

To many VC10 enthusiasts, Guthrie was the villain of the Vickers story: although not absolving him from his actions, we should perhaps see a wider BOAC and British picture before 'blaming' just one man, no matter how much we disagree with what he said! There is no doubt that Vickers, and the industry's relations with BOAC were soured by the airline's actions, and Edwards and Trubshaw were both less than polite about what went on.

There have been many rumours about BOAC's Board members, or influential others, having suggested alleged links and interests to, or in Boeing, but such claims, be they true or untrue, miss the point. It was government, successive governments, and BOAC Boards, that created the mess of which BOAC was party by design, not just by choice. BOAC seems to retrospectively have decided that it was 'forced' into the VC10, and then, having specified the VC10, decided that the VC10 was too expensive to operate. BOAC certainly did cancel a vast tranche of Super VC10s, but to simply blame Guthrie alone is to miss the point and the consequences of the Imperial and BOAC story to that date.

At least by 1965, BOAC had decided on going down the jet only route, but of significance, BOAC had by this time, decided to divest itself of its still young fleet of elegant and adored Comet 4s. The low-capacity, fuel-hungry Comet 4s were got rid of in very short time indeed and the reason was based on costs and capacity issues. As always, Comet 4, born of Comet 1, was too small, and Guthrie put aside national pride and ego and got rid of them p.d.q., with little emotion allowed.

Around the VC10 and BOAC, a degree of legend or myth has been created in opposing arenas. Surely we can observe that creating the VC10 was a very difficult task that would have defeated many men. But Vickers did not just deliver, they delivered something special. It might be rationally argued that by the early 1960s, BOAC had had its fill of British airliners being delayed in design and late into service, and the costs that BOAC had had to carry in dealing with such issues (securing interim aircraft and crews). But why should Vickers be tarred with that brush? Such design issues as seen in Comet and Britannia, were not Vickers's fault (nor BOAC's), but the overall and unique British airline circumstances surrounding fleet equipment procurement as not just, prop-versus-jet, but also in terms of size and capacity, allied to funding, operating and management issues, had been contributed too and co-created by BOAC. The airline's own identity, history and corporate culture encompassing all the issues previously discussed herein as historical, political, and societal issues of Imperial Airways and imperial Britain.

Guthrie's era revealed that BOAC could openly criticise the VC10's operating economics. BOAC demanded and got a subsidy for having to operate what it said were fuel-thirsty VC10s – a reputed £30 million. Yet those aircraft soon made a profit and BOAC was then very cagey about revealing its Super VC10 operating economics, and as we know from figures cited herein, the difference between Super VC10 operating costs and 707 operating costs by 1969, was minimal, and the Super VC10 fleet flew for more hours per day and required less cost in repairs and ground time and enjoyed a long-lasting load factor enhancing appeal advantage. Yet Guthrie publicly criticised the VC10, and in doing so, the VC10 and Super VC10 were damned in the eyes of the airline world and export market. The damage was probably incalculable. Yet no technical deficiency in the design or airframe was ever cited or evidenced. The nuances were more multi-layered. The likes of John Stonehouse and Tony Benn could do little to correct the Guthrie effect upon potential customers – it was all too late – the alleged misinformation had got out; yet it ignored the wider VC10 and Super VC10 benefits of passenger appeal, fuller load factor, slower, safer, take-offs and landings (also cheaper on tyres and brakes), and of real note, lower maintenance and repair costs.

Despite all its negatives, BOAC (even under Guthrie) threw a very large amount of money (£2 million) and reputational profile at promoting the VC10, and especially the Super VC10, creating a unique and innovative advertising and marketing legend.

The paradoxes of BOAC were obvious then and now.

1964: VC10's Service Begins

Hyperbole is easy, but persuading people of a truth is harder. Pilots were truly amazed at the flying qualities of the VC10 and its larger and heavier brother the Super VC10. Over-winged, over-powered and for accounting bean counters, over-designed, the VC10 offered reserves of handling and performance that were outside the experience of most civil aircrew at the time – or since.

Converting to a VC10 from a Comet was one thing, converting from a propeller powered device like a Britannia or a DC-7 was far more of a shock. Yet even jet experienced Comet pilots were amazed by the VC10's take-off performance, of the very slow take-off and landing speeds – at least 20kts slower than its rivals – followed by what must have felt like a near-vertical climb.

The few 707 pilots who flew the VC10 were simply staggered at the differences.

The VC10 pilots all agreed, saying things that reflected their genuine love of flying an airliner that handled, said some, like a jet fighter.

'Truly superb': 'Incredible to fly': 'Huge performance and safety reserves': 'You knew it would not bite you, and that it could also get you out of a nasty situation.'

'Simply the best handling and best performing four-engined jet this side of Concorde.'

'Wonderful, handled like a sports car, but built like a tank. Simply brilliant to fly': 'I transferred from VC10 to Concorde and felt well prepared.'

'VC10. It was utterly viceless. Engine out was easy.': 'Much easier to fly than a 707, especially if you lost an engine, and even more so if that occurred shortly after take-off.': 'Felt like it was carved from solid.': 'Stable in turbulence and so reassuring.'[8]

Such were the comments of VC10 pilots – even Comet 4 pilots coming over to the new BOAC machine were taken aback at the ability and ease of the VC10.

At East African Airways, there were new VC10 pilots converting from Comet 4s, but also from DC-3s and Argonauts! Imagine the test of transferring from nose-down, prop-powered approaches, and changing from 5° or 10° take-off angles, to learning about how to fly four Rolls-Royce Conways and a high-lift VC10 wing – a machine that could go upwards at nearly 20° in normal use!

BOAC VC10 Captain Terence Brand recalled that: 'The VC10 was a lovely aircraft. It handled like a dream, being smooth and progressive. All that power gave you confidence and great safety reserves to get out of trouble. The landings were very flattering, and only in crosswinds was some caution required. The sound of the Conways on take-off was like tearing of calico, and the push of thrust, unique.'

One of BOAC's lead VC10/Super VC10 training commanders was the ex-wartime RAF bomber pilot, Tom Stoney. He said of the VC10: 'It was really terribly easy to fly. Only that narrow undercart needed watching in crosswinds. The VC10 was so safe, and almost flew itself down the ideal glide path to arrive at such a slow speed compared to the Boeing.'

Captain Ronald Ballantine recalled that the VC10: 'Flew like a dream, a fighter-type performance. Stable, safe, and with far less deep stall worries than other types. BOAC crews were rightly proud to fly it, and of course, we never lost one.'

Captain James L. Heron was a member of the VC10 development crew and co-authored the BOAC VC10 flying manual, yet his name is rarely cited in the VC10 literature. An Australian, he had flown the Consolidated Liberator for the RAF, Lockheed Constellations and Bristol Britannias for BOAC before transferring to the VC10 fleet. He was also on board the Super VC10 inaugural flight LHR–JFK on 1 April 1965, captained by Harry R. Nicholls. James Heron retired in 1971 with a BOAC seniority number of Three. Captain's Heron's son once asked his father which aircraft, of all the numerous types he had flown in a career which spanned forty-four years, was his favourite? James Heron answered without hesitation: 'The VC10. It truly was superb.'[9]

VC10 fleet captain, Norman Todd, loved the aircraft, he went on to fly Concorde and opined that the VC10 was not just utterly brilliant, but a good training ground for Concorde pilots.

VC10 and Concorde test-pilot (chief test pilot for BAC), Brian Trubshaw, was categoric: 'The feel of the VC10 flight controls was superb – artificially created, but utterly realistic and accurate. Despite the weight and the carved from solid structure, she was light to handle. A firm pull on the stick got her off and up very quickly. Then it was that amazing climb angle until you throttled back, the fuel gauges swung down to a better flow rate and once cleaned up, the VC10 and Super VC10 just cleaved along. Losing an engine was no big deal.

'Only at low speed, high weights, or at very high altitude, were some of the speed/stall margins a bit tight. Like any swept-wing device the VC10 would Dutch roll too, but not in airline service. We did insist on that high inboard wing fence to cure some low speed instability and it dealt with spanwise flow near the stall and helped the engines too. You could place the VC10 down with ease and great accuracy – ideal for short fields. The Super VC10 retained the excellent flying qualities at the deliberate expense of short runway ability.'[10]

Another well-known VC10 pilot was Norman Tebbit – latterly a leading politician in Britain's consecutive 1980s Conservative administrations under Margaret Thatcher, but in an earlier life, a BOAC pilot and VC10 admirer.

In 2003, in an *Aeroplane* magazine poll of pilots opinions as to which aircraft was the best pilots aeroplane under a context of 'pilot-thrilling' question (i.e.; in terms of handling, power and abilities), the readership voted not for a jet fighter or even Vulcan or Concorde – but for the VC10.[11]

A VC10 forte was its ease of control in asymmetric thrust conditions. Losing an engine in the cruise required minimal trim 'tweaks'. Losing an engine soon after take-off, or on the climb out, demanded far less effort than in an airliner with widely spaced, wing-mounted engines that lay further out from the centre line. A VC10 losing an engine at a critical early flight stage from the runway needed corrective rudder input, but no great drama ensued – those four engines were close to the centre thrust line. A Boeing 707 in the same condition – take-off or go-around – would require large rudder inputs and rudder pedal forces of over 100lbs from the handling pilot(s) to hold the 707 straight. The ensuing minutes of physical effort would test any pilot. Trim and power adjustments and a very reduced climb rate were all to be expected – especially in a heavily loaded 707 – where climb rates would be minimal and rudder induced drag, significant. The additions of a taller tail fin, and a lower ventral fin (ultimately in two sizes!) to the 707 was demanded by the British airworthiness authority prior to certification for British use of the 707 – directly reflecting the directional control issues encountered as certain weight and power configurations: the ventral fin later became production line factory fitments. The VC10 of course had three rudders.

Sometimes, exotic car and aircraft designs that look stunning and have power can be real handfuls to master – they can contain hidden vices to catch the unwary or the complacent commander. Often, with power and performance, there can be a sting in the tail. This was not the case with the VC10 which was vice-less in normal use and offered massive active and passive safety advantages. True, it had the potential to deep-stall as all T-tailers can, but the VC10 never suffered from a deep-stall related crash – due to its superb design and well trained pilots. The spectre of 'Dutch Roll' – a blend of twisting and turning in flight – might also afflict its rear-biased swept-wing and CG and polar inertia combinations, but again not in normal airline use. Pilots were trained to 'catch' 'Dutch Roll' with deftly applied aileron and rudder, and if necessary, a whiff of the spoilers.

For the pilot, the in-service passenger loaded VC10 could be flown off from very short runways in very testing airfield conditions of weight, altitude density and temperature (known as WAT-limited). Having rotated off the runway, the VC10 could then be hauled into a 15° + climb angle and rocketed upwards to achieve safe, positive climb and terrain clearance in a far quicker time than any rival 707 or DC-8. In the cruise, the controls were easy and responsive; on the landing approach the VC10 could be guided in at 20kts slower than a 707, and could buy its pilot time on the approach – very beneficial in bad weather and poor visibility, and safer onto the short tropical runways. Instead of crossing the runway threshold at 160kts+, as in the case of a heavy 707-300/400 series, a VC10 could be calmly guided down the approach path angle with up to six degrees nose-up attitude held, slats and flaps dangling, power protectively spooled up, and then placed confidently down onto the tarmac at 130kts +/-, which was 20kts or more slower than its 707 rival.

The heavier Super VC10 required a few more knots over the VC10s more usual alighting speed regime and a maximum weight approach speed of 137.5kts was cited – still much slower than the 707 and DC-8 – with all the inherent safety advantages and reduced tyre and brake distress. Very occasionally, lightly loaded VC10s might actually alight on the tarmac at 120kts, which was unheard of in a big four-engined jet (the claimed touchdown speed record is 117kts on a near-empty VC10). Once down, the raked main gear with its cranked main mounting beam, would soak up the touchdown forces; the cushion of 'ground effect' air under the main wing and Fowler flaps would further soften the landing – a bit like a Delta-wing!

The undercarriage (retracting into the body, not solely into the wings) was, however, narrower than the 707s stiffer-legged, wider-stanced main gear, and the VC10 had to be accurately held wing down into crosswinds – the bigger tail fin keel area also catching the crosswind. However, the much slower approach and landing speed of the VC10 offered significant safety benefits over the 707, DC-8 and notably, the Convair 990.

VC10 tyre and brake temperatures and wear would all be lower, and the risk of a wing scrape reduced.

The VC10 was quite happy to enter the landing holding pattern at under 230kts 'clean' – that is without flaps and slats – then deploy those high lift devices for a slower flight profile at circa 190kts. Putting the undercarriage down and offering full flap at 180–160kts was a bit more fuel thirsty, but the VC10 and Super VC10 offered great stability and safety at these speeds, and the ability to perform a very sprightly go-around manoeuvre from close to the runway. The thing to avoid, as with all T-tailed, rear-engined and rear weight-biased jets, was getting low, slow, and with engines spooled down and with up-stick being 'pulled' by the pilot – that way led to the high sink rate that could lead to disaster near the ground, as early Boeing 727-100 pilots found when they failed to follow the rule book, resulting in a string of crashes.

Once on the ground, the very low touchdown speed made stopping the VC10 with thrust reverse and brakes, an easy task, only the narrow track undercarriage required watching if a crosswind was running. Holding the relevant wing down into wind was soon learned and, of course, there was no risk of scraping an engine pod on the wing into the ground – a real issue for all, wing-pylon equipped aircraft at even moderate roll 10° angles. VC10 pilots held the into wind wing down, all the way along the runway to under 50kts and were alert for the big tail catching a crosswind and 'weather cocking' the machine on its wheels. In a crosswind approach a VC10 liked to be flown 'crabbed'; that is nose into the wind angle and held on the rudder. Just before touchdown the aircraft was to be straightened up – 'kicked' with rudder, and then the into wind wing held down. The alternate crosswind method of cross-controls, one wing held down, and large amounts of opposite rudder, was an option, but it caused higher drag and loads on the tail.

Just like Boeing's high-tailed T-tailer, the 727, the VC10 needed a special technique if it was subjected to a bounced landing – the power had to be reapplied to regain effective airflow speed or 'control authority' over the elevators, so that the aircraft could then be re-pitched. Loss of airspeed meant loss of elevator effect at very low speeds, so a bounced touchdown required decisive action rather than the old technique of avoiding a pilot-induced effect (or oscillation) and letting the aircraft 're-land' itself.

Cabin Comfort & BOAC marketing

The new airliner brought in new standards of cabin services and fittings. Originally designed to have a 'classical' blue and gold interior featuring the Speedbird emblem, a late change was made to see softer, more muted tones, and of significance, checked seat coverings for the new Economy Class seat design. For the later Super VC10, a further revised interior palette was created by Charles Butler Associates of New York, led by Mr Alex Howie, with designs by Robin Day, RDI, ARCA, FSIA, were featured in the interior – with BOACs views of what they wanted framed by BOACs VC10/Super VC10 project manager Mr Jack R. Finnimore.

For the interior, BOAC wanted something new and bright for its shiny new airliner, yet paradoxically, the interior needed to be restful for long flights. The design brief was, therefore, difficult. The answer was to create muted cabin walls and carpets, populated by bright colours and patterns for seats and trims. Latterly, BOAC/BA spent money on a Super VC10 interior with slightly psychedelic 'pop-art' designs for the cabin bulkheads and new seat trims, this was put in along with large overhead bins in an interior upgrade for the 1970s. Sadly, for technical reasons, in-flight film screens could not be installed – whereas they could on the 707 fleet.

A VC10 hallmark was the superior quality and comfort of the Economy Class cabin – a new seat design built with a forwards, single spar, with a one-piece moulded construction that could be wiped clean and was light in weight – much lighter than normal seats, yet still safe with a near-15g rating, well over the 9g standard rating and very comfortable due to having 'proper' cushioning and lower back support that moulded itself to the occupant (all sadly missing from today's ultra-thin seats which promise more legroom, but offer less cushion comfort); the better cushioning (using Italian Pirelli neoprene webbing) really did mark a change from existing standard class interiors. The seat had a hiduminium alloy-constructed forward cantilever support beam, another new innovation of the VC10 design that was latterly copied. BOAC spent over £300,000 on its new seat orders to the Aircraft Furnishing Company, and took full page adverts in the UK and overseas media proclaiming the excellence of the standard class seats – even citing the 7ft tall American basketball player Wilt Chamberlain as being a man who could get comfy in a VC10 seat. For the Super VC10, BOAC wheeled out no less a celebrity than the venerable Marlene Dietrich and her legs, to proclaim the comfort of the seats and quietness of the ride.

The VC10's new (30 ton volume capacity) advanced cabin air conditioning could also cope with extra cabin demands of more passengers in tropical climes.

BOAC's adverts also stated that the VC10 was a 'great step backwards in air travel' due to the rearwards mounted engines and consequent quiet cabin. Another BOAC advert proclaimed that the airline had its 'nose in the air' – apparently this was not a reference to British snobbery, but to the VC10s excellence and its take-off abilities. Early BOAC launch adverts for the VC10 featured an oil painting of the VC10 and a strapline stating that the VC10 was: 'Triumphantly Swift Silent Serene'. Today we might think such an approach a bit pompous, but then, it was the context of the time, as were shots of pretty blondes looking alluringly into the camera in BOAC VC10 advertisements.

The VC10s interior cabin was at its widest mid-aisle, half-width to side wall radius point, 69.3in wide; Boeing's 707 was 69.0in and the DC-8s 69.25in. Maximum VC10 internal cabin width was 11ft.6in, external 12ft.4in.

Five toilets (six for Super VC10) were built in, although those at the rear were placed aft of the rear galley – which cabin crews found annoying when they were trying to work due to passengers walking through the galley.

Thanks to clever operational management under men like Ross Stainton, the BOAC cabin service was of the highest quality, as were the food, beverage, and amenities – especially on Super VC10 transatlantic runs. Entering the VC10 was like entering a calm oasis for beleaguered passengers and as the engines were at the rear, most of the cabin was very quiet with none of the vibration and noise associated with the Comet's underfloor wing root engines, and considerably less noise, vibration and harshness and jet efflux fatigue on the rear cabin walls – particularly in the seats aft of the wing where the VC10 was free of the 707s engine reverberations against the fuselage. Outside and underneath the VC10, those Conway Co12s at full thrust were somewhat noisier.

First Service and the Only Way to Fly

Six years after the VC10 design and build process had begun, on 29 April 1964, the first commercial VC10 service was launched. After months of route testing, BOAC polished up it's, by now well run-in G-ARVJ 'Victor Juliet', and launched it from London Heathrow towards Lagos, Nigeria via Kano. At the helm were top BOAC Comet men who had become the early core of VC10 experienced commanders and senior first officers. The first flight was commanded by Captain A.M. Rendall. G-ARVI 'Victor India' followed on down to West Africa on the 30 April. BOAC used stops at Frankfurt or Rome on the Nigeria service, and from such beginnings, VC10s began to replace Comet 4 and Britannia 312 equipment on BOAC's routes in Africa – notably down to Nairobi on the lucrative Johannesburg service – with a stop at Salisbury en route. Services to (Southern) Rhodesia were terminated under the political crisis and BOAC VC10s used Lusaka, Lilongwe, and then Blantyre as new stops instead of Salisbury. Accra was also served and the old Imperial staging post of Tripoli retained. VC10 services soon tracked eastwards to Beirut, Bahrain, Karachi, Calcutta, and Delhi. Soon Singapore saw VC10s and Hong Kong was VC10 country too.

BOAC deployed its 707-436s as premier services across the Atlantic and also on the Pacific routes, and it would not be until the Super VC10 debut that such routings would switch to the VC10 family. From 1965–1969, BOAC used its

Standard model VC10s to build up a Middle East route network to service the growing economies of the region – much money was earned by BOAC. Some VC10 routes from London went to Rome or Zurich, thence to Tel Aviv or Beirut, then onwards to the Gulf States and India. In doing so, Imperial's operations were being mirrored in the new, post-Comet, second jet age. It would be 1973 before BOAC VC10s opened up Addis Ababa service to Bole Airport, which was 7,625ft above mean sea level and also subject to temperatures in excess of 35° C – true 'hot and high' operations. The delay in servicing Addis Ababa was down to the state of the existing runway (an EAA Super VC10 had 'sunk' into the tarmac). From Addis Ababa, the BOAC VC10/Super VC10 route scythed down across the Indian Ocean to the Seychelles and Mauritius. Visits to very difficult runways at Entebbe and Ndola were also regularly undertaken by these large jets.[12]

The BOAC branded 'Super VC10' entered service on 1 April 1965 with Captain Norman Todd at the controls on the daily premier Heathrow to New York JFK run. G-ASGD 'Golf Delta' opened up the route and soon extended it down to the Caribbean BOAC destinations. Boston, Bermuda and Toronto were all Super VC10 destinations – with service to the US West Coast planned, but at that time, still the preserve of the longer-ranged BOAC 707-436 machines. The 707s were replaced on the runs to Chicago as early as 1966 by the Super VC10. In 1969, BOAC's existing Far-East 707-operated service was modified; 707s still served Los Angeles and Tokyo, but the Super VC10 was used on a round-the-world routing westwards from London Heathrow to the USA, thence to its western seaboard at Los Angeles, then across the Pacific to Honolulu, Fiji and Sydney. Going the other way, a service via Africa and the Seychelles would range up to Singapore and Hong Kong to link up with BOAC service on an east-bound Pacific route.

Often forgotten were the BOAC VC10/Super VC10 forays into South America – Lima and Caracas being favourites prior to the British Government's 1974 handing over of BOAC's South America services to BUA and British Caledonian. BOAC also lost its Nigeria route too. The BOAC VC10 fleet also played a major role in developing long-haul routes from Manchester and Prestwick as those airports grew in importance.

BOAC trained its VC10 and Super VC10 crews at Shannon Ireland and then at Prestwick Scotland. After having gained consistency of excellence under the watchful eye of senior BOAC captains such as, Dexter, Field, Fletcher, Futcher, Gray, Goulbourn, Harkness, Hoyland, Knights, Lovelace, Rendall, Stoney, Walton, and others, the new pilots were sent out onto the new VC10 routes. Of note, BOAC's senior captain – admired by colleagues as a 'gentlemen of the old school' – Cyril Goulbourn, would later be the commander of the Super VC10 hijacked and destroyed at Dawson's Field on 12 September 1970. Captain James

Futcher would command the Super VC10 that was hijacked on 21 November 1974 at Dubai and flown to Tunis prior to the hijackers surrendering (another Super VC10 was to be hijacked on 3 March 1974 and destroyed at Amsterdam Schiphol).

Throughout 1963, Vickers began to deliver the BOAC VC10s, and over 10,000 hours of route and airframe testing flying hours were flown by early examples of the BOAC fleet prior to the aircraft's 1964 service introduction. Day-return trips to Africa – with minimal jet lag due to only a one or two hour time difference – allowed the crews to work through any snags or operational issues prior to service launch. J.R. Finnimore was BOAC's top VC10 project and development manager from 1958 onwards and truly understood the machine, its concept, and its application.

BOAC launched the heavy publicity and marketing campaign for the new VC10 (and one year later the Super VC10) with advertisements in the national press and trade publications. TV and cinema adverts set to 'emotional' music with trumpet fanfares of Purcellesque nuance were broadcast, as was the new golden Speedbird imagery. BOAC even mentioned the new airliners very slow and safe landing speeds. Much was made of the VC10s power and style, and those new Economy Class seats which were of a new design and cited as the 'most comfortable' Economy Class seat in the world (most people agreed). The seat pitch was a generous (by today's standards) 34/35 inches (45 inches in First Class) and the cabin fittings and furnishings were of the highest quality. Fine food, great cabin service, and much better air-conditioning than used on the Comet, ensured that the new cabin environment and service offering were of exceedingly high quality. The BOAC VC10 cabin comfort and service, be it Economy or First Class, was a defining marketing tool for the airline and the cabin crews were rightly popular for their attempts to 'take good care of you' – as BOAC's publicity spin promised. By 1965, BOAC were offering First Class Super VC10 passengers Dunhill cigarettes, quality brands of food and alcohol, very fine wines and a prestigious First Class service in its serene twelve or sixteen seater cabin on North Atlantic and other runs.

With low noise levels, an air of British reserve, and featuring classical etched murals of London and the Thames, as seen in 1647 by Wenceslaus Holler, depicted on the cabin bulkheads, the BOAC VC10 cabins soon became the preferred way to travel.

Load Factor Facts

After the Super VC10 debuted on the New York run, passengers were wanting a Super VC10 booking only – 2,000 seat bookings were taken in the first eight weeks and 100 passengers a day were choosing the Super VC10 service over the BOAC

707 service. Load factors were up to 90%, rarely below 70%, and they stayed that way for a very long time – just as they did on the original VC10 services to Africa.

It might be argued that load factor as an economic calculus is an unwise component, not least as load factors tend to decline after a new airliner's novelty value wears off. However, in the case of the VC10, the aircraft's passenger appeal created a long-lasting load factor related operational component. A tough marketing sales type would surely argue that, who cares how it was achieved, but if an aircraft displayed consistent passenger appeal as a booking preference, then that added value should not be denied to the aircraft type responsible: money is money however it is earned. The truth was that the VC10 and Super VC10 sub-brand within BOAC's overall brand *did* attract preferential bookings over the other types such as the 707 – for years, not just months of novelty. Within twelve months of the Standard VC10s commercial launch, BOAC were recording a 40% VC10-only booking preference from customers. BOAC upped its cabin service offering to capitalise upon that. The VC10 and Super VC10 were a marketing man's dream and BOAC should be credited for having made the most of the imagery and quality.

Figures from the International Airline Transport Association (IATA) for April 1965–May 1966, show that the BOAC Super VC10 services, in comparison with a 'basket' of fourteen other airlines that operated 707 and DC-8 services, had a load factor advantage of 20–25% on a consistent basis and even a lowest advantage of 10% (November 1965). Such was the stuff of the appeal of the by now 'Swift and Serene' BOAC Super VC10. Even after BOAC introduced its first 747-100s on the transatlantic routes, passengers still preferred the 'gold standard' Super VC10 service – despite the lack of in-flight visual entertainment. The VC10 and Super VC10 built an enduring passenger appeal that was worth millions to BOAC in seats sold, yet rarely accounted for in accountant's figures, amortisation formulas, and BOAC criticism of the machine it had requested to its own demands.

VC10 flight crews were a happy band – after all they were not paying for the fuel! However, early over-powered days were soon controlled by a VC10 step-climb procedure to conserve fuel and engine life. Still, faced with a hot day and a loaded VC10 at Entebbe, Ndola, Lusaka, Nairobi, Karachi or somewhere similar in Africa, Asia or South America, the answer was simple: 'Full power on all four!' Whereupon the VC10 would leap off the line, blast down the runway and begin to fly in about a 25+ seconds timed take-off run, perhaps having used less than 6,000ft of runway, then clawing nose up as the Rolls-Royces pushed for all they worth as their exhausts went nearly supersonic with over 40 tonnes of thrust pouring out the back.

Out of vital Nairobi, as the main mid-route stopover on BOACs major revenue earning route to South Africa, and as a port for other operators VC10s and Super

VC10s (BUA, EAA), it was obvious that underpowered 707s, such as those of BCAL or Lufthansa, were limited in their take-off weights. Some suggest that even the turbofan 707-320B/C had a weight-limited take-off figure of around 125 tonnes – which was a massive 22 tonnes below permissible maximum weight and often requiring off loads of fuel or passenger/freight payload. In comparison, Standard VC10s could manage to take off at about 142 tonnes, which was only ½ tonne below maximum allowable weight. A VC10 or Super VC10 ex-Nairobi could therefore carry a full load to Europe, a 707, even a fan-engined 320B/C, simply could not.

When Nairobi's runway was extended to 13,000ft in the late 1970s, the 707s gained a little extra in payload ability at the expense of a longer, faster and riskier take-off run (in terms of speed, tyres, brakes and rejection distances). Over-boosting the engines might also be required – with consequent costs, and operating risks. At such a 'hot and high' runway, a 707 might require a 40+ seconds take-off run and at least 10,500ft of tarmac; a later long bodied DC-8 or early 747-100 might require a fifty seconds take-off run of 11,000 ft +. Only at somewhere like Kano or Nairobi, with a take-off temperature of 35° C, would a heavily laden VC10 require over 6,500ft of runway to 'Vr' – to get airborne. In many locations a VC10, at reasonable local air temperature, could get airborne in around twenty-five seconds and use perhaps a third less runway distance than other types to 'Vr' – a unique performance for a very big airliner. Using less thrust on take-off to save fuel did, of course, mean using more runway tarmac. Lightly laden VC10 take-offs in just over 2,000ft were recorded and the author witnessed a partly fuelled RAF VC10 rotate in under 2,000ft at Kemble airfield. Try that in a 707!

Even in temperatures of 20° higher than those set by the international rules for safe runway length calculations, a VC10 could get airborne with a full load in much less distance than a 707 or a DC-8 carrying a reduced load could manage. The Super VC10 did, of course, trade runway performance for payload, but was still able to offer unique take-off and payload performance, and could get off the ground and to 35ft 'screen' height datum' in 2,000ft less than a 707-320B.

In the early days, the BOAC Standard model VC10s were also a regular sight across the Atlantic, then the Super model took over. Of note, after the phased VC10 withdrawal, British Airways kept a spruced up, low-hours, Standard VC10 (G-ARVM) in reserve at London Heathrow in case the Super VC10 scheduled for a Blue-Riband service to JFK, went technical.

Cool Command Post

Although perhaps an 'elite', the fact was that the VC10 was easier to fly than a 707, and so the claim by 707 crews that *they* had been chosen to fly the more difficult machine due to their superior abilities, gained a bit of footing. Again, we can say that both aircraft were different and required different pilots who developed different skills. One thing was for sure though, the tightly cramped confines of Boeing's very narrow and hot 'cockpit', with its shallow windscreens and 'view out of a bath tub' feeling, was far exceeded in terms of pilot comfort, air conditioning, fatigue resistance and visibility, by the vast space of the VC10's deep-windowed command post with shoulder room to spare – a true flight 'deck' of maritime proportions. Crews were not up close and personal in the VC10 control post, whereas the two pilots sat close side by side in the 707, with the engineer behind.

VC10 pilots were also an early example of multi-type rating, as they were allowed to qualify for the Super VC10 too, both aircraft sharing nearly everything in common. Only the longer front fuselage of the Super VC10 needed to be cautioned over during taxying – with the nose wheel placed well back, the long nose had to be steered deep into turns, often hanging out over the grass. There were some minor speed differences and flap/slat/gear behaviours that were changed for the Super VC10, and of course the uprated Conway 550 engines had more power, the aircraft itself was heavier and the doors were in a different location. None of which could stop a 'Standard' model VC10 pilot from piloting a 'Super'.

BOAC built up a pool of over 180 VC10 captains and senior first officers, with young trainees from the Hamble flight college being guided along their VC10 career path.

BOAC Boeing 707 cabin crews thought they were the elite – and on long-haul round-the-world sectors lasting three weeks, with rest days spent in five star hotels, who could blame them. The early celebrity culture of California and the USA saw film stars and pop stars as regular BOAC 707 guests across the Atlantic. BOAC used the 707 on the Tokyo and Sydney routes, but the Super VC10 got to Sydney in the end.

The Standard model VC10 flight and cabin crews knew that they were operating the special aircraft and made Africa and Asia their own, and soon began to enjoy postings on the Super VC10 and the new trans-Pacific routes and stop-overs. In general, it was a friendly BOAC 'club' atmosphere, although amongst both flight and cabin crews, there were a few people on the flight deck and in the cabin with that British 'attitude' as a snobbish sense of self-entitlement and grandeur. They were, however, often brought back down to reality.

L.R. 1, L.R. 2 and Super VC10

The VC10 was ripe, not just for engineering development, but also for swish marketing and the targeting of premier transatlantic routes. VC10s had traversed the Atlantic, but a bigger, or rather a longer VC10, something even more 'super deluxe', painted in blue and gold and loaded up with high fare paying corporate 'fat cats', cigars, booze, smoked salmon and stylish stewardesses, was an airline executive's and marketing man's dream.

The Vickers Advanced Project Office was full of fertile minds and a longer, high capacity version of the VC10 had been considered early on in 1959 – as a stretched 'Vanjet VC10' iteration. But could the 'stretch' of the airframe be made to create an almost new version of the original? Could the VC10 contain enough reserves of performance and lifting ability to be reconfigured into a 200-plus seater for use on the much easier transatlantic long-haul routes to New York and to Los Angeles, San Francisco, Vancouver, or across the Pacific – or on Polar routes? Surely a bigger VC10 could sell to many airlines, and make a valid base for a pure-freighter? Either way, the bigger VC10 would, along with the DC-8 63, be the longest, single-aisle, non-wide-bodied airliner in the world.

The idea of a bigger VC10 grew inside Vickers – to sacrifice some of the VC10s over-performance to add weight in the form of a much longer fuselage and extra fuel tankage. This would reduce the VC10s 'hot and high' runway performance yet gain payload and improved economics. A longer, heavier VC10 variant might need 8,000ft or more of runway to get airborne fully loaded on a warm day, but that did not matter, as the aircraft was not intended for short runway routes in the tropics – the VC10 itself catered for that role. The runways at Los Angeles and New York then offered 14,000ft+ for 707s and DC-8s!

So it was that a bigger, heavier, long-range (L.R.) VC10 – as 'Super' VC10 – was conceived; the range would be 4000 miles and the cabin might seat 212 or even 220 passengers, and the aircraft would, with the advanced wing design, still have better runway performance than the 707-320 or a proposed 'stretched' 707, or the DC-8-60 series, as long-bodied rivals.

Vickers funded a series of stretched, Super VC10 design drawings and models as project studies – as early as 1960 – and BOAC would soon order a large fleet of Super VC10s as longer-bodied variants.

Vickers were also working on a 265 seater VC10 'Superb' iteration – with a double-deck fuselage suggestion – a vastly expensive retooling of the entire forward and under fuselage design.

Unlike other 'stretched' airframes, the VC10 did not need a larger tail fin, or major changes to its aerodynamics to cope with the effects of increased fuselage length and subsequent potential handling and performance issues in flight. As the engines were closely grouped, increasing the thrust levels had no effect on the aircraft's behaviour in the manner that might afflict a wing-pylon mounted engine design with issues of wing strength and the asymmetric handling case of a failed engine. No expensive structural reworking would be required. In other words, the basic design was so good it contained all the reserves needed for more to be asked of it and retain most of its payload and runway performance.

Early on Vickers wanted to extend the VC10 fuselage by 30ft, but then settled on 28ft (Douglas were planning a 38ft stretch over their original DC-8 fuselage). Fitting the developed Conway engines, each with 22,000lbs thrust (24,000lbs was mooted), would allow a max-payload range formula to carry enough weight from London to New York, Washington D.C., or Boston, with 200 or even 212 passengers in a dedicated route-specific Super VC10 specification. Vickers also reckoned it could add underfloor fuel tanks and leading edge or trailing edge wing fillets housing 250 gallons or 500 gallons of extra fuel, and these ideas were initially the VC10 ' L.R.1' and 'L.R.2' types. Wing tip fuel tanks were also considered, but in the end the idea of making the large tail fin area 'wet', by filling it with over 1,000 gallons of fuel, was the route followed. The only issue here was the extra weight it inflicted upon the Super VC10's centre of gravity. Vickers drew up plans for a 200 seater 'Super VC10 200' (to become 'Super VC10' as nomenclature) and the more specific 212 seater option. Larger cabin doors were suggested to aid passenger handling and emergency evacuation. With the benefit of much lower seat per mile costs, surely even BOAC could see the advantages of a non-Africa, non-'hot and high' VC10 re-engineered iteration for easier routes where weight, altitude and temperature were less crucial? The stretched VC10 would also make a superb all-cargo freighter.

BOAC were indeed interested in a more economic variant of the VC10 – something less 'hot rod' and more of a liner. The issue was that the 212 seater still might not be able to fly from London Heathrow to the US west coast. Could the 200 seater Super VC10 200 manage it? LR1 and LR2 could have. But then BOAC suggested a more modest Super VC10, and had the idea of watering the concept down so that the new, higher seat capacity Super VC10 could still be used on more difficult BOAC routes. It seemed to be another BOAC paradox, wanting a more economic, higher capacity Super VC10, but then demanding that such a formula was watered down so that the new airliner could still retain capabilities on routes that it was specifically designed – or redesigned – *not* to perform on! Vickers were frustrated again; here was the bigger VC10 to tackle the transatlantic routes that BOAC had wanted, but BOAC wanted a smaller, bigger VC10!

What one earth was the point of a dual-ability Super VC10 that was neither fish nor fowl? Such a machine might not tackle the seat per mile cost operating economies of the larger 707 and DC-8 as well as could otherwise be managed.

It will come as little surprise to know that exactly such a VC10 variant became the BOAC production-specification Super VC10.

Vickers met the BOAC demand and added a lesser 13ft (as opposed to Vickers planned 28ft) to the Standard VC10; this was done via two fuselage plugs – one

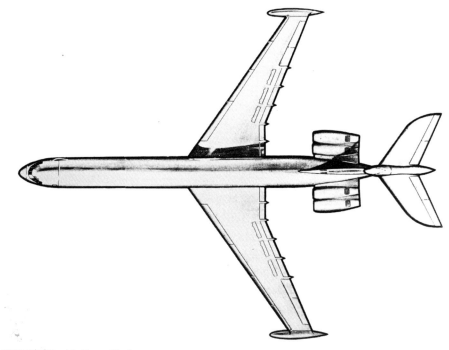

SVC10 LR with Extra Tanks.

behind the wing and one in front of the wing and the only significant structural change was the repositioning of the existing cabin doors and inserting a rear cabin door. The details of the Super VC10 design changes were fundamentally simple.

Super VC10 Design Changes

- 156 inches fuselage extension
- 75 inches between forward fuselage and 81 inches at rear fuselage
- Structural 'Keel' member stiffened to take longer forward fuselage loads to avoid 'nose-nodding'
- Top skin fuselage panels thickened in strategic locations
- Curvature changes to nose-fuselage joins
- Increases to metal gauges in wings and wheel well locations
- Strengthened landing gear side-stay frame and reinforced landing gear
- Fin fuel tank structural skin 'wet' fin with 1,350 gallons/6,173 litres capacity with force-feed ram air
- Change to outboard wing fence and additional mini fences and vortex sections
- Maximum speed for 45° flap increase to 184kt
- Addition of rear fuselage cabin door: deletion of mid-cabin door

- Forward cabin doors and service doors repositioned
- Rear cargo door relocated
- Minor cockpit and crew station layout changes
- Forward galley and toilet location changes
- Engine nacelle angle changed by 3° and four thrust reversers (two alter deleted due buffet to tailplane)
- Uprated Conway 'B' engines on wider stub wing to 11in and re-shaped pods
- Interior trim changes
- Up to sixteen First Class seats

At 171ft 8in/52.32m long and a maximum take-off weight of 335,000lbs/151,958kgs, the Super VC10 was the biggest and heaviest airliner ever made in Europe at that time. It was also the most powerful until the later model Boeing 747 with RB211 524 engines. The VC10 and Super VC10 were the fastest airliners of their era with a high-speed Super VC10 cruise speed of 505kt/582mph/936km/h at 31,000ft/9449m. Higher altitudes (36,000ft+) saw both VC10 and Super VC10 exceed the 600mph/966kmh figure. The Super VC10 was up to 15kts faster in the cruise than the 707-320B thanks to the aerodynamic advantage – but the Super VC10's added weight meant a touch more fuel burn once settled into that long-range cruise.

After the Super VC10 went into service with BOAC, it was discovered that by managing fuel flow demand between wing tanks and the fin tank, and causing a weight shift that markedly improved performance because it affected the aerodynamic stance of the airframe – its attitude (longitudinally). Through this the Super VC10 could be trimmed nose down or nose up – a bit like the old prop-liner 'on the step' attitude trimming. Previously, the VC10's tail plane incidence setting (TPI) was used to trim the attitude prior to take-off, but the new fuel weight trimming by fuel transfer allowed a more variable in-flight trim updated. Concorde latterly used fuel weight transfer tank management for trim improvements between subsonic and supersonic flight.

Super Days Out

BOAC ordered the Super VC10 design as their definitive Super VC10 and used it to create a marketing offering for the transatlantic runs, but the chance of 200 seats and even lower costs had been lost (the DC-8 60 series would fill that gap). The first Super VC10 test flight was on 7 May 1965; just one month after the Standard VC10 had entered service. By 1 April 1966, Captain Norman Todd flew the first Super VC10 revenue service to New York JFK and the gleaming dark blue and gold aircraft then wowed US customers in a series of North American sales tour and PR flights – real red carpet affairs where the Super VC10's quiet cabin, smooth flight, and soft landings astounded the industry and travelling public alike. It was in 1965–1966 that the short-lived 'BOAC-CUNARD' liveried Super VC10s plied North Atlantic skies – reflecting the commercial tie-up between the two great organisations. By the end of 1966, the idea had been quietly dropped and full BOAC titles returned to the smart blue noses of the fleet.

By the end of 1965, Super VC10s were serving Kingston, Nassau, Montego Bay and Bermuda. The Caribbean service also featured an often forgotten, once-a-week extension to Lima. Soon, San Francisco via JFK and Colombo, were all soon Super VC10 territory and, by early 1966, Super VC10s had replaced 707s on BOAC's Chicago service. New Super VC10 routes were opened up into 1966–1969 with services to Perth, Western Australia (Sydney came afterwards), Pacific routings, and a vital new service from Manchester and Prestwick to North America – including Antigua in the Caribbean. The 21 September 1968 saw the Super VC10's longest non-stop flight sector of 4,420 miles being launched from London to Barbados. October 1969 saw the launch of BOAC's true, round-the-world by Super VC10 service – being westbound from London to New York, Los Angeles, Honolulu and Fiji, then to Sydney.

However, even the Super VC10 lacked the range for a non-stop Heathrow to Los Angeles routing, but that did not stop BOAC routing them via Chicago to Los Angeles and thence across the Pacific on the round-the-world service though. A Super VC10 Vancouver routing via Montreal was an occasional delight – it usually being the preserve of a non-stop 707.

Standard model VC10s were in regular movement across the Atlantic in the early days – then the Super model took over. The shortest scheduled VC10 service operated circa 1970 on the connecting service from Bahrain to Dhahran. The two airfields were twenty-five miles apart, with the runways more or less in line. This was one of the shortest flight timed sectors of just eight minutes airborne. If a BCAL VC10 diverted into Heathrow from Gatwick due to weather, or BOAC did the same into Gatwick from Heathrow, the (direct) flight time to recover back to base would be about ten minutes. The author witnessed two very short RAF VC10 flight sectors in 2013 – Brize Norton to Fairford, four minutes flying, and Kemble to Brize Norton with seven minutes flying at minimal fuel weight after a 1,850ft take-off run!

In terms of the longest VC10 flights, the Super VC10 could manage over nine hours in flight with a nine hour fifty minutes endurance in typical flight conditions – depending on winds and allotted heights (but with possibly lower fuel reserves). One Super VC10 (G-ASGO), on the popular run from London Heathrow to Barbados, was airborne for nearly ten hours (9h 55m) in January 1971, with the aircraft having step-climbed to 41,000ft and effectively saving fuel over the planned route and avoiding a 'tech' stop. In the winter, the route would more normally operate via New York or an eastern seaboard runway.

The Super VC10 London to Seychelles came on line in 1972 and was one of the last new BOAC Super VC10 routes. This was developed into an Entebbe-Nairobi-Mauritius-Seychelles service with an onward, trans-Indian Ocean crossing to Colombo-Hong Kong-Tokyo service on a twice weekly basis. It was very popular with crews and passengers alike. A joint South Africa-Seychelles-Hong Kong service was created with South African Airways code-sharing on BOAC machines (SAA would later lose one of their 747's over the Indian Ocean on this service). BOAC's Super VC10s were hard worked by this time with a twelve hour flying day being the norm. Yet, as early as the spring of 1972, Super VC10s were being usurped across the Atlantic on the Chicago service by the 747-100 in BOAC colours.

According to BOAC's own official statement of accounts in 1971, the Super VC10 fleet had worked twelve hours a day, every day (in the air), by flying 70,347 hours at an average of 4,387 hours per airframe. Super VC10 costs per capacity-ton-mile were lower than the Standard VC10 fleet, but BOAC did not publicise a mixed-fleet cost per fleet comparison. In 1971–1972 we do know, however, that the BOAC Super VC10 fleet achieved an annual utilisation rate of just under 4,500 hours per aircraft (4,397 hours) which was seventy-five hours more than the best ever figure achieved for the Standard VC10 fleet and several hundred hours more than the VC10 fleet average figure.[13]

We also now know that the Super VC10's hourly flying costs were, on occasion, less than the BOAC's 707s; we should recall that unlike the 707 fleet, the Super VC10 could not rely on other airlines having operational and maintenance/repair support facilities. The Super VC10 was on its own and needed to achieve better reliability than its rival. From 1970–1974, two Super VC10s were lost (on the ground) to acts of air piracy and the type suffered a rash of hijackings in 1974 – maybe terrorists or freedom fighters, call them what you will, preferred the Super VC10!

The VC10 and Super VC10 fleets were integrated with dual-type crew ratings and cross-working by cabin crews. Over 300 VC10/Super VC10 fleet pilots, 120 engineers, 260 stewards and 250 stewardesses were employed by BOAC. A final fleet of twelve Standard VC10s and seventeen Super VC10s was reached in early 1969. Vickers had delivered the machines in a very short time indeed.

From 29 April 1964 to October 1976, the BOAC/BA Standard VC10 flew a revenue-earning 409,405 hours, and the Super VC10 fleet, from 1965 to March 1981, flew 797,791 flying hours and never caused injury or death. VC10 G-ARVM was the last of the fleet to be built and the last to remain in BA service beyond 1976. The Super VC10's last scheduled commercial airline flight was from the Indian Ocean islands to Dar-es-Salaam and Larnaca to London Heathrow with Captain Sanders making the final landing, and took place on 29 March 1981 with

G-ASGF ending the BOAC/BA VC10 and Super VC10 story. There followed at least two chartered enthusiasts flights around the UK airports and BAC factory sites over the next few days. On board one, was Ernest Marshall, VC10 chief project engineer, who had been there at the aircraft's birth pangs.

The BOAC Super VC10s (Type 1151) were registered G-ASGA to G-ASGR. East African Airways (EAA) were the only other Super VC10 operator and their (Type 1154) Super VC10s had a forward fuselage cargo door and a reinforced floor – so they were heavier. They also benefited from every tweak and upgrade learned during the VC10 and BOAC Super VC10 production series, and as they were fully painted, were a touch more smoothly finished – but paint weighed extra! The EAA machines were lavishly trimmed inside and out and carved their own niche in African aviation history. The fact of the Nairobi-Zurich-New York Super VC10 service being seen at JFK alongside the BOAC Super VC10 service would have been a sight for the men of Vickers as the 1960s ended and the decade of the 1970s began.

But all this was in the afterwards. Before, in 1965, BOAC was carping and cancelling about the VC10 and Super VC10 – the machines *it* had requested to its *own* needs – effectively setting the design parameters by default.

Maybe the resulting Vickers products, the VC10 and Super VC10 *were* 'Rolls-Royces' of the air – or a sportier version like a Bentley or an Aston Martin! However, it seemed BOAC had now decided 'after the fact' that what it really wanted was a Ford Cortina, or should that be a Ford Galaxie.

Chapter 8

Boeing's Big Beast: Deltas, B-52s and Stratotanker to Stratoliner

T he precursor airframe to the Boeing 707 was the narrower bodied, Boeing 346-80 or 'Dash 80' prototype for a military jet transport and potential air refuelling tanker. Designed in a very short time – off the back of the military requirement, the new airframe took its swept-wing inspiration from the success of Boeing's B-52 and B-47 jet bombers – their wings having been informed by German research. These two airframes had taught the company much about wing design, engine location and structural issues. Unlike the Valiant of Vickers, there was little that could be transferred over from a B-47 or B-52 in direct structural terms, but there was much that was beneficial to informing the new four-engined design. Critical in the mix was wing design and engine pylon expertise.

The men of Boeing did not, however, just wake up one morning and decide to design a transport variant with jet engines and B-52 or B-47 inspired motifs – although using the B-52 wing featured in the early Boeing jet transport design sketches – just as Vickers had first suggest a Valiant-derived wing and airframe for its transport design suggestion.

As a result of Operation Paperclip and the migration of German design research and its designers to the United States of America after the Second World War, swept-wing design became a lead theme of thinking. Just as with de Havilland's first highly swept all-wing jet transport ideas (that became the Comet 1), Boeing's early designs for a jet transport were based in the all-wing configuration. As design for a Boeing 'All Delta-wing Transport' Model 473-19A, first drawn in 1949, Boeing's designers came up with a four jet engined, delta-wing, tailless all-wing device.[1] The span was 110ft, gross weight was 145,000lbs and passenger capacity was sixty people. The large delta-wing gave ample room for massive fuel tanks and superb payload range figures – along with cargo capacity. But low-speed handling concerns scuppered the Boeing delta – designers (including Northrop) had not, in 1949, solved the delta and all-wing handling issues, although Alexander Lippisch and the Horten brothers, might have disagreed with such a claim. But lessons learned during the studies for this machine did percolate through to Boeing swept-wing aerodynamics knowledge and thus the 707 itself in 1959 – a decade later.

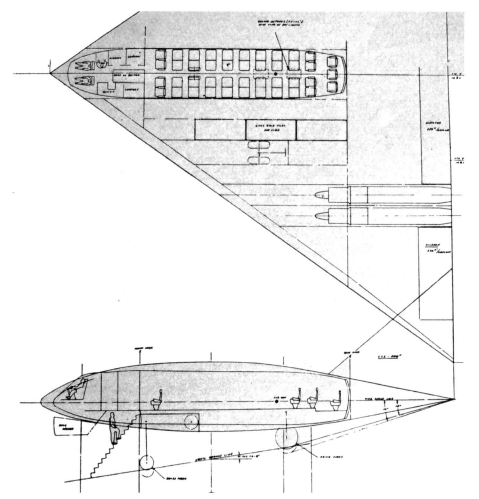

Boeing's Delta Idea.

In 1948, Boeing's design team had (like de Havilland's) realised that the military jet fighter and bomber types might not be the only application for the jet engine. The perceived wisdom was, however, that jet engines were expensive to build and operate, required huge maintenance resources, and were inefficient at lower speeds and altitudes – the domain of the airliner. Thus the 'luxury' of the jet engine was acceptable in military aviation, but not yet in airline transport – despite Comet 1. So in America and Great Britain, the propeller driven, piston-powered airframes continued to dominate, with even the turbine engine concept being perceived as applicable as a prop-turbine not a jet-turbine. It took the airlines and the airframe builders a decade to throw off the erroneous perceptions about the jet engine and to deliver jet airliners.

Jet engine turbine blade and combustion process design developments led to the realisation that while the thrust of the propeller-driven aircraft decreases with higher speed, the thrust of the jet-driven aircraft delivers constant and increasing gains with higher speed. Jets do not suffer from performance-sapping drag when an engine fails – unlike a propeller engine. Such drag at high airframe weight on take-off, or at high altitude, can have very serious consequences – leading to what some quaintly call a, 'gross height excursion', or a 'failure to proceed at the allotted altitude'.

The airlines were concerned that fast new jets would play havoc with air traffic control and their management of slower prop-liners, notably in the landing pattern. What of ground handling and maintenance? Little did the airlines realise how much money they would save with jets and not having to constantly rebuild piston-powered turbocharged prop-liner engines? And with suitable low-speed wing devices, the fast new jets could be slowed down on the approach so as to fit into the air traffic pattern – or that was Boeing's promise.

Jets (notably as turbofans) were quick off the ground, faster to climb, and more efficient (economical) the higher you went. Jets had to be the answer, but it took years to overcome the prejudices of perceived 'prop' wisdoms and military turbojet legacies.

Yet the men at Boeing were convinced of the efficacy and effect of a tanker or transport airframe using jet engines and swept-wings – the B-47 would prove this. Led by Edward C. Wells, Vice President Engineering: George S. Schairer, Chief of Technical Staff: J.E. Steiner, Preliminary Design Engineer: Maynard L. Pennel, Chief Project Engineer Aircraft, Boeing's team explored the idea of high-wing and low-wing jet transports, latterly using the highly-swept B-52 wing and its pylon mounted engine configuration.

Radical Evolution?

In a step-by-step design research process – evolutionary rather than revolutionary, yet still radical in concept and speed of execution, a Boeing 367 Stratocruiser fuselage was drawn up with a 20° swept leading edge wing and prop-turbine power (as a 367-60). Then came a 367-64 design, still using the Stratocruiser fuselage as a jet-powered version with B-52 type jets paired (two paired under each wing on a single pylon respectively), a new vertical tail surface, swept-wing, and a planform that looked like a Boeing 757 from four decades later! Yet this was Boeing's first four-engined jet design (if we ignore the delta proposal of 1949). The next step in the drawings was a completely new fuselage, and with the four jet engines spaced individually on their own pylons across the wing span. This process, beginning as

367-60 and leading through to the 367-70 series, became the defining military air tanker-transport 367-80 prototype – the genesis if the 707 itself.

Along the way, circa 1947–1952, Boeing had toyed with high-wing jet transport airframe designs with swept-wings and paired and pyloned jet engines. One such was the 1947 Boeing Model 473-1 – the first to be seriously studied by Boeing as a proposed jet transport. It looked like a curious blend of jet-type swept tail treatment, high-winged freighter, and Stratocruiser nose design. The suggested span was a mere 79ft, with a total gross weight of 48,000lbs, two 6,000lbs thrust engines and twenty-seven passengers – was it an early dream of domestic feeder liner type? Whatever it was, it represented a beginning of Boeing jet transport design psychology – as early as 1947 – as de Havilland's were doing the same thing.

So Britain's 'revolutionary' jet transport thinking may have achieved the Comet 1, something that Boeing did not in 1949, but we should not believe the hype that 'only' Britain was thinking of such or capable of such.

But Boeing was a military airframe supplier – a minnow when compared to the might of the Douglas Company and its heritage of brilliant and profitable civil airliners from DC-2 onwards. However, the Douglas pedigree and airline reputation was built around propeller driven airliners – the paradox was that it was the military minds at Boeing who had more jet airframe experience than the airlines favourite that was Douglas. So Boeing knew more about jet engines, swept-wings, and the relevant structural and aerodynamic factors, even if that was in a military airframe context. The technological leap from Douglas DC-7 to DC-8 was to prove far more difficult for the Douglas in California than it was to be from B-47 to B-707 up in Washington State at Boeing. Boeing was far more innovative than some like to admit. In the 1930s it had come up with the 247 airliner, and in 1948 the B-47 Stratojet was the world's first all-jet, swept-wing, high speed bomber (albeit with some wing design issues).

Boeing engineers Ed Wells, George Schairer, and John Alexander, began further thinking about a swept-wing jet transport type – an airliner. Boeing was an innovative company and its military aircraft were supreme, yet its 1940s airliners less than well received. Boeing had lost money on its airliners, including its last 1940s piston-engine design, the problematical 377 Stratocruiser. But Boeing had advanced the art of wing pylon-mounted jet engines in military applications and studies. Yet the idea for having the engines slung from pylons off the wing was a direct knowledge transfer and a feature first conceived in Germany in 1943, and soon scooped up in 1945 as the Allies plundered German design bureaus and unique high-speed wind tunnels and their findings.

Boeing had studied the seen high-speed German wind tunnels and soon had a state-of-the-art wind tunnel of its own. There, under the leadership of E.M. Storwick, Wind Tunnel Operations Engineer, the designs for the 367-80 were explored and honed in the mid-1950s. Soon, Boeing had defined a 35° swept-wing, four-engined, low-wing jet transport idea that would change the world and give birth to the 747 itself. Boeing threw $15,000,000 of its own money at the 367-80 design at Renton, Washington State. Suddenly, a near 200,000lb airframe (fully fuelled) with a span of over 130ft, capable of 550mph, was a tangible reality.

Strangely, Boeing itself named the 367-80, the 'Stratotanker-Stratoliner', which was hardly catchy. The legend of a marketing tag '707' was much smarter.

Following the design process from 367-6 to 367-79, the four-engined Boeing swept-wing tanker device as 367 – 80 for the USAF first flew as early as July 1954 and it took the US Government less than two months to then order a fleet of these airframes. It would not take Boeing long to create an airline transport version, albeit not yet with the wider fuselage section to allow for six-abreast seating. So the early Boeing airliner idea had a four-abreast main cabin not that much wider than the Comet's – whereas the Vickers V1000/VC7 paved the way for a six-abreast concept. But adding length, aerodynamic tweaks, and an advanced and wider cabin to the Boeing, would create the definitive original '707' airliner. However, the decision to expensively modify the fuselage toolings to make it wide enough to take six-abreast seating, came late in the day and *after* the airliner version had been announced in October 1955. The DC-8 was offered with an overall fuselage width of 147 inches, sufficient for six across seating, while Boeing wanted a common airliner and tanker fuselage width of 144 inches (to economize on tooling costs), which was too narrow for the airlines.

It was Boeing's president, in the form of William Allen, who made the costly decision to widen the 707 for six across seating. At 148 inch fuselage width, the 707 design would become one inch wider than the DC-8. And Boeing was, like the American car manufacturers, more than happy to modify and adapt the basic marketing specification airframe to individual customer needs – with many variants possible. Such options were costly in terms of toolings and manufacturing costs, but highly lucrative in terms of gaining orders and customer loyalty.

So when BOAC, at political behest, wanted British engines in a 707, Boeing were quite prepared to 'dump' Pratt and Whitney right in it and mount British Rolls-Royce Conway turbofans on a 707-420, launching it into the air on 20 May 1959; it was a Douglas DC-8-40 using similar engines that entered airline service first on 1 April 1960.

Pan American (Pan Am) ordered twenty 707s – Pratt and Whitney powered – opening the floodgates to not just 707 orders from American carriers, but also to the great 707 versus DC-8 sales race. With United Airlines as the DC-8 launch customer, Pan Am soon found itself in the bizarre situation of having ordered both the 707, and twenty-five of the DC-8 – with the consequent doubling of training, maintenance, and operating expenses from a mixed-fleet.

However, it would be late 1958 before either launch airline actually got hold of their equipment. In theory, V1000 as VC7 was circa 1955, intended for early 1958 delivery – being ahead of the game in so many respects. A BOAC Comet 4C did, of course, beat Pan Am across the Atlantic for the world's first commercial jet liner service across the Atlantic in October 1958, but this was a one stop refuelling service in all reality, not a non-stop transatlantic service. The first, true non-stop 707 service across the Atlantic only took place the following summer, in August 1959, and it would be a further two years before a refined iteration of the DC-8 made it across the Atlantic in one hop. Meanwhile, Comet and 707 services often had to replenish fuel at Shannon, Prestwick, Gander, or Reykjavik, if the winds were adverse.

Wing Design

For the 707, and taking lessons from its earlier military big-jets, especially in terms of wing pylon-mounted engine structural design in terms of bending relief, spar strength, flutter, aileron and flap performances, the Boeing design team created a strong, efficient, and easy to manufacture, true swept-wing of 35° sweep and thin aerofoil. The only real aerodynamic issues surrounded the effects of the engine pylons upon leading edge and upper wing surface airflow due their 'plume' effects on lift patterns and the fact that any leading edge devices would be interrupted by the engine pylons – thus reducing their lift-coefficient enhancing abilities. Of note, the original engine pylon design was changed between the 367-80 prototype and the production series 707 – with a shortening of the pylon length and a change in angle, both made to accommodate 'fatter' engine pods, specifically the later turbofan engines. A 12ft wingspan extension was also added to the later model 707.

The earlier, longer, cleaner pylons may have been more aerodynamically advantageous with the thinner early pure-jet pods. Another significant difference between 367-80 prototype and the productions series 707 was a change to the aerodynamically crucial nose – the point of airflow penetration. The 367-80 had a curved, slightly bulbous nose profile, yet the wider fuselaged 707 derivative had a sharper, less curved nose. Subtle, but vital development work took place right up to the last minute, and the tail design would be subject to some later questions.

The 707s leading edge devices seemed somewhat crude compared to what was known and possible – slats had been around since the 1920s and G.V. Lachmann's patent and application to the British Handley Page *Gugnuc* wing as the first slat-equipped design success. Despite Boeing's assurances to airlines that the new 707 would slow down on the approach and not upset air traffic control procedures, the 707 remained a fast 'hot-ship' of restricted effect in its leading edge devices. This was an area where the VC10 would greatly improve on over the 707. Did

Boeing lack leading edge device knowledge? Or was it just that the subject deemed a lesser design and sales issue than hindsight and the revised Boeing 720 wing would prove? Development would be the key to the 707s advance.

Strong, twist resistant, and simply flapped, the 707 wing had crude, 'swing-out' leading edge flap panels, and of concern, a non-streamlined wing to fuselage root section – both issues that Boeing would seize upon in early production years and change for the better. Of note, the Boeing 'Dash-80' 707 prototype had oval cabin windows, and significant tooling changes were required to alter the window belt line and related fuselage skin design to accommodate the production-standard square-shaped, but rounded-cornered windows of the definitive and wider-bodied 707: these windows themselves being much smaller than the DC-8s windows – but with more of them.

Contrary to the usually received view or perceived opinion, the 707 was not North America's first jet airliner – that honour went to Avro Canada and its four-engined C-102, which took to the air on its maiden flight as early as 10 August 1949 – only a few days after the de Havilland Comet's first flight. But for issues of design, funding and politics, Avro Canada's smart little jet liner might have changed history, but it was still-born as a non-swept, jet-powered piston-shaped iteration of 1940s design – not a swept-wing wonder for a new age.

The maiden flight of the Boeing 367-80 was on 15 July 1954, but it would be four years before that idea became the true 707-100 series, to become the -120 or as in Pan Am's launch order, the -121. In the intervening period, major design changes took place, not least a new, wider fuselage and new windows at the expense of new tooling costs. The 'KC' series USAF tanker airframes would, of course, provide Boeing with great opportunity to cost and develop the joint civil-military airframe.

With 150–180 seats, a range of 3,075m/4,949km, a 570mph/917km/h cruise, and those sharp wings swept at 35°, the new Boeing was far more capable than a Comet 4 – although not in terms of runway performance at tropical airfields where the Comet's large wing-area and lower wing loading allowed it a much more sprightly climb once off the ground – albeit under the caveat of the very careful rotation technique demanded by the Comet's aerofoil design (Comet had originally been equipped with leading edge slats on the outboard wing section and they had been regretfully, and perhaps in hindsight, unwisely deleted as they were apparently deemed ineffective).

It is a noteworthy point that Boeing did not consider 'hot and high' performance of the airframe as a major consideration, and the manufacturers later aerodynamic modifications and power plant upgrades to improve runway performance of the 707 might suggest that this was an original decision of some error. Although many of America's runways were long, low and surrounded by flat terrain, not all of them were, and many were not at low altitude, and not all of them were 14,000ft long like the runways at New York Idlewild/JFK or Los Angeles. Many American states featured high summer runway operating temperatures of +30° and the need for less than lethargic runway performance and climb-out was *not* invisible.

Denver (5,300ft elevation), San Diego, and other airfields, notably in the midwest, provided challenges to a heavily loaded early 707, even one with water-injection. But there would soon be the 727 to cater for such domestic services – which did offer spectacular take-off abilities under its 'parasol' high-lift wings and could then climb very steeply away – a 'mini' VC10 in fact. To get the runway performance required, the 727 followed the Vickers T-tailed, 'clean wing' theory; proof then of its correctness.

In retrospect, in terms of the original 707 and DC-8 with both Boeing and Douglas seemingly less than over-concerned with 'hot and high' take-off performance, we might fairly ask, why did they not consider the sales and marketing implications of such a policy with overseas customers – notably those airlines in South America, Europe and Asia with tropical routes? Surely they were not so arrogant as to think solely of the American market? The revisions to the 707 and the creation of the 720 and 720B must indicate that such needs had been less than fully addressed and that Boeing did indeed have to take steps to meet such customer demands.

Vital Wing Upgrades

A key point to remember is that the 707 did not have advanced, slotted, or 'slat' wing leading edge devices, not even a 'droop', but relied instead on crude, swing-out, part-span 'fence' sections. By the time the 707-320 appeared, the 707/720 wing update had been redesigned with a leading edge 'glove,' more efficient 'lift-booster' wider-span leading edge (Krueger type) panels, revised flaps, and new streamwise wing tips. All this cost time and money to re-engineer into the existing 707 airframe design. The American assets of speed and skill at rapid development were key to turning the early 707 airframe into an altogether more viable machine.

Boeing's later 707 derivative, the 720, not to be confused with the earlier 707-120, offered significant aerodynamic changes to the main wing with a leading edge root-section 'glove' to improve inboard lift and drag rates and higher Mach number cruise capability. Better, full span leading edge devices, trailing edge flap section improvements, and the placement of localised aerodynamic improvement devices on the wing span created better lift performance. The 720 was shorter, lighter, and had many expensive structural and tooling changes. The main body profile was the same, but shorter in the forward fuselage than the stock 707, and the wing was lighter gauged and the fuel tankage reduced. The 720 was cheaper than the 707 too, and had much improved short runway performance – if less ultimate maximum payload range ability.

Engine Issues

Boeing had added water injection to even US domestic specification early 707-120 series machines, but removed from the early, pre-'fan' 720s. In early 707-120 days, a basic 13,000lbs/5896kg from a JT3C two-shaft jet turbine was only just enough in terms of combined four-engined thrust. Remember, a Standard model VC10 had four engines of 20,000lbs thrust on offer. When BOAC ordered 707s, such turbojets were its specification – fitting Conways would initially be a BOAC specific event prior to Lufthansa, Air India and Varig optioning the engine. The decision by Boeing to carry water tanks (water being heavy) for Pratt and Whitney powered variants was taken in order to cool the engines and increase thrust on take–off by direct water injection into the combustion chamber process.

The 707 in later guises would, of course, reach 18,500lbs of thrust per engine – via the JT3 being repurposed into a (inlet) fan driven turbofan, but those developments would be several years away. This clever piece of re-engineering was hardly a dedicated by-pass design in the terms of the Rolls-Royce Conway, but it did offer a thirty per cent increase in rated thrust, with figures going up from just under 13,000lbs/5,440kg, to 17,000lbs/7,710kg and another 1,000lbs being latterly added. Noise levels were very considerably reduced and exhaust pollution less. The larger fan mouth at the front of the engine did increase aerodynamic frontal area drag at the front of the engine pod. So the Pratt and Whitney's 'development' of their early engine was a brilliant and noteworthy piece of engineering which had an effect far greater than might be expected upon the 707 as a machine and as an earner for Boeing. Here was a true northern hemisphere all-rounder viable on many airways; a quick update of the 707 as the 707-120B and –320B airframe aerodynamics mated to the new engines, then also gave us the separate, lighter model 720B. The 707-320 Intercontinental model soon became the turbofan 320B.

So a new 'fanjet' era was born! American Airlines converted every turbojet 707 in its fleet to the new fan engine specification, as did Qantas and others.

Qantas Jets

Boeing had sold over 2,000 examples of its 707 model by 1972, and amongst that total, of particular interest, were the especially built Qantas 707-138 variants from 1959. These machines were the result of a demand by just one customer – Qantas – for a special performance variant with greater runway and fuel range abilities on that airline's more demanding 'hot' routes. With the option of going with the Boeing 707 in 1959, or waiting until 1961 for the Douglas DC-8, or 'doing' a BOAC and buying expensive stopgaps such as the Bristol Britannia or the Douglas DC-7C, Qantas had to get the correct advice and the correct decision

– it might go bankrupt otherwise. The difference was that within Qantas and within its Australian Government's overseeing structure, were men with expertise, knowledge and decisive abilities who were allowed to manage the airline to the best outcome. As BOAC sent prop-powered Britannias to Sydney on premier services, Qantas was going jet powered.

In 1958, Qantas took a bold decision to go with the 707, but the truth was that the early-model 707s lacked ability in the temperatures and conditions of Qantas Pacific region operations. The most demanding route segment on the Qantas network was the long Nadi (Fiji)-Honolulu (USA) sector. The problem was compounded by the relatively short 7,000ft runway at Nadi and the prevailing high temperatures. Qantas wanted something special; a bespoke Qantas 707 performance was needed.

The 707s payload range formula was not a true trans-Pacific formula for Qantas. But Boeing had already suggested taking forward fuselage length out of the 707 to create a 720 domestic variant – latterly the simpler, and much changed, turbofan 720B model. Qantas realised that a shorter 707 fuselage (more akin to the -120 original) would, with latterly added 720 model tweaks, notably better leading edge lift devices, create a uniquely capable tool for long-haul and trans-Pacific use. So Qantas reached agreement with Boeing to take ten feet out of the rear fuselage for a Qantas-specific aircraft, and the special Qantas 707 was built to the original length of 128ft 10ins instead of 138ft 10ins. This version was, confusingly in terms of nomenclature, designated the 707-138 model and became widely referred to as the 'Qantas Boeing 138' – this being the Qantas Boeing customer designator , not an indicator of any dimension.

Through the elimination of a ten foot section from the fuselage behind the wing, the empty weight of the aeroplane was reduced by 2,500lbs. Thus, with the same wing and engines, this weight saving could be utilised for fuel uplift. Forward fuselage length had also been removed in the 720, so the Qantas 138 was very slightly shorter in front of the wing compared to the main production 707-320 series.

Boeing were quick to respond to the Qantas requirements – and a team of Qantas engineers were based at the Boeing factory and were given freedom by Qantas to create their own very special machines. This Qantas aircraft was also to be fitted with a version of the Pratt and Whitney JT3C-6 that allowed the use of additional 'overboost' take-off thrust at Nadi only. Even so, the performance of these early aircraft, on occasion, was marginal. The Qantas 707-138 arrived in Australia as early as 2 July 1959, when *City of Canberra* completed its delivery flight.

So it was that in the summer of 1959 – ahead of every other airline outside the US – Qantas took delivery of the first of seven Boeing 707-138s. Services to the United States began within weeks, and two months later the service was extended to London via New York – a Qantas 'first'. A Sydney-London service via Mexico and Caribbean stops was a short-lived, but glamorous Qantas routing; Sydney-London services via India, on the old traditional 'Imperial' route, began in October 1960. BOAC's competing prop-turbine Britannias suddenly looked serene, but slow and outmoded, no matter how good the cabin service.

Four of the new Qantas 'B' versions of the -138, and fitted with turbo-fan engines developed by Pratt and Whitney, were purchased in 1961 to complement then to be 'fan' retro-fitted original Qantas -138s. These 138Bs offered lower fuel consumption, shorter take-offs, larger payloads over longer distances, and a faster cruising speed of 960km/h. And they could cruise over the Pacific at FL41 – 41,000ft, high above the 'washboard' undulations of clouds and turbulence. Boeing's willingness to tweak the 707 for a special Qantas order made any chance of selling VC10s to Australia a forlorn hope.[2]

With its extended range and speed, the 707-138/B (and then the -338/B models) reduced travel times between London and Sydney from forty-eight hours to twenty-seven hours – a figure only just above today's one-stop route timing – so the 707-138/B was a massive marketing tool for Qantas. For Qantas, its 707-138Bs, the famous 'V Jet' (for Vannus) branding offered the best of all worlds and provided stiff competition to the BOAC trans-Pacific round-the-world services. The -138 also showed just how flexible Boeing were prepared to be on the production line with bespoke specifications – whatever the production costs.

707-versus-VC10 and the Max-Payload Range Formula Argument

Maximum payload range can define the success of an airliner. It constitutes the distance the aircraft can fly with its loaded weight of fuel and passengers – as opposed to a simple fuel range fuel consumption based figure for an empty airframe. The vital payload range formula defines the actual in-service combination of fuel capacity and load by weight to range. The crucial question was just how much total weight as payload could be carried for how far. From knowing all these parameters, the airline accountant can arrive at the 'maximum payload range' formula.

Of note, fuel consumption 'improves' as fuel is burned off and fuel weight lessens – passenger and cargo weight staying the same in-flight. But carriage of weight can be limited by available runway distance and local 'hot and high' conditions. No matter how good an ultimate maximum payload range an airliner might have, it might have to offload tonnes of fuel and passengers and freight in order to actually leave the ground in such circumstances. This was the 707s weakness in Africa and other tropical locations – and the VC10's gain. However, on the easier BOAC North Atlantic runs, the resulting VC10 design did not let the

VC10 or Super VC10 fly from London to Los Angeles in one go – as the later 707 320B/C could with a standard airline configuration load.

What made the Boeing 707 so attractive – once it had been developed a bit into the turbofan 320B/C – was its lower cruise-flight fuel demands and commonality with other operators. The Standard VC10 *was* heavier than 707 and VC10s performance capabilities effectively became redundant on the easier North Atlantic routes – the Super VC10 regained some of the loss. The VC10, of course, took off in a shorter distance and climbed like the proverbial bat out of hell; a loaded turbojet 707 clawed its way up to its cruise height, even a turbofan 707 was less than sprightly. A heavily loaded 707 turbojet, or turbo fan, could really struggle to make a decent rate of positive climb from a difficult airport like Nairobi or Kano. A marginal 707 'tropical' initial climb rate of 350 feet per minute (ft/pm) might contrast with the more usual temperate zone 1,500ft/pm to be expected. However, once (slowly) up there, the turbofan 707-320B used less fuel. But who defined the VC10's operating requirements and consequent costs in the first place?

BOAC, of course!

For the vital max payload range worst case scenario as cited at the time of the mid-1960s, it was suggested that a Standard VC10, after the first year of commercial operations, had an average cost per flying hour of £475 alongside a 'best case' scenario for the (turbofan) 707 as a cost of £371 per flying hour. This difference was so large that many questioned it. And did that figure include the fact that the VC10 was achieving notably higher daily hours-in-flight times and much higher load-factors? The VC10's costs would come down as experience and daily flying hours built up. The Super VC10 improved things and BOAC were strangely reluctant to reveal their Super VC10 versus 707 economic forensics, which at one stage would see the cost of operating the 707 exceed that of the Super VC10. BOAC reported in 1972–1973 that its Super VC10 fleet were averaging 11.09 hours flying per day against the their 707-436s flying much less – 8.7 hrs per day. So the Super VC10s earned more in the air every day! BOAC's full cost figures for revenue flying hour were cited as £486 per hour for the Super VC10 and £510 per hour for the 707-436 – a complete reversal of the so often claimed perception of 707s better economy. Things were a bit closer for the Pratt and Whitney JT3D fan-engined 707s that joined the BOAC/BA fleet. Given that BOAC had secured a reputed £30 million State subsidy for operating VC10s due to their higher fuel burn, what formulas applied to the bigger Super VC10 versus the big 707-436/707-320 in BOAC service?

What of the issues of the VC10 and Super VC10 superior load factors (often at eighty per cent on some routes and up to ninety-eight per cent on others, at a time when the airline industry average load factors hovered in the fifty-five to sixty-six per cent zones).What of the better maximum payload range on tropical route sectors? What of its lower maintenance and repair costs? And of the Standard model VC10 fleet operating at a daily utilisation rate of eight hours per day (and a best rate of 10.1 hours per day) and the Super VC10 fleet ultimately delivering twelve hours per day? Few airlines had achieved this with any new airframe, nor the remarkably high, on-time despatch rate the fleet quickly developed. Such issues were not framed in the BOAC headline publicly cited figures in the VC10 versus 707 debate – to the detriment of the VC10. Later Super VC10 operations saw the gap in flying hour costs narrow considerably. And of the Super VC10 surpassing the 707 figures (as cited above)? Where was *that* in the story?

We should also recall that when the VC10 entered BOAC service, the BOAC Conway-powered 707-436 had been in service for over two years, yet BOAC achieved VC10 despatch reliability (after some initial issues with brakes and flaps) to exceed the 707s.[3] The Super VC10s maintenance schedule also reduced non-flying time and costs, achieved in a claimed, one third of the time that the 707-436 achieved. Nor had the 707 stemmed BOAC's massive long-haul operating losses by 1963.

According to published figures, the operating costs of the 707-320B and the Super VC10 across the Atlantic were far closer than the statements and legends portrayed at the time. Contrary to the so-called BOAC 'Boeing' boardroom, the Super VC10s could be within about six US cents of the slightly cheaper to operate 707-320B, it was not always the couple of dollars difference per-seat- mile that was the headline claim. And as we know, latterly, the Super VC10 ended up being cheaper to run.

Also 'missing' from the numerical costs headlines was the fact that the VC10 was so well designed and so well made, that it did not need major structural and metalwork replacements such as spars, wing skins, fuselage skins and support beams, that according to the American Federal Aviation Administration (FAA) and British Civil Aviation Authority (CAA) airworthiness bodies, were the new standard for large jet airframe inspection and replacement schedules – as framed by 707 and DC-8 experience.

As an example, in April 1966, cracks were found in tailplanes of high-hours Boeing 707 aircraft and an expensive spar and panel replacement programme ordered. Then, fuselage skins of some 707s were reputed to be suffering corrosion. There were also reported problems with doors, and hairline cracks had been reputedly found in 707 tail fin support spars and there were problems with skin panels and fasteners, notably in the aft fuselage region of jet efflux effects. These issues cost their operating airlines much money to address.

The VC10, while not problem free with early, entry-into-service brake, axle and oil seal issues that were quickly rectified, suffered no such major structural issues in the 1960s, although the decision was taken to only operate with two outboard thrust reversers as the buffet from inboard reversers had been found to cause distress fatigue on tailplane skins after several years' service. It would be 1970 before the VC10 fleet (by then up to seven years into their hard lives on rough surfaces at 'hot and high' runways, in sweaty conditions) would require a service bulletin requiring inspection and/or repair to tailplane pivot bearings and, some potential reinforcement in the wing box area. In 1972, inspections of high-cycle airframes would reveal some fatigue effects on rear under-fuselage skins – and if you had witnessed the intense and repeated battering a VC10's underbelly took from stones, dirt and dust, when alighting in the Sahara at Kano, or on a rough field in East Africa, such effects could hardly be blamed on manufacturing standards. It would be twelve years into VC10 service life before any local corrosion issues would be noted – notably in undercarriage supports.

Tropical airliners in humid conditions are also affected by fungal sludge in the fuel tanks and the VC10 was not immune. After a decade or more in service, some level of Super VC10 metal distress problems had become evident in certain areas of a few high-time, high-cycle aircraft subjected to use in hot and cold climes of humid-freeze-defrost effects. Yet as a general factor for the VC10, avoiding costly structural repair regimes early in its commercial life meant that the VC10 and Super VC10 kept flying – earning money and costing less in on-the-ground and material and manpower costs.

Coach Class and More

In terms of seat per mile costs, as a retrospective aside, we should not forget that at the launch of its 707 fleet, Trans World Airlines (TWA) was operating it's early 707-120s with a high number of premium seats – forty-six seats in First Class (including four in a front cabin lounge) and just sixty seats in Coach/Economy Class; what did that do to 707 costs per flying hour and seat per mile costs? TWA would feel the financial pinch and soon cram in over 130 Coach Class seats. A few niche operators might offer an all-Economy Class 707 with 190 seats, but with prestige airlines offering spacious First Class cabins, circa 1961, the typical 707 passenger layout provided 150–170 seats. Pan Am operated several cabin layouts and passenger accommodation before – 179 became a later – standard two-class configuration.

BOAC's VC10 offered Economy Class accommodation from 135 to 151 seats, dependent on how many seats were First Class and the overall seat pitch. The Super VC10 seated 163 to 174, but BOAC offered sixteen seats in First Class – soon reduced to twelve or less if the front cabin mail/freight cage was included. Other operators could get up to 180 seats into a Super VC10. The VC10 seat per mile costs could also look worse than they were, if, as in the case of British United Airways (BUA) or East African Airways (EAA), a number of seats were removed in order to prove a mixed 'combi' type cabin that accommodated not just passengers (in reduced numbers) in two classes, but an in-cabin freight hold. EAA's Super VC10s so equipped, offered just 111 Economy Class seats, divided from a fourteen seat First Class cabin by a large freight hold. BUA sometimes operated with just eighty-four Economy seats in its VC10s – the front fuselage taken up by a large freight cabin accessed via the large forward freight door.

These are the very details that need to be considered when making a 'big picture' costs assessment of VC10 and Super VC10 operations within and beyond BOAC, or anyone comparison to the 707.

Factors such as tropical runway lengths may well have changed on the geopolitical stage, and not at BOAC's behest, but perhaps the airline should have thought of that before ordering and dictating the design and delivery of an airliner to meet their own previously held views and certainties of short lengths and required performance therefrom? And if such certainties were wrong, that was BOAC's management's fault – not Vickers.

Can Vickers be 'blamed' for too closely meeting its customer's specified performance demands? Of course not!

As Brian Trubshaw always said: 'BOAC got what they asked for.'

Boeing's 707 and the Douglas DC-8 all benefited from the runway extensions that national governments and operating authorities funded in the USA, Africa and Asia to accept those new airliners. For example, Nairobi's original runway at 5,000ft length soon grew to 8,000ft and then a new 13,000ft strip. Singapore's 'postage stamp' of a short runway suddenly became the longest in the region. The big 707s and DC-8s demanded up to and over 10,000ft of runway in less than worst-case tropical conditions. The VC10 had been designed to serve a previously existing runway length scenario. The inherent design legacy penalty is obvious.

Early 707s-120s, and even the later 220s, 320s and heavily revised 720s, were all turbojet JT3C and JT4A powered: they simply failed to match the VC10s combination of lift and fan-jet power. The fan-powered DC-8 was also looming over Boeing's 1960-delivered 707 turbojets. No wonder the rush was on get a turbofan onto new-build 707s and to re-engine older, in-service 707s with fan-engines *before* the VC10 became a marketing threat. Before that occurred, a thirsty 707-320, with JT4 turbojets, was the 'Intercontinental' flagship sales tool for Boeing; fan engines could not come in soon enough in the 'B' series.

So here lies an argument made at the time of the VC10's launch and still made to this day – one about payload and range and a sometimes 'invisible' factor – performance – and its effect on payload being lifted off the ground.

The VC10s heavy gauge construction added a weight penalty of a suggested 7tonnes at the aircraft prepared for service (APS) specification in comparison to the more straightforward and lighter gauge 707 structure (specifically as the 707-320B long-range model).

In design terms, there were pros and cons on both sides of the Standard VC10 versus 707-320B airframe ethos argument, with many features and issues to consider, but the VC10 scored where it mattered for its application – safety, durability, passenger appeal and tropical conditions flight performance.

The B707 as the 320/B series offered a touch more rear fuselage internal cabin length over the VC10, and this allowed the fitting of up to two extra rows of seats. This aided the Boeing's seat per mile costs, but the lesser ability of the 707 to lift such a payload on key tropical routes was 'missing' from the debate. In comparison to the bold headlines of a simple airframe analysis, or even a manipulated one, a combination of specific VC10/Super VC10 factors, creating better value for money for the operating airline, allied to higher load factors due to the VC10s passenger appeal, all combined to create an underlying economic picture that was hidden from the accountants headline figures and subsequent claims and perceptions about the VC10s economics.

Given such diverse added value considerations as outlined herein, comparisons between the VC10 and 707, or DC-8, are thus unwise, if not incongruous, unless proper and detailed full account is taken of such factors when painting the overall fiscal picture.

During the VC10s life, and to this day, critics' heap blame upon it for headline issues of economics, yet those issues do not reflect the full story – they have been cherry-picked.

The Boeing 707 could not do what a VC10 could do, so the reverse argument – that the VC10 was a failure because it could not do what it was not designed to do, be a 707 rival on 707 routes – seems perverse in the extreme. The fact is that the arguments about the VC10s economics did not tell the whole 'cost' story; there were the hidden factors that played in the VC10s favour.

Just as the early turbojet 707 and DC-8 operating costs are separated out from the later versions respective costs, should we also try and delineate between the BOAC type 1101 fleet that was minus the wing improvements aerodynamic package and the revised Standard model VC10 1102/1103+ models that did incorporate such changes. Early 707s and DC-8s also went without aerodynamic changes to their wings, in fact, 148 DC-8s were let out of the factory with a performance penalty wing and resultant payments to airlines. And for the VC10 it remains fashionable to cite it (and the Super VC10) as cast in comparison against the most-developed and best performing 707 – the 707-320B turbofan series – although early BOAC fleet-specific comparison must cite the 707-320, 320B, and the BOAC-ordered 707-420, as the

-436 with its Conway engines. More than a few mainline, turbojet-powered, 707s were still about when the VC10 entered service. But the VC10 was rarely compared to such competitors in the accountants' long-running arguments over costs.

The Vickers and Boeing airframes were nearly the same length, within five feet of each other's wing span and with similar wing areas – but different wing loadings. The VC10 had larger rear cargo holds. Of significance in many respects were the thrust differences, with static thrust of the ultimate Super VC10 measured at a total of 87,200lbs from the four Rolls-Royce Conway 43/550s, and 72,000lbs total thrust from the 707-320B's four JT3D-3 fan engines. That is like having almost one extra engine worth of thrust!

The in-service max take-off weight for a BOAC Super VC10 was up to 8,000lbs more than that of the Boeing 707-320, yet the Super VC10 used at least 2000ft less runway length to get airborne 'over the fence', or screen height. This was a figure of significance. The Standard VC10, when loaded with passengers and at set IATA /FAA normal temperatures, used even less runway than that – often well over 2,500ft less than a 707. Thrust and wing lift advantages in the VC10/Super VC10 design were the answer, despite their higher structural weights. And the hotter and higher the airfield, the more the VC10 (loaded for service) advantage became over a 707 or a DC-8.

The '10 Tonnes' Issue

Supporters of the 707, often make a lot of noise about technical paperwork that showed the 707 to be able to lift 10tonnes more than the VC10. Such a broad claim was a selective one and in some senses a game of smoke and mirrors. The 707 was a term than needed definition; in this case it did not mean all the 707s as a generic label or family, it meant one, latterly developed 707-320B/C variant, but of course this has been twisted by legend into 'the 707' – as in *all* 707s, which is in error.

So the truth was that there *was* a single variant of the 707 that could carry its transatlantic payload further on a non-stop basis to America's West Coast – in terms of range in miles – than a VC10 or a Super VC10, but that 707 was the -320B/C model which came along just over half a decade into the life of the 707, and was the result of many upgrades and much learnt and spent. So, *one* major 707 model did have a max-payload range advantage in certain conditions on a cited northern hemisphere temperate zone route.

For Super VC10 to 707-320B comparisons, we can observe that the Super VC10 has a range of 4,720miles, but that the leaner Boeing 320B/C can stretch to 6,160miles (still air datum), carrying 1,200lbs more weight. But any such perspective of the 707-320B/C uplifting such extra tonnage, cannot be seen in isolation, because to do so would ignore the payload to range graphs, the requirements of runway length, operating temperatures and take-off run 'screen height' climb-out data. Getting a non-stop 707-320B/C from London Heathrow to San Francisco or Los Angeles or vice versa from the very long runways of those airports was one thing, trying the formula out of somewhere more challenging was another. The 707-320Bs payload range advantage was not just nullified at a 'hot and high runway'; it was turned into a payload deficit of up to 20tonnes!

Of note, even though the big turbofan 707-320B/C could fly from London to Los Angeles non-stop, it could only reliably do so in standard airline two-class seating configuration. A packed, heavyweight, charter configuration 707-320B/C with nearly 200 seats, would be challenged on such a long-range flight and be wind and cruise-level dependent.

Even the early 747-100 was compromised at ' hot and high' airfields when a Super VC10 was not. As we know, on a hot day at Nairobi, a fully laden VC10 or Super VC10 could take-off at high local daytime temperatures (+30C), leave the runway in a shorter distance than any 707 or 747-100, climb out at good pitch angle, clear local terrain, and then continue to a destination such as Rome, Zurich, Frankfurt or beyond with a full payload. Meanwhile, a 707, a 707-320B/C series (and even a 747-100), would have to avoid or off-load tonnes of cargo, fuel or passengers, to bring its runway length requirement down to fit within the available combination of runway distance and the effects of altitude air density and local temperatures. If, having achieved such a feat, the said 707-320B/C might lack the fuel payload to reach Frankfurt or other European airports, and would need to refuel en route – thus adding the costs of an extra landing in terms of risk, tyres, airframe cycles, engine use, time, crew hours, resources and fees – thus wholly undermining any theoretical ability to lift those extra 10tonnes from a challenging airfield; not the usual 10,000ft, or 14,000ft runway at near sea level that was the 707s American mainland and transatlantic forte.

The combination of the VC10/Super VC10 wing and engine thrust figures meant that it could climb safely away from a 'hot and high' runway at maximum take-off weight (MTOW). The effects of an engine failure soon after V2 upon the 707 in such conditions could be very demanding indeed, with the already minimal climb rate further denuded, and massive leg-rudder forces required from the pilot. In the VC10/Super VC10 such effect would be minimal.

Furthermore, we should again note the key safety factor of the VC10/Super VC10 having lower take-off speeds and notably lower approach and landing speeds with all the safety and costs benefits inherent.

Of example, the Conway 540 powered, launch model baseline VC10 offered 4 x 20,400lbs of thrust, whereas the equivalent launch model 707-120 offered 4 x 13,500lbs of thrust from its early engines. The Boeing's max payload at 23,587kg, was higher than the VC10s 18,335kg, but then came the fuel range and max payload range figures, which were massively in favour of the VC10, with the Vickers machine offering 5040mls/8,115km in max payload range; a contrast to the 707-120s figures of 3217mls/5177km for max payload range. Obviously, 3217m/5177km is much less than 5040m/8,115km, and represents a major commercial and operating issue.

An unfair turbojet-to-turbofan comparison?

Both types are cited as launch models. Even the 'fairer' comparison – from the Boeing's standpoint – shows a developed 707-720B with fan engines, and thus more technically comparable to the baseline VC10, could only get to 4110mls/6,514km as a max payload range; still short of the early VC10's 5040m/ 8,115km. So the picture was as clear as mud,

The Super VC10 traded performance for more seats, but still had a max payload range of 4,720mls/7600km (the fin fuel tank regained the weight-induced loss). And the uprated Conways each delivered a minimum of 22,500lb/10306kg of thrust, or 22,800lbs as B-spec engines. But 4,720mls/7600km *was* less than the 707-320Bs nearer 6,000miles range and far better than the original turbojet-powered 707-320 Intercontinental model which the VC10 was still up against.

So the bold '10tonnes more' claim applies to a later 707-320B/C and as can now be seen, has caveats relating to where that runway was located in terms of temperature and altitude and resulting payload ability.

Interestingly, the Rolls-Royce Conway 506/508 Co 12-powered 707-420 Intercontinental model (-436 at BOAC), with its lesser 17,500lbs of thrust and lower (0.3) by-pass ratio in comparison to the VC10/Super VC10 Conway 540s/550s, achieved a respectable balance trade-off between its figures:

- B707-420: Conway-508 engines: Range with max payload 4865miles/7830km
- Super VC10: Conway 550 engines: Range with max payload 4720miles/7600km.

Perhaps we should not focus solely on Africa as a 'hot and high' argument for the VC10 versus 707 comparison. Imagine a very hot sweltering day at Barbados, Chicago, Denver, Sydney, Nadi, Perth, Bombay, Rio de Janeiro, Buenos Aires, Caracas, Karachi, or Hong Kong. Some of these airfields may be 'hot', but not 'high', but the VC10/Super VC10 payload/range/performance advantage remained obvious against the 707 – even the 707-320B series at such locations.

Anyone in any doubt as to such performance issues, only needed to have stood at the end of an African runway in the 1960s or 1970s and seen a heavily laden 707-320B/C, or a DC-8 -60 series skim, alarmingly low, over fields or lakes after take-off, struggling to gain 500ft, to realise just what the VC10 advantage was – for a VC10 or Super VC10 would be nose-up, Conways thundering, and the clean-wing lifting with a good rate of climb to safety.

Across the 707 and 720 models, the later developments did improve the 707 performance figures, upping the cruising speed and allowing much improved 'hot and high' field performance, but fuel range, passenger and cargo capacity were decreased from longer-bodied 707 variants. It was a case of giving with one hand and taking with the other – once again, something very different from the sales and marketing hype used to attack the Vickers product. The revised 720B with fan engines offered a max payload range less than the original VC10's, and still without matching the VC10s 'hot and high' runway and climb performance. The 707 was also sold to the US Military Air Transport Service (MATS) as a 126 seater transport – the C135A- Stratocruiser, also available with turbofans as a C135B. The max payload range was just over 3,500 miles.

By clever and agile adaptation, the 707 developed. You can hardly argue with that, but you can remember that all this 707-development and tooling cost time and money on the production line. Interestingly, Braniff in America had 'hot and high' runway operating requirements and opted for the 707-320 series with the boosted JT4A turbojet engine – it was designated a 707-220. Braniff were the only major domestic customer for an airframe created by Boeing to counter the launch of the DC-8 family, but the advent of the JT3D turbo fan for the 707 as a B/C series was the sales advantage that proved Boeing's philosophy to be sound across a customer base beyond the type of operations BOAC operated.

Performance is one thing, payload lifting ability is another – the coin has two sides which cannot easily be matched, as the development costs of the 707/720 family proved, and which the DC-8 so clearly demonstrated in its performance-sacrificed-for-payload range trade off (requiring up to 12,000ft runway length for take-off).

The debate could be endless, but the facts are the facts, and fudged claims and selected debates fail to do service to the designers of the machines. More recently, the very lethargic take-off performance of the early Airbus A340 variants at 'hot and/or high' airfields, underlines the point about payload, performance and operating conditions.

In the course of the 707 airframe's life, Boeing built 1,010 707s from 1958 to 1978. Of the military type 707 variants, Boeing built 800 to 1991. In comparison, Douglas manufactured 556 DC-8s between 1958 and 1972. Boeing invested $135m on the 707 programme, Douglas even more. Both were massive gambles. Per-airframe profits on the 707 were adversely affected by the many specification changes, customer-specific options and on-going design, development and tooling costs, as Boeing refined the design post-launch. Yet the 707 was an earner and an employer across four decades, and had benefited from its military origins and amortised costs.

The 707 changed history, but to suggest, simply based on sales numbers, that it 'wiped the floor' with the VC10 would be unfair and untrue. The 707 was superb, but the VC10 advanced the art, and like Concorde, only sold in low numbers. The VC10's sales and development potential was killed by confusion and contradiction at political and state-sponsored level. As the last big, single-aisle four-engined jetliner, the VC10 came late to the market – no fault of Vickers who designed and built them in very quick time. Like all thoroughbreds, the VC10 was an expensive breed alongside Boeing's heavy horse.

BOAC's Bizarre Boeing Legal Action

In a bizarre long-running legal action by BOAC against Boeing after the airline lost a 707 on 5 March 1966 in Japan, due to what the final report said was clear air turbulence that had put the 707 over its design limits and caused the resulting crash and loss of all on board (the pilot had flown past Mt Fuji at a distance that was a point of discussion), BOAC and Boeing were at war!

In a dog-with-a-bone subsequent legal case lasting twelve years, BOAC (and then as its successor BA) alleged that pre-existing cracks in the 707s fin attachment support structure were related to the causation of the crash; Boeing countered with the findings that they were *not* and that the design was stressed beyond the known and certified design limits. BOAC, which owned and operated the plane, sued Boeing for damages, alleging actual negligent design and manufacture, breach of express and implied warranties and resulting liability.

Incredibly, BOAC had, it seemed, alleged a 707 structural design issue that it was prepared to go to Court over – for years!

There followed a long and very expensive legal 'dispute' regarding issues as facts or not.

The evidence of the accident reports was that clear air turbulence (CAT) off Mt Fuji was the causative event of the accident – whereupon any allegedly pre-existing or defective tail fin 'crack' or design issue thus became immaterial – *if* it was 'found' that the turbulence exceeded the design strength of the plane, and therefore, there would have been a crash whether or not the fin attachment fitting was defective or not. This was the defence case laid out and stated as a basis of judgement in the US Courts; BOAC formally appealed by contending that the (district) judge should not have granted such summary judgement, because there existed a 'genuine issue of material fact' which remained to be resolved at a trial, and because all discovery in the case had not been completed (surely that was down to BOAC to correctly provide and prove from 1966–1978?).

Interestingly, there *was* undisputed evidence of some degree of alleged minor fatigue failure in the fin attachment fittings on the Mt Fuji crash 707, but it was formally found that there was no evidence indicating that the crash resulted from, or was caused, in whole or in part, by such failure. Instead, the evidence supported the finding that cracks in the fin fittings were not a causative factor and that stressing beyond the design limits, was.

BOAC was found to have been unable to produce any evidence that a contributing cause of the accident was a defect in the aircraft. The court noted that BOAC had failed to meet its burden under Rule 56(e) to introduce 'specific facts' contradicting Boeing's contention that no genuine issue of material fact existed. After twelve years of investigation and litigation, all BOAC had come up with was allegedly suggested as, supposition, speculation, and conclusory argument of its legal counsel. BOAC, it is said, presented no evidence 'sufficient' to require a jury or judge to resolve the parties' differing versions of the truth at a trial.

Thus, on 23 September 1976, and then at a final date of 8 November 1978, BOAC's twelve year long case against Boeing was seen on appeal, and then was thrown out in law with the subsequent conclusion that the 'probable cause of the accident in question was abnormally severe clear air turbulence (CAT) which imposed excessive loads on the aircraft beyond its design limits.'[4]

The whole story of a decade-plus long legal case being brought by BOAC (then even by BA) against Boeing, and it seems, in the face of the accident and technical reports, is a bizarre and concerning spectacle. But why would an airline as technically competent as BOAC (post-1974 as BA), bring such a case and so doggedly pursue it for so long at such vast expense and risk, and be so apparently evidentially weak in proving its claims? This truly is a forgotten story and one that those who theorise some form of unhealthy relationship between BOAC and Boeing as having influenced BOAC's original orders for the 707, and later Boeing products, *always* forget to cite. Even more bizarrely was that BOAC was ordering 747s and 737s by the dozens from Boeing – as this litigation against the manufacturer was still in place!

We can of course opine that if BOAC's case had had any merits, the implications for the 707 and Boeing would have been catastrophic. As it was, 707 tails fins were not falling off – in or out of turbulence.

Other Contenders: DC-8 Delights and the IL-62

In 1955, the sales war took off; but while the early 707 was preparing to enter service as 1958 dawned, the Douglas DC-8 was behind in the race into service. It would be 1960 before the long-range DC-8 30 series first flew with Pan Am, and the Rolls-Royce Conway engined variant sold only to Air Canada, Canadian Pacific, and Alitalia. And how come BOAC were shy of a Conway-engined DC-8? After all Pan Am had ordered both the 707 and the DC-8. Curiously, in the machinations of 'engines on the wings' preference at BOAC, the DC–8 did not get a look in.

The DC–8 has been called a 'beauty' by many, and it certainly was sleeker and smoother than the 707, notably with more dihedral, sharper engine pylons and a more curved nose and windscreen treatment. Above all, the DC–8 is oft-quoted as being fast (even touching Mach.1 in test flight) but, contrary to perceived wisdom, the DC–8 actually had a major aerodynamic problem and it was one that the airlines carried the cost for whilst Douglas spent five years tweaking, redesigning and modifying its main wing and engine pylon designs for the airliner. The VC10 and the 707 may have undergone changes to their original aerodynamic specifications, but such alterations were carried out early on both cases. The DC–8 issue was that Douglas had built and delivered thirty airframes before invoking metalwork changes, and 148 airframes before implementing major wing and pylon design alterations. And that was not an end to it.

Inside Douglas, a faction of engineers wanted an advanced new wing, but a dominant group wanted a wing with less sweep that would allow pilots to transfer more easily from straight-winged prop-liners to the new swept-winged jet. Boeing was known for swept-winged military jets, but Douglas was known for its airliners. The new Douglas jet would, said the proponents, have an 'easier' wing and be less unforgiving and have lower approach speeds. But for the new jet's high-speed cruise, Douglas ended up choosing a new super-critical aerofoil with a flatter top than Boeing's more swept, but more old fashioned and heavily cambered 707 aerofoil.

Inside Douglas, the machinations of management over the wing went on for years and had a financial cost. Douglas's top engineers, such as A. Raymond and I. Shogran, were keen to create a jet that matched the prop-liner DC–7's handling behaviours – surely a very difficult challenge. The DC–8s wing designer was K. Kleckner, and his DC–8's wing had 30° sweep, not 35°, as favoured by the rival 707. With less sweep, the DC–8s wing was supposedly less 'foreign' in handling or behavioural terms for old school-prop-liner pilots in comparison to that of the new highly swept 707.

However, paradoxically, the DC–8 lacked the protective leading edge aerofoil camber changing devices that make a swept-wing safer at low speed – notably from ground stall upon 'Vr' rotation at take-off, and from upset and dangerous sink rate on final approach – 'low and slow'. So the DC–8 wing was not as benign at low speed as it would have been if it had been given proper leading edge devices as lift enhancers and protectors. The DC–8 10 series first flew on 30 May 1958, but flight testing revealed a drag problem that was 13% over estimates and 10% over customer performance contracts. Of interest, given the speed-related claims made ever since for the DC-8, the first machines had a maximum economical cruise speed below Mach. 80 – at Mach .79. The drag rise at high Mach numbers (Mach.75 and above) was greater with the DC-8 wing.

The DC-8's wing began to become a problem.[5] This was really serious and Douglas had to throw vast resources at a 'fix'. In fact early DC-8 customer airlines received a compensation package of approximately $230,000 per airframe due to the failure to meet design specifications as per contract. Unlike the 707, the DC-8 was envisaged from the start to have a six-abreast (3x3 seats) cabin – as had Vickers V1000. The DC-8 also had longer undercarriage legs and, greater ground clearance for body and engine pods – permitting massive fuselage 'stretchability' front and rear and better roll angles close to the ground before a pod would strike the runway.

The DC-8 family was a well-built and superb aircraft that was developed into the world's first ultra-long-range 200/250 seat airliner, yet never given proper, extendable wing leading edge devices. This was its significant design issue. DC-8s were great and loved by many, but handled incorrectly, the big Douglas could, say pilots, bite back. Heavily loaded, iced up, or in very hot air, the DC-8 needed careful handling on take-off. Yet for the likes of United Airlines, Air Canada, Scandinavian Airways System, KLM Royal Dutch Airlines, Swissair, and Japan Airlines, to name some major operators who loved their DC-8s, the max range-payload of the DC-8 -50 and -60 series delivered serious financial operating advantages. But there came a point where performance was limited, and more seats meant almost halving the max payload range in the -60 series, whereas the shorter DC8-50 series offered a max payload range of 11,260km (7,000m) – far in excess of the 707-320B or the Super VC10 – but in differing operating conditions and runway performance and at great cost in terms of fuel consumption at take-off and climb. Such aircraft were rarely seen at difficult 'hot and high' airfields, and when they were, they were massively payload and fuel limited. The DC8-60 series was the most demanding machine in terms of runway and operational restrictions – not that that showed too much on a cold day at JFK's or LAX's longest runways.

Douglas invoked significant leading edge/aerofoil 'glove' and pylon improvements to all new DC-8s, but less well known was Douglas' earlier production changes to the wing. This included a 2ft 8in span increase and fitting small, minimal span-width (2ft-3ft) open channel 'slots' in the wing – cited inboard beside each engine pylon – with the small slots opening at flap selections of 10°. This was a simple void opened up behind the leading edge, not an extending device: its effect was deemed minimal. The later post-airframe 148 changes added speed (adding 0.02 to the Mach number) and range to the DC-8, with a claimed 2% cost-per-tonne mile benefit, but take-off performance was still challenging outside normal conditions. All this made the development of the Super VC10's wing look far more benign.

Later, modified DC-8s were indeed, fast, but this was more due to its new cleaner design, and notably its further wing-pylon and full-length engine pod aerodynamics refinements – also latterly adding completely new pylons – rather than its wing sweep factor and original specification. The later DC-8 61 could accommodate 259 passengers – a stunning figure for the 1960s.

In a rebuff to Boeing's 707, it was the DC-8 that became a reborn 1980s 'tool' through the idea that led to the fitting of CFM 56 turbo-fans to late model long bodied passenger and cargo configured examples of the DC-8 family. Thus, from 1980, appeared the DC-8 73 series with each engine giving 22,000lbs of thrust – the same as a Standard model VC10 with Conways in 1964!

Ilyushin Il-62: The 'VC10-ski'

Despite some exaggerative stories about spies, stolen plans and political intrigue, the Ilyushin Il-62 was a Soviet design story that endured. First flown in 1963, the Il-62 was a large beast and highly capable, yet it was in its aerodynamics that the Il-62 had its main issues. Despite much work and suggestions of piracy of knowledge from Britain, the Il-62 wing lacked the advanced low speed and high lift capabilities of the Vickers aerofoil and its leading edge devices. Indeed, the Il-62 had to be flown very accurately indeed in order to avoid potentially disastrous handling problems; the climb-outs were slow and at reduced pitch angles until the speed built up. Weights, loadings, and centre of gravity, were all critical factors in operating and flying the Il-62. Ilyushin also failed to adequately protect the close-coupled rear-mounted engines from the effects of turbine disintegration and engine failure, or fire spreading to the neighbouring engine and the main structure; such problems lay behind several of the Il-62 tragedies – so too did a series of deep stall events.

Despite such issues, the Il-62 was rugged, and over the course of over twenty years in manufacture, was re-engined on numerous occasions to provide more power and more fuel economy. The airframe also featured some milled-from-solid panels and strong construction – the landing gear was particularly robust, as in the Soviet design bureau tradition. An Il-62 could be operated from rough runways and in terrible winter conditions.

The Il-62 featured a rear under tailfin support wheel that betrayed its poor CG, and need for rear fuselage relief at rest (Tupolev's 154 T-tail tri-jet, in long-range variant, needed six tonnes of ballast in the nose to stop it falling over backwards!). A lack of leading edge devices on the main wing also revealed shortcomings of knowledge. An Ilyushin wing design team is said to have even asked Vickers for assistance in solving some of the aircraft's issues. And was it really true that activists on the British political Left had handed a set of VC10 plans to Moscow?

A similar rumour was to come about Concorde's plans. Did a set of Super VC10 manuals go missing from an East African Airways captain's luggage? Of such speculations we know little truth. Surely the history of Soviet airframe design was seen as such a threat to the West at this time that actual Soviet design bureau achievements needed to be undermined. After all, it was the Soviet system than got into orbit first, and as the Comet 1 failed, and no other western jet airliner flew, the Tupolev Tu-104 and Tu-110, as two and four-engined jet airliners with heavily swept-wings, further rattled the western complacency of assumed technological superiority.

It was the same much ridiculed Soviet system that created the world's largest, fastest, swept-winged airframe (yet prop-driven) as the Tu-20 bomber, and its airliner derivative in the form of the Tupolev Tu-114, which in 1957, was the world's largest commercial aircraft, and in 1959 shocked American designers with its brilliance when it took N. Khrushchev to Washington D.C. In April 1960, the Tu-114 took a series of F.A.I. world records, notably attaining 877.21kph with a 25t/kg payload over 2,000km; not bad for a prop-propelled airframe. By 1961, the Tu-114 had lifted 30,035kg to an altitude of 12,073m. Whereas the lumbering Bristol Brabazon had been an utter failure, the bigger Tu-114 was an incredible success. Japan Airlines even borrowed one to serve Moscow from Tokyo across the vast wastes of the Soviet Union. In 1960, no western airliner existed that could match the turbo-prop Tupolev Tu-114 series. Now that *was* bad PR for Washington and London. The Tu-114 remains the ignored and obscured piece of 1950s Soviet airliner genius and should be more widely recognised by aviation enthusiasts.

Soviet civil aviation was too often underestimated and a particularly noteworthy aspect of the Il-62 story was that Ilyushin did succeed in creating a larger, longer, developed turbofan version that in fact matched the idea of the true, original Vickers Super VC10, 212 and 265 seaters – which BOAC so stupidly curtailed. The 6.5m fuselage extension long-bodied Il-62M of 1972 had extra range and seating for 160–204 passengers in two or three-classes. Developed Il-62 variants with even longer range gave good service on ultra-long-haul routes such as Moscow-Havana, Moscow-New York, and Moscow-Singapore. In 1978, a final Il-62 version offered much newer, high-bypass engine technology and other refinements, it could transport 195 passengers on very long-haul routes, but the day of the large rear-engine airliner design was over and Ilyushin created the Il-62 and Il-82 designs that resembled a Boeing 707 crossed with an Airbus; convention had won – again.

East German (DDR) airliner Interflug, made great use of its Il-62s and upon the retirement of the Il-62 fleet from Interflug service, a most remarkable feat of flying took place. Interflug donated an Il-62 to an aviation museum based at the location where Otto Lilienthal first flew. There, a 1,500ft/500m long grass runway was the only access for aircraft. In October 1989, Interflug's Captain

Heinz-Dieter Kollbach flew the Il-62 low across the surrounding countryside and came in over the farmland and made a typical Il-62 high-speed approach. He then expertly landed the giant Il-62 on the short grass strip. A firm, decisive, 'on point' touchdown was needed to stay within the small field. Kollbach had to raise the nose high up to create aerodynamic braking from the airframe, lowering it before it slammed down of its own accord, then the thrust reversers started venting grass and soil! The airliner was then taxied over the grass to its final museum resting place. This event proved the strength of the Il-62, but of course a VC10 trying the same thing would have touched down much more slowly and more gently.

Russia's VC10 'copy' was, in fact, a reliable yet flawed favourite of the Eastern Bloc airlines, and had its own club of admirers, notably the late 1990s IL-62 operations of CSA, the Czech airline. Aeroflot and Cubana also stretched the Il-62 glide across the Atlantic very successfully, but the IL-62 was no 'hot and high' performer and its take-off resembled a gentle act of linear levitation. It suffered a number of engine related mass-fatality accidents and deep stall events. In a way, the benefits of the T-tail rear-engined configuration were not needed on IL-62 routes and the advantages of the design concept wasted.

Chapter 9

VC10 Beyond BOAC: Other Operators

Vickers, or BAC as it became part of, needed to recoup its costs. The company might have made over £70 million from the 400+ Viscount sales, and had had good turnover from the Valiant project for the RAF, but the costs of the V1000 and the solely Vickers-funded VC7 studies had not been recouped. Without Vanguard orders, Vickers would have been in trouble. But VC10-from-Vanjet had, by 1960, become a very expensive undertaking. The company's sales team worked to market and sell the VC10, and had already thought about marketing the Super VC10 to a wider global audience. Getting ex-British colonies to look at a prospective purchase was easier than getting Pan Am, or other organisations beyond the legacy of the Empire, to consider the VC10. But approaches to Asian, Middle Eastern and South American carriers were all made.

A lesser known airline – Varanair of Siam (to become Thailand) – was targeted and liveries and a model Super VC10 created; Vickers sales teams made presentations to Egypt's Misrair, Aerolineas Argentinas, Lan Chile, and there was a little-known approach to PLUNA of Uruguay in June 1961. In July 1961, Poland's airline, LOT was also targeted. A Super VC10 sales model in the colours of Greece's Olympic Airways was also created. As late as 1966, CSA of Czechoslovakia were approached (despite the politics inherent) and a demonstration flight in Prague took place, yet to no avail.[1] As late as 1971, amid suggestions of selling DH/HS Tridents to China, a BAC sales team spoke to the Chinese about a possible VC10 licensed production series to be built in China, or re-starting the Brooklands production line for an order of 120 airframes, but the British Government failed to secure the project.

The Pan Am VC10?

A formal proposal to Pan American World Airways (Pan Am) was made in New York in 1960 of not just the Standard VC10, but also the proposed freighter variants. Vickers printed up a joint logo Pan Am/Vickers brochure and technical review booklet. Clearly depicted therein was a planform view of a VC10 with wing leading edge root fillets as an 'LR1' and with trailing edge fillets in an 'LR2' version – both fillets housing extra fuel tanks! Wing tip fuel pods, as seen on the

Comet 4, were also cited. Removable cylindrical extra fuel tanks in the cargo hold could also add a safety margin for winter operations.

The 'Pan Am Spec' VC10 could have carried 20,625 imperial gallons of fuel and might seat 196 Coach Class passengers for transcontinental US long-haul flights, or less in a two-class cabin for intercontinental flights. The BOAC Empire-route flight deck and its need for several extra officers could also be dispensed with – two crew operations being a new idea.

The Pan Am-spec Super VC10 would boast 196 Economy Class seats, or 175 with a small First Class cabin included. Here too was seen the idea of an underfloor compartment behind the flight deck – an early crew rest cabin proposal, but also a possible six-seater cocktail lounge. Vickers General Sales Manager (USA), Geoffrey Knight, made a clever and detailed technical presentation to Pan Am as early as 1960 and lightly developed engines with better cruise fuel consumption could be secured (as suggested), the 'Pan Am Super VC10' with large main cabin, two crew, and extra max-payload range, was quoted by Vickers to deliver a seat per mile cost of US\$ 2.83 dollars (average) and US\$2.59 dollars on a 4,000 mile non-stop sector. These highly competitive figures did break the US\$3.45 dollar cost on a short 500 mile sector. The airline took a serious look at this original 'Super' VC10 proposal, but alas, it was not to be.

An internal Vickers memo dated 28 October 1960 and featuring the view of Geoffrey Knight, categorically evidences that Pan Am were impressed by the VC10s abilities, particularly for their South American routes.[2] Yet Boeing's stranglehold and its ability to quickly revise the early 707 were key reasons why Pan Am avoided any further VC10 approaches.

Sadly, it was all, not to be. BOAC took the longer, but shortened Super VC10, and it was Africa that would provide the VC10 and Super VC10 with a brief but vital extension of life. Ghana Airways took just one VC10, but EAA took four Super VC10s – with the cargo door option.

Ghana Airways

As is known, the influence of empire and colonialism lived on in the new independent Africa of ex-British colonies. While ex-French colonies purchased Caravelles, the ex-British colony of Ghana did not need much arm twisting to purchase its first jet airline – a Type 1102 Standard model VC10 – that incorporated the improved wing leading edge and new wingtips that Vickers had readied early in the development process to improve lift and reduce drag.

A hiccup along the way had been Russian influence in West Africa and the troubles brewing in Nigeria. Ghana had briefly flirted with Moscow and Ghana Airways soon found itself flying Antonov 12s, Ilyushin IK-18s and a DC-6s! A leased Bristol Britannia sounded like a better idea, but in fact it was an ageing ex BOAC Stratocruiser – G-ANTZ – known in Africa as 'Ants', that BOAC arranged for the start-up new airline to operate between Accra and London via Rome, Frankfurt and even Barcelona.

Ghana Airways had been born in 1958 and was part-capitalised by BOAC and it was natural that the Britannia flew in Ghana Airways titles.

By 1961, under a new President, Ghana could see larger air traffic numbers between Accra and London, and the airline ordered three VC10s in 1961. The latter two were to have the forward cargo door that Vickers had come up with. By November the first 'GH' – Ghana Airways VC10 Type 1102 – had been delivered in a smart new livery designed at Brooklands. This aircraft – 9G-ABO – would shuttle between the two cities of Accra and London for sixteen years without fuss or accident. An initial period of using British crews ended when Ghanaian pilots were to become fully qualified on the VC10. The three VC10s seemed to suggest over-enthusiasm and routes to America and the Middle East failed to materialise, the two further GH VC10s were excess to the airline, with 9G-ABP being sold off and leased to MEA, where it was damaged by munitions in Israeli military action at Beirut Airport in 1968 – a nearly new VC10 lost. The third 'GH' machine went to BUA as G-ATDJ and an after-life with the British RAE/MoD. Yet the sole 9G-ABO was kept so busy that it had to be repainted by part process during scheduled maintenance and so often appeared in non-standard colours even after a bright new livery was created in 1976.

The Ghana Airways machines became legend in Ghana – even far out in the countryside, the national airline's VC10 was famous and copied for the extravagant coffin designs popular in that society. Ghanaians were justly proud of their VC10 operation, and even buses in downtown Accra sported murals of 9G-ABO. Crowds would cheer from the roof of Accra airport when 9G-ABO thundered down the runway and rotated up and off to London. Was not this exactly the operating environment and effect that Vickers had intended for the VC10 in Africa?

Laker and BUA to BCAL

No one could ever call Frederick Laker (Sir 'Freddie' Laker) a snob. Laker was a sharp character, a clever businessman; above all he was quick – he had to be to survive. Not everyone loved him, but you had to admire his verve and tenacity. So while BOAC vacillated and pondered, Laker leapt on the VC10 bandwagon and made the most of the opportunity. In fact the re-manufactured VC10 Type 1100 prototype was the subject of a Laker lease to become a BUA /BCAL airframe.

Laker's British United Airways had been talking to Vickers during the VC10 production stage and therefore can be given some credit as an important contributor to the VC10 story.

As the airline world's great cartels of established airlines lost their grip in the early 1960s, as new routes deemed perhaps far too menial for flag-carriers to bother with, people like Laker snapped at the heels of expanding civil aviation – not least the charter flight market which Laker and his BAC 1-11 fleet would be part of creating. Laker flew cargo, people, in fact anything anywhere, and that included troops on military charters. But in bidding for premier route licences, Laker and his 'on-paper' Laker Airways and nascent 'British United' entered a new world – one where they needed a smart, new jet. BUA had used second-hand Britannias and DC-6s. After being granted route licences to South America where Comets and 707s reigned (even Aerolineas Argentinas had Comet 4s), Laker did a deal with BAC (the Vickers name having by this time being subsumed into the new conglomerate) to purchase the modified G-ARTA – modified to Laker's personal theories.

With route licences awarded to South America and West Africa (at BOAC's expense) Laker began to make good profits. He did so by offering a combination of flexibility of product and offered mixed cargo/freight and passenger opportunities by getting his VC10 equipped with the forward cabin cargo bay and a large upwards-opening cargo door leading into a reinforced cabin floor. His VC10 could thus be a 'combi' configuration with eighty-four Economy Class seats and a large cargo bay, and he could offer a small First Class cabin too. Alternatively, rearwards facing seats could be fitted throughout the whole cabin and Laker could service his Ministry of Defence trooping contracts. And if a Russian or Asian crew of fisherman or super tanker crews wanted to be taken from Sydney to somewhere obscure, Laker could fix that too because a VC10 could get in, and out, of almost anywhere.

Laker's first production VC10 order for BUA was G-ASIX and it entered service on 31 July 1964 – not long after BOAC's 1101 model VC10s. Laker's machine had the revised wing leading edge profile, 4% chord increase and new wingtip profiles. This specification was his VC10 Type 1103 and made the most of the improvements that BOAC had ignored, and which Ghana Airways had accepted on their first Type 1102 VC10. By October 1964, Laker's BUA had received G-ASIW and that entered service just in time for Christmas of that year. Ghana Airways were very pleased with their first VC10, 9G-ABO, but did not take up the option of their second VC10, which would have been registered 9G-ABQ. Laker seized the machine off the production line and it received an out-of-sequence registration as G-ATDJ.

BAC (still referred to in the trade as Vickers) decided to try and recoup some of the money it had laid out on the VC10 programme and took the decision to fully renew its prototype VC10 airframe G-ARTA, that had appeared in BOAC's colours, but never been flown in BOAC service. After a refit that in part was a

184 VC10: Icon of the Skies

rebuild and reconfiguration, a refreshed G-ARTA emerged – Freddie Laker smelt a bargain on offer and pounced, but Laker had to accept that it would not have the forward cargo door to his 'BUA' specification. This aircraft was immediately leased to Middle East Airlines and wore their full livery as OD-AFA. It was later written off in British Caledonian colours during an empty landing at Gatwick in windy conditions in 1972. A heavy landing had kinked the fuselage and stressed the rear end; it was deemed not economically viable to repair.

BUA's VC10s crossed the Andes, dropped in to Nairobi, toured the shipping ports and cities of the Far East, and on occasion even performed short haul holiday charter flights in Europe. BUA VC10s also appeared in 'Sierra Leone' titles serving the far west of West Africa's arc of history after a 1960 agreement to set up that nation's new air service. Laker seized the opportunity to serve Sierra Leone Airways with a Britannia and then a BUA VC10 carrying very large Sierra Leone titling. In 1961, Britannias had served a Freetown- Gatwick- Freetown schedule, in late 1964, the VC10 G-ASIW, embarked on a leased 'Sierra Leone' titled service that lasted into 1965.[3]

Freddie Laker took his Rolls-Royce Silver Cloud on a sales and marketing tour of East Africa and to South America in his 'personal' VC10, the Rolls emerging from the cargo cabin and descending on a lift to be driven away across the tarmac. The Union Jack featured large in BUA's original livery, but was smaller in the airline's new 'BUA' logo typed colour scheme of 1966. BUA served Argentina, Chile, Peru, Brazil and Uruguay – this was the oft-forgotten domain of BUA's all-white VC10s in remote corners of South America. Many are sure that if he could have, Laker would have used his VC10s in cargo mode to haul beef from the outback cattle stations of the region! Such a task was, and remained, the home of ancient prop-liners that were once prestige beats for major airlines.

Laker and BUA worked their VC10s hard – with two airframes clocking up 3,000 flying hours in just 390 sectors. And if BOAC could offer passengers various in-flight mementos and a 'Junior Jet Club' book for children, Laker could do the same thing – producing a very attractive certificate for those crossing the equator by BUA VC10. With BUA you could also get of one of its short-haul BAC 1-11s and then onto a BUA long-haul VC10 in a seamless transfer.

In 1970, with Laker having 'left' BUA, the airline was absorbed by British Caledonian, and the VC10 fleet soon reappeared in Caledonian's attractive blue livery with a large lion rampant upon the tailfin and with Scottish names applied. 'B-Cal', as it was tagged, used 707-320s on its long-haul routes, but continued to use the ex-BUA machines on South American and other services including to West Africa. After just under five years' work, the high-cycle and hard worked VC10s were sold off.

Air Malawi VC10.

Nigeria Airways and '5N-ABD'

Ghana's neighbour, Nigeria, was also an ex-British colony, but one with a more troubled history. Again, it was natural that the emerging Nigeria Airways, so long a previous Imperial Airways, West African Airways arena, and a BOAC premier route, should be a VC10 application. BOAC and Nigeria Airways operated a joint service on the Stratocruiser and Argonaut runs from London to Kano and Lagos with BOAC providing the machinery and flight crew and Nigeria Airways supplying some cabin crews and ground services. The Nigeria Airways logo would be applied via adhesive stickers to the aircraft deployed to the route. Britannias took over this route too – jointly titled with Nigeria Airways stickers, and the airlines airline code 'WT' being applied to the flights to and from London.

The Lagos run was a pot of gold for BOAC and for Nigeria Airways (WT), and soon a BOAC was also jointly titled up for the BOAC/WT flights to West Africa. BOAC's G-ARVA and G-ARVI received the smart green and gold Nigeria Airways stickers on their noses as part of a wet-lease agreement and this led to a fully painted Nigeria Airways VC10 in green and white stripes. In 1969, this then led to Nigeria Airways purchasing BOAC's G-ARVA – that airline's first VC10. It was registered as 5N-ABD and operated by a mix of ex-BOAC crews. Sadly, it crashed on final approach to Lagos on 20 November 1969, in circumstances of a let-down procedure and runway/air traffic control events that led to disaster, with all on board perishing in the impact, or worse, having survived that, in the ensuing fire. Nigeria Airways would go on to bigger things – including a brief Boeing 747 affair. British Caledonian would also pick up the old BOAC links with Lagos.

Air Malawi and '7Q-YKH'

After Rhodesia's little local political difficulties and a declaration of independence from London's reach, BOAC served Malawi (Chileka Airport) with the VC10, as an alternate port of call. BUA also used Malawi instead of Salisbury and EAA served the destination. So the shape and ability of the VC10 was familiar to Malawians and their leadership. The nation had also been part of colonial British history and been familiar with Central African Airways and Vickers Viking airliners.

By the early 1970s, the idea of Malawi having its own jet airliner service to Europe, in order to serve its growing trade and international status, manifested in early 1974 in the lease of an ex-BUA, BCAL Standard VC10 service in which a BCAL-liveried VC10 operated an Air Malawi service from Gatwick to Blantyre and return on a weekly basis. By the end of that year, BCAL had sold a Type 1103 ex-BUA VC10 (G-ASIW) to the Malawi Government as 7Q-YKH. Painted up at Gatwick in a rather old fashioned red and white livery, the machine became the flagship of the Malawian regime under Dr Hastings Banda. The initial services began in December 1974 and saw good load figures. By late 1976, the idea of stopping en route at Amsterdam Schiphol was framed and that service began in early 1977.

A twice-weekly Air Malawi service to Gatwick and a local schedule to the Seychelles and other East African airports led to the sole VC10 accruing sixty hours a week in the air. This was asking a lot from a second-hand airframe, but 7Q-YKH did, in the main perform well, and had the benefit of the forward cabin cargo compartment and door. Freight traffic soon gained a place in the economics of the service. Sadly, with rising fuel costs, engine and airframe overhaul events, the Air Malawi VC10 chapter closed in September 1978. The aircraft went into storage at Bournemouth Hurn (where 7Q-YKH's tail had been built at the Vickers facility) for a long and expensive fallow period. With no buyer found, 7Q-YKH was flown back to Malawi after sitting for three years at Hurn. Plenty of fettling, adding oils, changing tyres, running the electrics and hydraulics and days of ground runs, let an Air Malawi crew remove the VC10 on a Malawian airworthiness certificate back to Chileka field via Athens.

There, the VC10 sat for nearly a decade, deteriorating and becoming a hulk. She tipped over backwards, falling onto her tail, and had to be righted.[4] Then, in 1995, she was chopped up for scrap. It was a sad end to the VC10 as part of African aviation.

Gulf Air and the 'A40' VC 10s

Aviation in the Gulf stemmed from the efforts of Imperial Airways in the region in the 1930s. So the British were closely linked to the development of airlines in the Gulf. Today's major carriers can all trace their origins back to early aviation in this hot arena.

Gulf Air began with DC-3s, yet expanded rapidly into jet aviation. By 1975 the convenient opportunity of BOAC becoming British Airways (BA) and the availability of its waning Standard model VC10s, which although a decade old and hard worked, were in excellent condition, well maintained and still had plenty of flight cycles left in them. Gulf Air had, of course, an Imperial Airways and BOAC history – BOAC owned shares in the company. Transferring its VC10s was not a huge challenge.

Having done a deal in 1972 with BOAC for a VC10 to operate with 'Gulf Air' stickers applied to its noses for scheduled services to Bahrain from London Heathrow, in 1974, Gulf Air purchased five of the BOAC VC10 fleet, and these came with a contingent of BOAC/BA VC10 pilots who were either transferred or directly employed on short-term contracts on lucrative terms. Some RAF and EAA pilots also went to work at Gulf Air on the VC10 fleet. British cabin crews also found a happy home on the Gulf VC10s. The VC10s gave up their dignified BOAC colours and emerged as all-white with a triple coloured stripe running from the nose and up the VC10s stylish tail. With a Gulf 'A-40' registration added in front of the former BOAC (British) registration, the original BOAC sub-registration lived on, as an example G-ARVC became A40-VC. Four 'A40' VC10s followed on.

After just three years of operations (which included a sublease of A40-VL to Air Ceylon to operate on Heathrow to Colombo services), Gulf Air went wide-bodied and ordered Lockheed TriStars. The VC10 fleet had just begun to appear in the Gulf's new 'Golden Falcon' livery, and two of them sported the new paint scheme, but most of the fleet were wound down and were not painted – instead they were sold off to Dismore Aviation (brokers) in December 1977 and January 1978, prior to conversion to RAF K2 Type. Gulf's A40-VL was, in early 1978, the last Standard VC10 in scheduled airline service.

So popular was the VC10 in the Gulf States that no less than three airframes became the personal transport of local leaders.

The Government of Qatar purchased a lease on BOAC's G-ARVJ for the ruler's personal flight and the aircraft was eventually retired in 1981 and went to the RAF for conversion.

BOAC's G-ARVF was sold for the very healthy sum of just under £700,000 to the United Arab Emirates Government in 1974 and served with Sheikh Zayed as a stunning executive jet until 1981 prior to being preserved at the Hermeskeil aviation museum in Germany.

The Sultan of Oman Royal Flight purchased G-ASIX from BCAL as A40-AB (he donated it back to Brooklands Museum at the end of its career on 6 July 1987). Equipped with lounges and double-bedrooms, this was a VC10 with a unique history.

Middle East Airlines

MEA had flown DH Comet 4s and Viscounts, so the VC10 was natural territory for the Beirut-based airline. MEA had big ambitions – even transatlantic routes – but failed to secure the licences it wanted. MEA was unable to secure trade agreements with the British Government that would have leveraged the funding for purchase of two or even three VC10s in 1966. MEA became a Boeing 707 customer, but did lease two VC10s for a brief period. The second Ghana Airways machine was registered in Ghana as 9G-ABP and leased to MEA two years later in 1967, but was destroyed by military action at Beirut Airport on 28 December 1968. So was lost a nearly-new, low-hours VC10.

The ex BUA/Laker VC10 remanufactured prototype, G-ARTA, was sub-leased to MEA and registered as such. It was used for 11 months in 1968 as OD-AFA, then going to BCAL as G-ARTA again.

East African Airways and the '5' Star Supers

There may be some irony in the fact that the final, ultimate Super VC10s – the last built – were operated by East African Airways (EAA) rather than the originating order airline; BOAC itself. BOAC had by this time walked away from its original larger Super VC10 order and the forward cabin cargo door equipped 'Combi' version.

EAA ordered its new fleet in early 1965 and took rapid delivery with the first Super VC10, 5X-UVA arriving in 1966. Boeing 707s had been looked at by EAA, and they had ordered DC-9s for regional use in Africa to replace its prop-liner fleet, but the company already had de Havilland Comet 4 experience. EAAs chairman, Chief Fundikra, was convinced of the Super VC10s abilities out of hot and high Nairobi and its 5,320ft altitude runway. With the forward fuselage cabin cargo door added, along with all the aerodynamic refinements added, and with 'B'-spec Rolls-Royce Conway 43/550s that pumped out at least 22,500lbs thrust each; the EAA Super VC10s were the largest, most powerful and sleekest sight in African skies. Like BOAC had done, EAA threw an expensive advertising campaign at the Super VC10 and its potential customers all over the world. EAA decided to make the most of everything about the Super VC10 being just that – Super. Direct flights to and from African and Europe – fully loaded – were possible and the planned EAA service to New York, just one refuelling stop away. EAAs 'Supers' beat BOAC's Super VC10 into African skies – the latter's machines eventually tracking down to South Africa and the Seychelles/Mauritius service – also crossing the Indian Ocean up to Singapore and Hong Kong.

EAA ordered a fourteen-seat First Class cabin and an eleven-seat Economy Class; between the two lay the lucrative freight cabin that so added to the export economy of East Africa.

Everything Vickers had learned went into the Super VC10s and for the EAA machines a new bold white livery was designed. The addition of multi-coloured side stripes made the Super VC10 look even longer than the dignified blue of BOAC, and the EAA blue lion emblem was positioned just behind the cockpit windows. On the tail fin could be found the flags of each of the three 'East African' consortium nations which had created the jointly owned airline of Kenya, Tanganyika and Uganda. Each nation had a new post-colonial registration prefix and the EAA Super VC10 fleet was therefore labelled with '5Y' (Kenya), '5H' (Tanganyika) and '5X' (Uganda). Inside the fleet, very expensive-looking murals of African wildlife and safari scenes were moulded into the bulkheads and cabin sidewall fittings. Seat covers were in bright blues, greens and yellows.

EAA's Super VC10 crews came from Comet 4 and prop-liner (Argonaut and DC-3) experience in Africa; they too formed a close-knit 'club'. The EAA Super VC10 fleet flew east to India and Asia – notably a Hong Kong service, and transited Zurich for London Heathrow and a crew base at the Skyways Hotel where much fun was had. The Super VC10s also provided a high-quality service across Africa to Lagos and Accra. EAA used its Super VC10s to numerous European holiday destinations and in early operations tended to make the airliners stop more often than the task for which they had been designed – to the detriment of fuel and crew costings. This practice was soon modified. The concept and sight of a direct link between Nairobi and New York with a bright and shiny new Super VC10 was perhaps the greatest operational achievement of the EAA Super VC10 story – 5H-MOG flew the inaugural service on 10 December 1970 under the command of Captain G. Leslie. EAA also achieved the first sight of the Super VC10 in Australian and New Zealand skies in 1974 – carrying the Kenyan team to the Commonwealth Games in New Zealand.

The Super VC10 fleet was crewed by local, ex-pat, and increasing numbers of indigenous African flight deck crews and, in the main, was one big happy family that was close to the hearts of many East Africans – whatever their race or creed. Sadly, EAA lost a Super VC10 at Addis Ababa in tragic circumstances, a difficult decision at high speed on take-off that was a reaction to events that were not the fault of the crew, and neither were the immediate events that followed, as the machine failed to properly slow down due to braking maintenance issues and airfield topography and placements.

The power, safety, and sheer style of the EAA Super VC10s carved a niche in African history; EAA also made money with its fleet of Vickers jets, and yet the new 'open skies' policy subjected EAA's key routes to strong competition. International, Ugandan, and domestic Kenyan events and policies doomed the airline and as its financial position floundered, it eventually went bankrupt on 27 January 1977 after several years of cash flow problems and unpaid bills and refused fuel carnets. The still-young fleet was promptly grabbed on account of overdue airframe payments and repossessed straight back to the UK, where they then sat dry-wrapped for a number of years prior to conversion with fuselage fuel tanks for the RAF air-to-air tanker fleet (BOAC's Super VC10 lacked the cargo door and did not receive the full cabin tank layout).

So ended the final chapter of the VC10 family, Vickers aviation in Africa and an African airline operating a Super VC10 jet that had been 'Super' in every way.

EAA's Super VC10, 5X-UVA, was EAA's first and flew from 12 October until it was written off in the take-off accident at Addis Abba on 18 April 1972, when a punctured nose wheel and subsequent events caused it to crash off the runway and burn out, with many casualties but some survivors – the only Super VC10 accident. 5H-MMT entered EAA service in October 1966 and upon EAA's bankruptcy in

SVC10 'Superb' Double Decker.

1977, was repossessed and ferried to Filton Bristol, latterly to be converted to RAF Type 1164 K Mk3 – 5Y-ADA. 5X-UVJ arrived in Nairobi in April 1969 and was repossessed in May 1977; it was sold to the RAF for conversion. 5H-MOG was the last ever built VC10 of any type – as a Super VC10 – and was a child of the 1970s, being completed in February 1970. It served just seven years with EAA before being repossessed to Filton in August 1977 and thence to the RAF as Type 1164 K Mk 3, joining 101 Squadron in February 1985.[5]

The RAF and the VC10: T-tailed Transport to Tanker

RAF Transport Command (or Support Command) was, in fact, the RAF's de facto 'airline' and, as the jet age changed military aviation with the fighters and bombers of the era – notably, the Hunter, Lightning, Vulcan, Victor, Valiant, and other wonderfully named devices – the RAF needed a large and fast transport aircraft to supply and service the materials and men such machines demanded. As the Cold War developed, the RAF would also be required to uplift cargo, soldiers, and all the plethora of Britain's end-of-Empire era.

A big RAF transport jet was needed, and just as was the case for BOAC, the Comet 4 was too small and the Britannia – however brilliant – too slow and to small, but nevertheless enduringly useful. The fact was, however, that uniquely, a fleet of RAF VC10s could, in one go, rapidly deliver for deployment over 500 troops (armed infantry), a mix of men and freight including armour to 14tonnes weight (with bombs and vehicles in the cargo hold) to a combat or tension zone, non-stop over 4,000 miles away (or further with refuelling) in well under one day. Alternatively, an RAF VC10 could rescue a large number of casualties with seventy-six stretcher 'Casevac' cases and an onboard medical set-up with operating facility.

For Vickers, developing the Valiant into the V1000 for just such a new RAF 'big jet' demand had led to the civilianised VC7 airliner. As we know, that died, but not before it had left a legacy upon the Vickers Vanjet studies and the final outcome as the VC10 itself. The Boeing 707, of course, began life as an offshoot of military airframe procurement process.

So the VC10 for BOAC was also born from a military airframe process – if less obviously. It was natural then that the VC10 project should include an RAF variant from the start. Indeed, Sir George Edwards cited the RAF as the VC10's most nationally important user. In the record of VC10 and BOAC history, we cannot ignore the RAF VC10 story and a charting of it – not least as BOAC shared with the RAF some aspects of VC10 crew training and maintenance.

The RAF's thirteen C Mk1 VC10s were 'tweaked' airframes and the original variants were 'hot-rods' of the air because they had the more powerful Conway engines from the Super VC10 and the revised wing of the developed Super-Type

Super VC10 – itself stemming from work on the aerodynamics of the VC10s wing first seen on the Type 1102 VC10 airframes. With the forward cargo door added and a stronger cabin floor designed to take such cargo loads using a 'roller' movement system, the RAF VC10s were heavier, more powerful, and therefore the RAF VC10 was thus less focused on seat per mile costs and long-range operating economics.

At maximum weight, the heavier and more fuel thirsty VC10 Mk1 has a shorter max-payload range than a Standard model VC10 – 3,185nm – but a higher 59,000lb payload, which might include vehicles in the cargo cabin. However, provided it was not heavily loaded up to MTOW, an RAF VC10 C Mk1 with a reasonable load and with the extra tail fin fuel tank full could, with high altitude cruise levels, achieve a range of over 5,000 miles. This despite extra weight – even the seats (rearwards facing) in the RAF VC10 were heavier. Numerous other production changes included an auxiliary power unit, a standard fit HYRAT emergency hydraulic generator to complement the electrical ELRAT, and these differences created the distinct RAF VC10 C Mk 1 – or Vickers Type 1006. But it was not until Christmas of 1965 that the first RAF VC10 took flight – just over a year after the first BOAC VC10 entered service. RAF acceptance and first service flight came in May 1966. Interestingly, BOAC helped the RAF with VC10 pilot conversion training – after all, both BOAC and RAF pilots came, in the main, to the VC10 from the same aircraft – Comet and Britannia.

Vickers received its RAF VC10 orders in September 1961 – for an initial five airframes – and the team set to work to create the RAF specification VC10. A total of fourteen RAF VC10s were ordered, but the fleet was reduced by one airframe when it went to the Rolls-Royce fleet as a test bed for the RB211 high-bypass ratio development testing programme as G-AXLR.

The key C Mk1 design developments were in wing, engine and structural changes.

The stronger floor, which could take a load of 1,000lbs/sq ft, added weight which allowed a near-6,000lbs maximum load with spreaders – more than enough for a vehicle or bomb rack, but by this time, VC10 and Super VC10 aerodynamics work came together which recouped some of the weight-related performance loss via lower induced and wake drag achievements. So the RAF VC10 was more aerodynamically efficient with the new Super VC10 wing, and also boasted the wider and revised incidence engine mounting stub wing. The forward fuselage cargo door and its mechanism added weight and a very small local aerodynamic penalty around its frame. The Super VC10 engines – the Conway 550s – had also by this time been uprated from 22,500lbs to 22,800lbs thrust as a 550B, by inserting an extra intermediate compressor stage. The Super VC10 tail fin fuel tank of 1,350gallons was also added. An RAF-specific option was a self-starter for the VC10 – ideal in non-airline locations – so was added the Bristol Siddeley 'Artouste' auxiliary power unit (APU) and the revised tail cone to house it. The sheet metal at the nose was altered too – to allow provision for the addition of an in-flight refuelling probe.

All-White VC10s

Painted in the all-white RAF livery with a bright blue cheatline 'flash' the RAF VC10s looked very different indeed to the BOAC versions and performed with even more panache. BOAC's cancelled Super VC10 orders meant that the RAF could jump in and get quicker VC10 C Mk1 built slots for its Type 1106 airframes and the first RAF VC10 registered as XR806 took off from Brooklands on 26 November 1965, entering RAF service with the reformed No. 10 Squadron in July of 1966, but not performing its first full RAF 'airline' Transport Command duties until early 1967 after months of crew training and route proving all over the world – where on occasion, local BOAC VC10 knowledge came to assist.

The home base for the RAF VC10 years was Brize Norton in Oxfordshire. Its single runway saw continuous VC10 operations up to 2014 and with some poignancy saw the ex-BOAC/BA, Gulf Air and EAA civil airframes return to service from a base deep in the English countryside.

From 1966, RAF Transport/Support Command received twelve of its own distinct VC10 'hot-rods' and used them to build the RAF's equivalent of a daily, worldwide air transport service. With room for 150 troops, or a lower seat number of 139 in airline standard comfort, and/or a mixed load of cargo or medical/casualty evacuation accommodation the fleet (all named after RAF Victoria Cross holders) began the legend of the VC10 in RAF service. This included the British withdrawal from its old colonial outposts on what were once Imperial Airways routes. At its 1970s height, the RAF's own 'airline' at Brize Norton carried nearly 10,000 passengers a month and operated an airline style check-in facility. Some of the VC10 fleet were averaging 200 flying hours a month. Daily, or several times a week services to Aden, Cyprus, Gan, Germany, Hong Kong, Singapore and Washington ran with VC10 precision. The 'Base' Hangar was kept busy fettling VC10s round-the-clock.

A principal role for the RAF VC10 fleet had been Royal and VIP/Diplomatic flights all over the world for over thirty years. The first use of the VC10 being in May 1965 when her Majesty the Queen visited Ethiopia by BOAC VC10. However, arriving by RAF VC10 with the flag flying always made its mark. RAF C Mk1s for Royal or VIP duties could be converted into a VIP cabin arrangement with tables, sofas and beds.

Inside the massive VC10 'Base' hangar, they carried out the repairs and maintenance of the RAF fleet, with up to six VC10s being accommodated at the same time inside the building – this was where the RAF also experienced an unfortunate VC10 'jacking' accident, as had BOAC, BUA and EAA.

BOAC had had their VC10s in service for nearly three years, and Super VC10s in service for two years, when the RAF VC10 full in-service 'airline' schedule began towards late 1967. This meant that the RAF could benefit from BOAC experience and RAF crews were trained by BOAC on its simulators at Cranebank and also fly 'live' sectors on the BOAC routes. We should note that like BOAC, the RAF never lost a VC10. This speaks volumes for the quality of design and pilot training and behaviours of both organisations.

Latterly, the RAF and BOAC shared maintenance knowledge with the RAF VC10 fleet.

There is some irony that the VC10 itself was born from a military project with a civil airframe offshoot, only to end up as a military airframe born as an offshoot (and a latter day conversion) from a civil airliner. Both roles demonstrate the excellence of the VC10 design and build quality. The RAF C Mk1 VC10 fleet achieved excellent reliability figures and where problems arose the RAF developed its own techniques for solving those problems – in fact it implemented a schedule of preventative, rather than reactive measures. This included coming up with a new, quicker, cheaper way of changing the tailplane by chemically freezing and shrinking the main mounting pivot and inserting it 'cold', thus ensuring a lower stress level during fitting.

As in airline service, the VC10 could develop problems with axles and brakes, and the RAF experienced several such events. A fleet-wide axle replacement programme stemmed from an incident of axle failure. The RAF's high utilisation rates revealed a need for a different grade of engine oil, and a limitation on nose wheel tyre degradations due to the dangers of the engines ingesting thrown tyre treads. The RAF VC10 maintenance team at Brize Norton developed a VC10-specific, travelling spares package of vital items which could be accommodated in the main hold. This ensured that en route issues could be dealt with rather than having to wait for spares. Just as with BOAC service, the lack of many other operators en route meant that the VC10 had to look after itself – although the RAF could always ask BOAC!

VC10 K Mk 2, K Mk 3 & K Mk 4

Before BOAC's successor, British Airways, 'dumped' its just-retired fleet of Super VC10s in a field in Oxfordshire at Abingdon (and at Prestwick Scotland) in 1981– where they would be stored for over five weather worn years, in some cases badly rotting away – there were the remaining early BOAC Standard VC10 airframes to be disposed of. By 1976 they were being considered for sale and Gulf Air purchased five. It was the ex-Gulf Air fleet of standard BOAC Standards that were first ferried to Bristol Filton to enter into an inspired idea – rebuilding VC10 airliners as RAF air-to-air flight refuelling tankers, formulated by government in 1978 under 'ASR 406' schedule. Next up would come the four remaining East African Airways Super VC10s, the last machines built, which had been repossessed in 1977 and were relatively still 'fresh' in age, but had endured more short-flight 'cycles' of take-off, pressurisations and landing (all of higher fatigue), than the BOAC/BA long-haul machines which, although they had spent between eleven and twelve hours a day on the wing every day they were in service, had experienced fewer 'cycles' from take-off to landing.

The 'K2' label applied to the ex BOAC/Gulf Air machines as a new Type number of 1112, and the K3 name applied to the ex EAA Super VC10s as Type 1164. The whole rebuilding project was ordered via the Weybridge-Bristol Division of British Aerospace (latterly 'BAE'). A principal upgrade was the fitting of the developed Conway 550 B engine with 22,800lbs static thrust across all the airframes – requiring some expense. Each wing had a flight refuelling pod with a 50ft trailing hose and localised reinforcement of the outer wing was required for the mounting points. A third, central drum-type 'HDU' 81ft hose refuelling point was applied under the tail of the K. Mk2, and this required revised metalwork to the lower fuselage lobe. The extra fuel tankage was applied inside the old passenger cabin and featured five, double-skinned, cylindrical metal tanks on bearer frames, with flexible membrane cells in each tank. The external venting of fuel vapours was a vital consideration. Fitting a nose-mounted flight refuelling probe also added to the range of the tanker itself, offering good flexibility wherever the deployment. Only the oil-capacity of each engine could be the limiting endurance factor.

A whole new array of electronic systems for control, navigation and communications were also added to the old analogue 'clockwork' VC10 flight decks. CCTV would be fitted to enable the fuel operator to closely monitor the receiving aircraft.

The ex BOAC/Gulf Air machines had had to have holes cut in their roof panels to insert the tanks – but the ex EAA machines were equipped with the cabin cargo door – making conversion easier and cheaper in terms of metal and man-hours.

For safe conversion and a new 'zero-timed' parts replacement programme to be effective, the VC10s and Super VC10s were stripped bare, down to their keels, cleats, and under skin structures. Everything was forensically examined, microscopically sampled, and replace or repaired where necessary. From fin-supports to wing ribs and wing boxes, from engine struts to tailplane skins and to windows, the airframes were effectively re-manufactured; at least there were plenty of spares lying about!

The first K Mk2 was ZA 141 (ex G-ARVG), first flying as a tanker on 22 June 1982 and wearing a camouflage livery not common to subsequent airframes; the first K Mk3 was to be ZA 148 (ex 5Y-ADA) and first flown as a tanker on 3 July 1984.

The 1981 withdrawn BA Super VC10 fleet had been assessed and six had to be scrapped due to very high hours and corrosion after nearly twenty years' service and over five years storage in damp conditions. Others (five) were salvageable and they would form the fleet of five K Mk4 RAF machines registered as ZD 235 to ZD 240.

After years in damp, external storage, wrapped in 'sweating' plastic, and then coated in oil, the ex-BOAC/BA Super VC10 fleet from Abingdon were in a sorry state and had to be flown over to Filton with their flaps, slats and gear locked down in a series of flights that represented some risk. Much expense was required to deal with the effects of years of static storage in British winter and summer conditions. This included new skins to the top of the structurally vital, centre wing torsion box, a very complicated job because it 'opens' up the monocoque of the hull and risks consequent twisting or misalignment. A series of jacks, stays and supports all had to be used to keep the airframes 'true'.

The conversion of these airframes did not include any fuel tanks being inserted into the fuselages, instead relying on the original aircraft's wing, body and fin fuel tanks of 17,925 gallons capacity and an air-to-air refuelling ability to perform a more limited task. The first of these conversions to Type K Mk4 was to be ZD 242 (ex G-ASGP) and it first flew on 20 July 1993, but was not in RAF service until April 1994.

The RAF's original fleet of C Mk1 VC10s were also subjected to a multi-million pound refurbishment programme (carried out by BAE/FR Aviation Hurn), which extended their lives and added the refuelling capability with just two underwing refuelling pods. They lost their all-white livery and emerged in the grey hue that became the later-life RAF VC10 standard. The refurbished C Mk1s became C1.K types.

Brian Trubshaw was the director of the K Mk1-K Mk4 project, and despite cost overruns resulting from unforeseen works and delays, the idea and the outcome was a great success and added over a decade to the VC10s life and benefited the nation's military ability and its economy. The cost overrun resulted *not* from bad project management, but from an alleged pre-project initial under-estimate of the work required to the VC10s that had been stored, and the costs and time required – so found a Parliamentary Select Committee that looked at the issue of the bill for £130 million.[6]

The RAF reformed an original ex-Royal Flying Corps bomber squadron – 101 – to create a VC10/Super VC10 tanker nuclei at Brize Norton – initially termed as a Tanker Training Flight – the 'TTF'. No. 101 Squadron had last operated the mighty Vulcan in 1982 and been disbanded in 1982. Officially reforming on 1 May 1984, the squadron existed alongside No. 10 Squadron at Brize Norton and made the most of that squadron's three decades of VC10 operational and maintenance expertise.

With its high T-tail, the VC10 proved a popular in-flight refuelling tanker, as it allowed manoeuvring receiving pilots more room to move and less danger of collision with a low-set tailplane, as found on other tanker types. There was also no exhaust streams or buffet from wing-mounted engines to contend with for pilots flying close up behind the VC10s wing-mounted and under-fuselage refuelling hoses, a major plus for reliable refuelling. However, for the VC10 to refuel from another VC10, care had to be taken, as the receiver's tail plane and fin could be buffeted by exhaust and airflow from the donating VC10 – the receiver's high T-tail being in-line and at the nearly same height with the four Conways of the 'mother' ship!

Across the Gulf Wars, Afghan, Libyan and other conflicts alongside normal global military deployments, the RAF tanker fleet have racked up an envious accident-free record of service to a number of other nations air forces, as well as to RAF types. The RAF VC10s provided over 25% of the in-flight refuelling for the US Navy during the original Gulf conflict. Of interest, No. 101 Squadron have performed a number VC10-to-VC10 in-flight refuellings that have allowed events such as flying from the UK (Brize Norton) to Perth, Australia with just two in-flight refuelling sessions across a 9,000 mile non-stop routing on a 15 hour 53 minute flight. The weekly VC10 service to the Falkland Islands also provided numerous challenges to the RAF crews, and again, no major accident ever occurred.

Far from providing over a decade's planned service up to 2000 as planned, the RAF VC10 fleet flew on until 2014. By this time, however, the costs of keeping the Conways maintained and fuelled, and of addressing the fatigue issues of these very hard-worked airframes, with their flight cycles beyond original design life, begun to become prohibitive. Major expenses, such as wing-skin, fuselage panel and structural section replacement have, quite expectedly, had to be performed.

No. 10 Squadron operated its VC10s for an astonishing thirty-nine years.

RAF VC10 Finale

After forty-seven years of RAF service, the VC10 made its final air-to-air refuelling operational sortie on 20 September 2013, and retired from service on 25 September 2013. Two VC10s, ZA147 and ZA150, flew together in a sortie that involved refuelling one VC10 from the other. The captain of ZA147 was Squadron Leader Jess Gannon. The VC10 officially had its last flight on 25 September, before landing at Bruntingthorpe airfield at 1602hrs after two very noisy go-arounds, when ZA 147 (ex-5H-MMT) shut the log book on forty-seven years of RAF service and fifty-one point three years of total VC10 flight.

So ended the VC10's incredible story in the sky. Who could have predicted back at Brooklands in 1958 that the Valiant, the V1000 and the Vanjet, could have led to such a meaningful contribution by one airframe design? Gladly, eight intact complete airframes have made their ways to various museums, and nose and forward fuselage sections litter the landscape.

Chapter 10

Full Flap: What Might Have Been and What Was

H ere lay perhaps the hardest part of the VC10's lost potential, the story of what not just might have been, but the story of what was dreamed, designed, drawn, and modelled for a great array of VC10 and Super VC10 derived ideas and airframes. Once again, thanks to Vickers, it was all there for the taking, but instead, it was thrown away by the men of power and politics.

Many airlines were canvassed and the VC10, Super VC10 and variants thereof, were presented notably to Pan Am, New Zealand National Airways, Air New Zealand, Varnair, Cathay Pacific, United, Eastern and CSA. But there came no more VC10 business. Yet the VC10 and its planned derivatives got close to major overseas sales. Letters of Intent for VC10 freighters were signed by United Airlines, Eastern Airlines, and Trans-Australia Airlines. As early as 1960, an advanced, ultra-long-range Super VC10 with two-crew, 196 seats and extra fuel tanks was framed for a presentation to Pan Am in New York. A high-capacity short-haul VC10, or VC11 Mk1 (not to be confused with the later, short-fuselage VC11 proposal), was also suggested to BEA and major world airlines. A later proposal saw the real possibility of restarting VC10 production for a Chinese order – that sadly came to nothing.

Having turned out Wellington, Viking, Viscount, Valiant, a host of smaller Vickers Supermarine military airframes, and having turned the V1000 into Vanjet, and into the VC10, the men of the Advanced Projects Office at Vickers had heads full of ideas. Anything was possible, so long as money and potential orders could back up the development of an idea. But with an airframe like the VC10 already firmed up, developing it was the natural thing to do; exploiting the VC10's civil and military potential was obvious.

By 1960 ideas were coming thick and fast. What about a VC10 that could carry passengers *and* freight in the main cabin, or just cargo as a pure freighter? How about a stretched VC10 to carry 200+? What about a double decked VC10 to carry 265 passengers? What about a 5,000 mile range, missile-launching platform for a nuclear deterrent – the new Skybolt missile? How about a clip-winged de-rated VC10 for BEA to use across Europe, or a smaller – back to Vanjet type – reverse-engineered VC10, a VC11 shorter range variant?

The projects included:

LR/1 and LR/2

These plans included adding trailing edge wing tanks, underfloor cylindrical 'quick-fit' fuel tanks and a potential leading edge 'fillet' to house a fuel tank to the basic airframe housing 250 gallons or 500 gallons+ of extra fuel, and these ideas were initially the VC10 'LR/1' and 'LR/2' types that were ingredients for a larger 'Super' variant of the Standard model VC10.

The LR/1 would have extra tanks in the baggage/freight holds at the expense of such capacities. Winter and summer tankage volumes as fitted, yet removable fuel tanks could adapt to weather and range demands on the routes. The LR/1 might also have a leading edge fillet tank. The LR/2 would see changes to wing metalwork to also add wing-root fillet cited tanks. Adding this extra tankage at minimum structural expense could put the VC10 range up to a level where it could manage a non-stop flight from London to the US West Coast, or on trans-Pacific sectors – a 707-320B speciality. The LR/1 saw an 8,000lb increase in fuelled MTOW weight and the LR/2, with both sets of wing tanks and tip-tanks, gained 14,000lbs. Fuel capacities rose to 163,000lb/kg and 167,000lb/kg respectively. A maximum weight of 342,000lbs was suggested and the LR/2 would have had a total tankage of 20,875 gallons; no major structural changes were envisaged, saving time and costs. Both the 'LR' ideas were rejected by BOAC.

Super VC10 '200' & 'Short Haul' VC10

With the original 120-seat VC10 expanded to its production size as Type 1100, ideas for a longer, higher seating capacity VC10 variant were drawn up early on in the VC10 design process in 1959. Vickers suggested several 'stretches' to give 200, 212 and 217-seat capacities dependent on configuration. Ultimately, a Super VC10-200 – as one with 200 seats was suggested. A 28ft fuselage extension also saw repositioned and larger cabin entrance and exit doors, the fin fuel tank and extra fuel tankage from the LR/2 proposals.

Thus was born the Super VC10-200 long-range airliner, yet which BOAC rejected (and thus terminated) in favour of the curtailed 'stretch' that created the production standard Super model VC10 as the Super VC10.

Yet it was from the earlier suggested Super VC10-200 that the idea of a long-bodied, clipped-winged, shorter-ranged VC10 'air bus' type domestic high-capacity airliner that would have been ideal for US eastern seaboard intercity and interstate use came. So were conceived the 'short-haul' VC10 proposals prior to the final VC11 reincarnation of Vanjet.

The record of this proposal has become confused over time. A later 1966 dated short-haul version the VC10 was presaged by a 1960 dated proposal for a 200-seater

Super VC10 that had, as an offshoot, a high-capacity short-haul derivation. Throw in a long fuselage four-engined short-haul VC11 and a much shorter fuselage, but later an eighty seater, VC11 Mk2 proposal, and the record is obscured.

With 221–230 passengers at 32–34in seat pitch respectively, a 44,000lbs payload, and yet still retaining performance at hot or high airfields, the long-bodied short-haul VC10/VC11 offered that intercity 'airbus' type efficiency. De-rating the Conway engines to 17,000lb thrust could have further reduced costs and still preserved an ideal 1,000mile sector range capability. This was a 'US$3 dollars a seat-mile' airliner – just what the airline accountants demanded. If this airframe could have been fitted with two-RB211 engines, it would have been much more economical and the world's first 'big-twin' airliner. Throw in automatic landing as 'Autoland' and the likes of BEA would have had the large, intercity express they always dreamed of, but never realised until the Boeing 757 came along (itself an apparent close 'lift' of a Hawker Siddeley HS 134 big-twin-jet design proposal). We might also notice the similarity to the original short-haul VC10 proposal of the later, very long-bodied 180-seat MD Super-80 series twin jet DC-9 derivatives, to see what can be done with an original airframe in terms of 'stretching' and high-capacity cabin configurations.

With more seats, lighter wings, less fuel weight and shorter range, a Super VC10 based intercity variant reduced operating costs – even with those thirsty Conways – but perversely, avoiding the Conway's more expensive long-haul, cruise consumption meant a cost-saving, despite the extra take-off and landing cycles of short-haul operations. Shortening the fuselage and either fitting new engines or deleting two-engines were latterly mooted for VC11 Mk2. Trans-Canada Airlines (TCA) and NCA New Zealand both showed interest in these proposals.

Super VC10 'Superb'

This was double-decked with Rolls-Royce RB 178 engines (as predecessors of the ultra-fuel efficient RB211 family). This saw the VC10 fuselage deepened and an eighty seat lower deck cabin forwards of the wing, leading into a re-profiled nose; 265 seats were proposed, and a variant, also with closer seat pitch, might offer eighty seats downstairs and 200 on the main deck. All doors, windows, wings, tail parts and main structural items would be carried over and the double-bubble lower deck would effectively be a multi-arc 'mirror' of the existing fuselage design. Could such an airframe – one that still retained a good degree of the baseline VC10's runway performance – have countered the developed DC-8 60 series and challenged the 747 and the wide-bodied tri-jets? The idea was fully planned and drawn up, but BOAC were against it, and at that time, there was much debate about emergency procedures and cabin evacuation from ever larger airliners and

VC10 Elevated Flight deck Nose-Loading Freighter Proposal.

some official views were aired about these factors in relation to the sheer scale of the Super VC10 '265' – or the 'Superb' as it has been tagged. In May 1965, yet another British aviation minister had the unenviable task of telling the House of Commons that VC10 funding – in this case up to £50million for the launch of the VC10 Superb '265' seater – was not to be forthcoming.

A more radical reinvention saw Super VC10 wings and fuselage re-modelled with four engines, two paired under each wing; not on pylons, but underslung. This design also deleted the T-tail and had 300 seats on offer – it too presaged the 'airbus' concept long before Airbus Industrie made it a reality.

VC10 Freighters: F3–F4 and More

Perhaps the most intriguing work concerned the VC10 freighter or cargo versions. Most observers know that a forwards-hinged fuselage design for the VC10 was created (the F4), but few were aware of the clamshell-type, upper lobed, nose-loading freight design was considered and a model made (see photo above). With its performance reserves, the VC10 airframe offered very good freight/cargo payloads. Removing the cabin seats, trims, galleys and toilets of the passenger specification VC10 reduced weight and added payload ability.

A VC10 F3 (F for Freighter) side-loading design proposal had made the most of the RAF-type reinforced floor and side cargo door; the F3 might carry an incredible 80,000lb payload. The further F4 freighter variant added a nose-loading facility by having a swing-nose section. It also used a hydraulically hinged and clamped forward section and 'plug' type controls and services mechanisms to ensure the flight deck was secured when closed and control runs protected. Vickers envisaged special loading ramps and jacking platforms to be part of a global freight network package, allowing quick loading and unloading of the F4. A fifteen minute turnaround was quoted if using the dedicated ground equipment. The F4 could lift 79,000lb over 3,500 miles. The maximum freight package size was 82ft – at that time the world's largest proposed air-cargo volume. A heavy duty 1000lbs/sq.ft + floor strength could also be specified – at weight penalty.

Lesser known was the VC10 clamshell-type nose loading freighter that featured a Carvair-type, or Boeing 747 style, upper deck 'bubble' and elevated flight deck station, below which a cavernous 95ft+ cargo deck was offered. Although it got off the drawing board to model stage, the double-decked, clamshell-nose required an expensive new fuselage structure, and although decades ahead of its time was not pursued. Only Boeing's 747F would rival it – over a decade later.

Other 1960s VC10/Super VC10 suggested iterations included the creation of a bizarre 'aerial yacht' that mated three VC10 fuselages together via interconnecting wings as a giant 450-seat transatlantic 'flying wing' device that would use the soon-to-be cancelled Rolls-Royce Medway engines. Military multi-role derivations

BEA Short Haul Clipped Wing VC10.

suggested, included maritime reconnaissance airframes, a bomber, and of course a tanker. Making the VC10 a three-engined jet (using Rolls-Royce aft-fan RB 178s), with a redesigned ventral fin engine (as per the DH Trident), was a more expensive suggestion, however, having seen the Rolls-Royce high-bypass ratio RB 211 tested on a VC10, the idea of re-engined VC10s and Super VC10s as twin-jets, using the RB211, was mooted, but deemed far too expensive,

Tailpiece

If we strip away the pomp, the national ego, and just look at the product, the VC10 and Super VC10 carry their own legends of success, their own achievement of engineering design brilliance, and Vickers Armstrongs excellence. The subtleties of the story may be lost on those who just look at numbers and compare the 707s sales figures with those of the VC10 family, for this story was not just about meeting a demand or a need, but in doing things by moving the state of the art forwards into a new arena – a real step into the untried and untested. The small production VC10/Super VC10 run does not indicate or evidence any issue with the design of the aircraft, it reflects the history, the political games, vacillations, power play, and ever moving goalposts of a turbulent period in post-war British history – factors far beyond the remit of an engineering company, or one man, no matter how illustrious or brilliant.

The VC10 (like the V1000) represented a massive financial risk to Vickers Armstrong as a trading entity. As an offshoot of the plot, from the VC10 came the VC11 as a short-haul jet design, and then, from the absorption of the Hunting H 107 design into BAC, came the Edwards-influenced 'son' of the VC11 – the BAC 1-11 twin jet airliner that sold well in America, not just to BEA. Indeed, Freddie Laker had been the launch customer behind the BAC 1-11 and the support for it. Without Laker and the BAC 1-11, the entity that was the British Aircraft Corporation might have died.

Cancellation of the Rolls-Royce Medway engine also had its roots in the VC10-VC11 saga, and in the DH Trident's downsize by BEA. Time has revealed the malevolent 1960s role of the European Union (EEC/EU) and British political supporters of its social science experiment, they had an effect on not just BAC, the 1-11, or 'One Eleven', but also the Two-Eleven and its wide bodied 'airbus' type 'Three-eleven' offshoot that BAC suggested in the midst of the 1960s story of the competing foundling child of the Airbus Industrie A300 and A300B gestation and re-birth, amid oscillating government positions over supporting it, or not. The name of the Europhile Roy Jenkins as MP and minister, can once again (as with VC10) be cited as a negative behavioural factor and a source of damage to Vickers, BAC and the plans of a certain 'GRE' – Sir George Edwards himself.

What of TSR-2 and any knock-on effects on that and BAC's viability? Time has revealed that politicians stabbed TSR-2 in the back, and that a certain man of power named Louis Mountbatten delivered the final blow to TSR-2's hopes of a sales break (in Australia). From V1000, to VC10 to TSR-2, it all seems like a very sorry saga indeed. Yet the aircraft, the Vickers /BAC designs, were potential world beaters, and all were ahead of the game.

The passing of time and the habit of the internet generation to get away with presenting opinion as fact, and gross error as truth, has impacted many historical events and stories. Some people believe what they read on the internet without question and then repeat it – often in print. Such a fate has, to a degree, befallen the VC10 story and debate; in doing so the VC10 design concept and its designers have, on occasion, been undermined by erroneous rubbish. We should clearly state that BOAC never evidenced any significant technical design problem with the VC10; nor any hidden, operational troubles. The VC10, to coin a phrase, 'did what it said on the tin'. Some people say that Vickers might, perhaps, have designed the VC10 in a shorter time frame; but that would not have been their way, and the high-quality forensic and safety-first test-by-test approach could have been denuded. Creating the VC10 from 1958, to first flight in 1962, was not a poor record, nor outside then acceptable boundaries, indeed it seems, in hindsight, quite a short time frame for such a massive undertaking. And would you really have expected Bryce and Trubshaw to spend less time than they did making sure the thing was safe to fly? As we know, BOAC, BUA, BCAL and the RAF, never lost a VC10 and there are reasons why that proud boast can be made. Great design, superb testing and wonderful training, all leading to consistency of performance, were the answers.

Some observers have stated that the reasons why BOAC's management 'publicly trashed' its own aircraft – that machine being designed to BOAC's exact orders – have not been fully forthcoming. Although there may be some hidden, 'smoking gun' of historical conspiracy theory plot hidden in the archives, it is more likely that the conduct, structure and behavioural psychology of BOAC (and its predecessor Imperial Airways) as charted herein, are the more likely explanations of the mess that surrounded BOAC, its fleet procurement, and its VC10 and Super VC10 story. But we must accept that in the end, the BOAC VC10s and Super VC10s made their mark and became global favourites – BOAC *did* realise that, and did invoke a VC10 family brand and customer product of preference, whatever the vacillations and machinations of past politics and corporate power battles.

We can also observe that the success of the RAF VC10 operations, as both transport and tanker, revolutionised RAF transport uplift and brought new standards and new capabilities across its British military tasks. Like BOAC, the RAF never lost a VC10.

The airliner also delivered superb service to other airlines such as British United, British Caledonian, Ghana Airways, and East African. All of which proves that the VC10 and Super VC10, in concept and design, were significant, advanced, and above all, correct. The VC10 and Super VC10 changed airline travel – notably in Africa – and gave a jump start to emerging independent African nations and their airline links and status upon the world stage. EAA's really super Super VC10 service, Nairobi-to-New York via Zurich, did, in the eyes of many, put BOAC's attitude under some focus. Sir Freddie Laker's brilliant promotion of his VC10 fleet and its flexible deployment also should not go unrecorded, particularly against the record of the national carrier that was BOAC. The British Royal family and many British politicians have also enjoyed an emotional relationship with 'their' airliner – the flag-flying VC10s that carried them around the world for several decades.

Safety First

Today we take air safety for granted. The crash of an airliner belonging to a major airline is a very rare event indeed. This was *not* the case in the 1960s and 1970s. Large airliners operated by serious 'safety culture' airlines crashed all over the world on a regular basis – several times a year – every year. Pan Am, Lufthansa, BOAC, KLM, United, Swissair – the leading quality airlines *all* had fatal crashes, often involving 707s, 747s, and DC-8s. Yet BOAC never lost a VC10 or a Super VC10 – not even when faced with a double engine failure on the climb-out at high weight or temperature.

We can suggest that the 'Andes Incident' was the closest we got to losing a VC10 in British airline service and that the VC10's design and build, allied to good piloting, saved the day. The VC10's inherent strength ensured that neither the tail, the wings, nor the engines, came off in-extremis.

The reason BOAC never lost a member of its VC10 fleets, and never injured nor killed a passenger on the Vickers airliner, was down to two factors – the significant and advanced safety features of the VC10 design, and the excellence and experience of BOAC/British Airways crew training and performance. The BOAC VC10 and Super VC10 fleet flew over 13 million passengers, made over 250,000 landings and accumulated over a million (1,207,106) flying hours covering an estimated 560 million miles and over 1.2 million revenue-earning hours. These statistics – free of serious accident, death, or injury – are remarkable. In an era when big jets crashed very often, the VC10 family's crash-free record at BOAC (and with the RAF) should never be underestimated.

Sir George – the VC10 Man

Given that Sir George Edwards is famed for the Viscount, Valiant and Concorde, events such as the loss of TSR-2 and the machinations around the VC10 might be seen by some as achievements that were flawed. If that is the case in some opinions, then we should add that any such underachievement *cannot* be laid at the doors of Vickers or its main man – George Edwards.

Edwards truly was a hero, perhaps a 'man of the Century', someone from humble upbringings who made good as a self-made man and who made life good for others – workers, pilots, passengers and the national benefit. George Edwards had a calm strength of character and integrity; he could, say some, be rather strict and forthright, but was always fair, unlike many men of certain beliefs or behaviours. Edwards had an open mind and had that global future vision that saw beyond the short term expediencies of politicians, or passing design fads and fashions. We might correctly conclude of Edwards' integrity, that his aircraft were designed and built the same way. The VC10 was designed by a talented group of men, but we should recall that the original sketches were made one weekend at home by Sir George Edwards himself.

On 29 June 2012, the VC10 celebrated fifty years of flight and a major event was held by the Brooklands Museum Trust at Brooklands to mark the event on that date. Many ex-Vickers veterans and civil and military pilots turned up, as did Sir George Edwards' daughter, Angela Newton. Hosted by Julian Temple, the museum's general manager, and highly respected aviation writer, Max Kingsley-Jones, a wonderful very British day was held and a series of lectures delivered.

Speakers included Mike Salisbury who had been part of the VC10 aerodynamics team under Ken Lawson, David Haward who had worked on the VC10's test systems rig, only subsequently to being an engineer at Boeing in Seattle. BOAC VC10 pilot and BA Concorde pilot Christopher Orlebar also attended (along with his MG BGT – blue of course). Fellow VC10 and Concorde commander Mike Bannister also paid tribute to the VC10. The RAF's VC10 story was framed by Wing Commander Kevin Brookes, as Officer Commanding No. 101 Squadron and a man with twenty years VC10 experience. Ex-RAF VC10 pilots, Richard King and David Parsons, who both went on to fly HM The Sultan of Oman's VC10, A40-AB, also spoke of VC10 operations. It was Richard King who was at the controls in 1987 when with Parsons, and engineers George and Wilkins on the flight deck, the Omani ex-BUA VC10 ended its twenty-five years life by returning back to Brooklands, having been so kindly donated by the Sultan of Oman, where it remains on display. Fond British Caledonian memories of the VC10 were presented by Alistair Pugh – the airline's former vice-chairman. Former BOAC VC10 stewardess Josie Payne retold the story of the Tunis VC10 hijack.

Despite its fifty year history, the fact was that however superb in every respect, the VC10 project did, through no fault of its own, signal the end of British, large civil airframe design and manufacture. Concorde came from the same stable of course, and we can see several VC10 design themes in subsequent airliners. The loss of the potential VC10 derivatives that were all ready to go from the Vickers/BAC drawing boards – from the true 200-seater Super VC10 proposals, the cargo and combi machines, and to the idea of an RB-2ll engined conversion – chart a failure of vision so typical of Britain in that era. In a way, the VC10 marked the end of a new beginning, and the story of a political and national process of far wider contexts and impacts than of just an airliner and an airline.

The VC10 project and its fifty-four production airframes was a unique, quality design product born into an age where accountants and corporate men did not want exquisite solutions, but rather an effective common denominator. To make an automotive analogy, the VC10 was like a Rolls-Royce, a Bentley, or an Aston Martin, or a perhaps even an early Saab, Mercedes Benz, or a Porsche; that is, as being an over-engineered device, a product with 'build-quality' created to the highest standards for a niche market that demanded clever performance and intelligent ingredients over and above the 'norm' that others in the marketplace knew would instead suffice and cost less to manufacture. In the world of the motor car circa the 1970s, Volvo, Saab, Mercedes Benz, all were built with thick steel that was corrosion proofed like nothing else, but a Ford Cortina, a Vauxhall Victor, or a Toyota Crown had thinner steel with no such protection – and were lighter and more nimble. Like the Swedish and German cars, the VC10 was thick-skinned and coated in anti-corrosion or anti-fouling paint like a liner – in true Vickers shipbuilding tradition.

That the inherent quality of the VC10 (or the cars cited above) would last longer, cost less in repairs, and retain both the performance and the hidden safety benefits, and create a loyal customer or user following, seems to have been forgotten. The VC10 was not consumer durable, it was not a short-life device, it was something different.

With the hindsight of history, we might wonder if BOAC realised just how high a quality answer Vickers would provide to BOAC's question. Did anyone in BOAC realise that in response to BOAC's demands, Vickers would turn out a pure bred beast that, if it was a car, would have been a cross between a Rolls-Royce and a Ferrari – one with Swedish-car standards of safety and build quality? No one else has ever achieved or tried it. And now we know why – it goes against the 'bean counters' ethos and lowest common denominators. Yet the fact was that in the end, BOAC's Super VC10s cost less to operate than its 707s – despite all the claims by BOAC to the contrary. But it took time for the truth to come out, and when it did, it was far too late – a sentiment Sir George was fond of expressing.

We should not see the VC10 solely as a product of the 1960s; as the last VC10, the final airframe, an East African Super VC10, was a child of the 1970s, being completed at Brooklands in February 1970. It flew on as an RAF tanker until 2013 after being repossessed in 1977 and re-manufactured prior to RAF delivery in 1985.

Boeing's 707 was, of course, a formidable device that Sir George Edwards respected, and it was re-engineered across the decades and served the world's airlines and their passengers brilliantly. But it was not a second generation, advanced aerodynamic weapon like the VC10. That the RAF has recently ordered and deployed ancient, but re-manufactured 707 airframes in an airborne surveillance role, and at vast cost to the British tax payer, is a sad and damning indictment of British political history and British politicians, many of whom, be they on the political Left or Right, should hang their heads in utter shame.

VC10 Excellence

Excellence was demanded and delivered by the VC10 and Super VC10. Strength, safety and style, all took wing in the ultimate subsonic airliner of an era now passed. Perhaps we should allow the late Brian Trubshaw, VC10 and Concorde test pilot, the last word, as spoken personally to the author:

> 'The VC10 was a beautiful aircraft to fly and its design and its designers went on to create Concorde. The VC10 provided a level a comfort not seen before. The 707 was indeed a fine machine, but it was not – in design, manufacturing or flight – the engineering and design advance that the VC10 represented. Many of the VC10's innovations are now seen in today's commercial airliner designs – for example in flight controls, aerodynamics, and even the introduction of a composite floor and tail fin researches. Concorde's low-weight carbon brakes were also a VC10 development. The VC10 did not need to be so extensively repaired or rebuilt during its airline life, true testament to its integrity and the men that designed and manufactured it. The VC10 used dramatically less runway to take-off than any competitor and climbed away more safely. Its slower landing speed addressed very real safety concerns over ever higher jet airliner landing speeds. In RAF service, the VC10 crossed the end of one century into another, and represents a remarkable story that few, if any, other types can rival. There is no doubt that the VC10 was remarkable, and the best of British.'

So sets the sun on a critical period in British aviation history and a remarkable product from a remarkable company. The VC10 and its fifty years of combined airline and national military service represent a huge achievement. The VC10 was born from the legacy of the British in Africa and their Imperial Airways and BOAC as airlines as instruments of national policy, and from that great lost historical opportunity that was the V1000/VC7 story. BOAC was not always wrong, and not always the villain, yet its hands do bear significant responsibility for what went on and what happened to the VC10 and the losses associated with it and the end game of British airliner production. We might level the same charges at BEA (another state-owned British corporation) and what it did to the potential of the de Havilland/Hawker Siddeley Trident. Successive British Governments of Labour and Tory rule, opportunistic MPs, political chameleons and the Civil Service, all have VC10 blood on their hands. A national saga seems to have evolved and much money frittered away.

However, if you never travelled in the brilliant VC10 or Super VC10, or if you never piloted one, you do not know what you missed. It is as simple as that. It was as superb as that.

The Greatest Tail.

The VC10 can only be called a unique triumph of British engineering and industrial design, the likes of which we are unlikely to see again. An accountant would say it was over-engineered, but a pilot or passenger would say it was brilliant and safe. All we need to do amid the new world of digital design, computational fluid dynamics, and composite construction, is to remember what the VC10 men at Brooklands and Wisely, achieved by brain power, by hand, and by superb craftsmanship. Thankfully, we have the Brooklands Museum Trust to remind us of what Sir George Edwards and his band of brothers did in designing and building the incomparable VC10 and the even sleeker Super VC10.

Notes

Introduction
1. Edwards, G.R. Sir, *'Looking Ahead with Hindsight'*, 62nd Wilbur & Orville Wright Memorial Lecture, Royal Aeronautical Society, London, 6 Dec 1973.

Chapter 1
1. Barfield, N.A., Dr, *Aircraft Engineering*, BAC VC10 Supplement, Burnhill Publ Ltd, April 1965. pp. 4–8.

Chapter 2
1. Cole, Lance, *Secrets of the Spitfire: The Story of Beverley Shenstone: The Man Who Perfected the Elliptical Wing*, Pen and Sword, Barnsley 2012. pp. 235–236.
2. Gardner, R., *From Bouncing Bombs to Concorde: The Authorised Biography of Sir George Edwards OM*, Sutton Publishing, Stroud 2006. pp. 50–59.
3. Cole, Lance, *Secret Wings of World War II: Nazi Technology and the Allied Arms Race*, Pen and Sword, Barnsley 2015.
4. Gardner, R., *From Bouncing Bombs to Concorde: The Authorised Biography of Sir George Edwards OM*, Sutton Publishing, Stroud 2006. pp. 190–191.
5. Cole, Lance, *Secret Wings of World War II: Nazi Technology and the Allied Arms Race*, Pen and Sword, Barnsley 2015.
6. Williams, Paul, MP, Hansard Vol 547, cc 665–670, The House of Commons, London. 8.51p.m., 8 December 1955.
7. Shenstone, B.S., Private papers.
8. Evans, S.H., Correspondence to B.S. Shenstone at Kyrenia, Cyprus, 1956–1957.
9. Benn, A.W., Personal communication at the Wyvern Theatre, Swindon 2003.

Chapter 3
1. Pudney, John, *The Seven Skies: A Study of BOAC and Its Forerunners since 1919*, Putnam, London 1959. p. 18.
2. Gunn, J., *Defeat of Distance*, QANTAS University of Queensland Press cited by John Stackhouse, *From the Dawn of Aviation: The Qantas Story 1920–1995*, Focus Publ Pty, Sydney 1995.
3. Pudney, John, *The Seven Skies: A Study of BOAC and Its Forerunners Since 1919*, Putnam, London 1959. pp. 100–139.
4. Pudney, John, *The Seven Skies: A Study of BOAC and Its Forerunners Since 1919*, Putnam, London 1959. pp. 53–99.
5. British Airways Archive London.
6. Simms, Phillip, E., *Adventurous Empires: The Story of the Short Empire Flying Boats*, Airlife, Shrewsbury 2000.

7. Coster, Graham, *Corsairville: The Lost Domain of the Flying Boat,* Viking, London 2000. pp. 37–43.
8. Allen, R., *A Pictorial History of KLM,* Ian Allan 1978.
9. British Airways Archive London.

Chapter 4
1. Higham, R, *Speedbird: The Complete Story of BOAC,* I.B. Tauris Publ.
2. Higham, R, *Speedbird: The Complete Story of BOAC,* I.B. Tauris Publ.
3. Raymond, A.E., 1958 Albert Plesman Lecture.
4. Pudney, John, *The Seven Skies: A Study of BOAC and Its Forerunners Since 1919,* Putnam, London 1959. pp. 131–139.
5. British Airways Archive London.
6. Cunningham, J.C., Grp Cpt, Personal communications, Buckinghamshire 1999.
7. Davis, P.J., *East African: An Airline Story,* Runnymede Malthouse Publishing 1993 and personal communications.
8. Barfield, N., Dr, Vickers Report cited by Cole, Lance, F., *Vickers VC10,* The Crowood Press, Ramsbury 1999 and Personal communications.
9. Evans, S.H., Correspondence to B.S. Shenstone at Kyrenia, Cyprus, 1956–1957.
10. Wood, Derek, *Project Cancelled,* MacDonald Janes, London 1975 & 2nd Edition 1986.

Chapter 5
1. Evans, Stanley, H., Personal correspondence to B.S. Shenstone, Kyrenia 1956.
2. Myhra, David, *Secret Aircraft Designs of the Third Reich,* Schiffer Books, Atglen, PA 1998.
3. Cole, Lance, F., *Vickers VC10,* The Crowood Press, Ramsbury 1999, cited from Vickers archives at Brooklands.
4. Ibid.
5. Ibid.

Chapter 6
1. Smallpiece, Basil, Sir, *Of Comets and Queens,* Airlife, Shrewsbury 1980.
2. Trubshaw, E.B., Personal communications, Gloucestershire 1998.
3. Hieminga, J., Personal communications and cited via M. Ungless at *'A Little VC10derness'* (www.VC10.net).
4. Vickers archives Brooklands Museum Trust.
5. Gardner, R., *From Bouncing Bombs to Concorde: The Authorised Biography of Sir George Edwards OM,* Sutton Publishing, Stroud 2006. p. 133.
6. Hieminga J., Personal communications and cited at *'A Little VC10derness'* (www.VC10. net).
7. Hieminga J., Personal communications and cited via M. Ungless at *'A Little VC10derness'* (www.VC10.net).
8. Cole, Lance, *Vickers VC10:* The Crowood Press, Ramsbury 1999.
9. Trubshaw, E.B., Personal communications, Gloucestershire 1999.
10. Aircraft Engineering, 'Vickers VC10', 1964.
11. Read, M., Personal communications, Wiltshire 2014.
12. Hieminga J., Personal communications and cited via M. Ungless at *'A Little VC10derness'* (www.VC10.net).

Chapter 7

1. Hansard, 22 July 1964.
2. Higham, R, *Speedbird: The Complete Story of BOAC*, I.B. Tauris Publ p. 15–47.
3. Hansard, 2 December 1963, Vol 685, cc 786–913.
4. Ibid.
5. Widely cited and of note at: Gardner, R., *From Bouncing Bombs to Concorde: The Authorised Biography of Sir George Edwards OM*, Sutton Publishing, Stroud 2006. p. 137.
6. Gardner, R., *From Bouncing Bombs to Concorde: The Authorised Biography of Sir George Edwards OM*, Sutton Publishing, Stroud 2006. p. 224.
7. Stonehouse, John, *Death of an Idealist*, W.H. Allen, London 1975, p. 55.
8. Cole, L.F., Personal communications, 1998–2014.
9. Hieminga, J., Personal communications and cited at 'A Little VC10derness' (www.VC10.net).
10. Trubshaw, E.B., Personal communications, Gloucestershire 1998–2000.
11. *Aeroplane Monthly*, May 2003.
12. *The Putnam Aeronautical Review*, Issue Number One, May 1989, Editor J. Motum. pp. 3–38
13. Ibid.

Chapter 8

1. Pennel, L., Maynard, 'Boeing Jet Tanker-Transport Design', *Aeronautical Engineering Review*, Vol 13, No 8, August 1954, pp 32–36.
2. Gunn, J., *High Corridors: QANTAS 1954–1970*, University of Queensland Press cited by John Stackhouse, *From the Dawn of Aviation: The Qantas Story 1920–1995*, Focus Publ Pty, Sydney 1995.
3. Finnimore, J.R., *VC10: 'A Niche in History'*, Putnam Aeronautical Review No1, May 1989. pp. 13–14.
4. British Airways Board, Appellant, v. The Boeing Company, Appellee. No. 76-3373. United States Court of Appeals, Ninth Circuit, Nov 8, 1978. George N. Tompkins (argued), of Condon & Forsyth, New York City, for appellant. Keith Gerrard (argued), of Perkins, Coie, Stone, Olsen & Williams, Seattle, Wash., for appellee. Appeal from the United States District Court for the Western District of Washington. Before Chambers and Hufstedler, Circuit Judges, and Renfrew, District Judge.
5. Hubler, R.G., *Big Eight*, Duell, Sloan and Pearce, New York 1960.

Chapter 9

1. Vickers archives at Brooklands Museum Trust and cited by Cole, Lance, F.
2. Vickers archives at Brooklands Museum Trust and cited by Cole, Lance, F.
3. Henderson, Scott, (with Walker, T.,) *Silent Swift Superb: The Story of the Vickers VC10*, Scoval Publ Ltd, Newcastle-upon-Tyne 1998, p. 68–69.
4. Henderson, Scott, (with Walker, T.,) *Silent Swift Superb: The Story of the Vickers VC10*, Scoval Publ Ltd, Newcastle-upon-Tyne 1998, p. 117. Also personal communications.
5. Davis, P. J., *East African: An Airline Story*, Runnymede Malthouse Publishing 1993.
6. Trubshaw, E., Brian, Personal communications, Cherrington, Gloucestershire 1998–2000.

Bibliography & Sources

Books, Publications, Lectures, Correspondence:

Aeronautical Engineering Review, August 1954.

Aircraft Engineering BAC VC10 Supplement, Burnhill Publ Ltd, April 1965.

Allen. R., *KLM: A History*, Ian Allan 1976.

BOAC/BA, Press, PR and publicity materials 1947–1982.

British Airways Archive Collection.

Cairncross, A., Sir, *Planning in Wartime*, Oxford University Press, Macmillan 1991.

Cole, Lance, *Vickers VC10*, The Crowood Press 1999.

Cole, Lance, 'The African Queen', *Aircraft Illustrated*, December 1994.

Cole, Lance, *Secret Wings of World War II: Nazi Technology and the Allied Arms Race*, Pen and Sword, Barnsley 2015.

Coster, Graham, *Corsairville: The Lost Domain of the Flying Boat*, Viking, London 2000.

Davis, P.J., *East African: An Airline Story*, Runnymede Malthouse Publishing 1993.

Edwards, G.R., (Sir) *'Looking Ahead with Hindsight'*, 62nd Wilbur & Orville Wright Memorial lecture RAeS, London, 6 Dec 1973.

Edwards, G.R., Sir, Correspondence with B.S. Shenstone at Kyrenia, Cyprus, 1962.

Evans, S.H., Correspondence to B.S. Shenstone at Kyrenia, Cyprus, 1956–1957.

Finnimore, J.R., *VC10: 'A Niche in History'*, *Putnam Aeronautical Review* No1, May 1989.

Frater, Alexander, *Beyond the Blue Horizon*, London, 1986.

Gardner, C., *British Aircraft Corporation*, Batsford, London, 1989.

Gardner, R., *From Bouncing Bombs to Concorde: The Authorised Biography of Sir George Edwards OM*, Sutton Publishing, Stroud 2006.

Gunn, John, *The Defeat of Distance*; Also: *High Corridors: QANTAS 1954–1970*, both by University of Queensland Press.

Gunston, Bill, *Early Jetliners*, Phoebus Publ, London 1980.

Headley, M., *Vickers VC10*, Ian Allan Publ, Shepperton 1989.

Hieminga, J., www.VC10.net as referenced content and personal communications.

Henderson, S., *Silent Swift Superb: The Story of the Vickers VC10*, Scoval Publ 1998.

Higham, R, *Speedbird: The Complete Story of BOAC*, I.B. Tauris Publ.

Hubler, R.G., *Big Eight*, Duell, Sloan and Pearce, New York 1960.

McGregor, G., *The Adolescence of an Airline*, Air Canada, Montreal 1980.

Pudney, John, *The Seven Skies: A Study of BOAC and Its Forerunners Since 1919*, Putnam, London 1959.

Simms, Phillip, E., *Adventurous Empires: The story of the Short Empire Flying Boats*, Airlife, Shrewsbury 2000.

Smallpiece, Basil, Sir, *Of Comets and Queens*, Airlife, Shrewsbury 1980.

Stackhouse, John, *From the Dawn of Aviation: The Qantas Story 1920–1995,* Focus Publ Pty, Sydney 1995.

Stonehouse, John, *Death of an Idealist,* W.H. Allen, London.

The Putnam Aeronautical Review, Issue Number One, May 1989, Editor J. Motum.

Trubshaw, Brian, Edmondson, S., *Test Pilot,* Sutton Publishing, Stroud 1998.

Vickers Armstrongs Archives (Brooklands Museum Trust), including design drawings, publications, and pamphlets.

Wood, Derek, *Project Cancelled,* MacDonald Janes, London 1975, & 2nd Edition 1986.

Interviews & Communications 1984–to date:

Norman Barfield

N.W. Boorer

Terence Brand

John Cunningham

Ronald Ballantine

Peter J. Davis

Sir George Edwards

W. Gunston

Jelle Hieminga

Mike Hutchinson

Angela Jeffreys

Albert Kitchenside

David Leaney

Christopher Orlebar

B.P.H. Shenstone

John Stroud

Brian Trubshaw

Appendix 1

Fleet Registrations:

BOAC/BA VC10 and Super VC10:

Standard VC10 Type 1101

G-ARVA
G-ARVB
G-ARVC
G-ARVE
G-ARVF
G-ARVG
G-ARVH
G-ARVI
G-ARVJ
G-ARVK
G-ARVL
G-ARVM

Super VC10 Type 1151

G-ASGA
G-ASGB
G-ASGC
G-ASGD
G-ASGE
G-ASGF
G-ASGH
G-ASGI
G-ASGJ
G-ASGK
G-ASGL
G-ASGM
G-ASGN
G-ASGO
G-ASGP
G-ASGR

Other operators:

Air Ceylon Type 1101:
A40-VL (leased from Gulf Air)

Air Malawi Type 1103:
7Q-YKHG

British United/British Caledonian Type 1103:
G-ARTA 'Loch Ness' (Remanufactured Type 1100)
G-ASIW 'Loch Lomond'
G-ASIX 'Loch Maree'
G-ATDJ 'Loch Fyne'

East African Airways Super VC10 Type 1154:
5H-MMT
5H-MOG
5X-UVA
5X-UVJ
5Y-ADA

Ghana Airways Type 1102:
9G-ABO
9G-ABP

Gulf Air Type 1101:
A40-VC
A40-VG
A40-VI
A40-VK
A40-VL

Middle East Airlines Type 1100/1102:
OD-AFA (As leased ex-Laker)
9G-ABP (As lease ex Ghana Airways)

Nigeria Airways Type 1101:
G-ARVI (leased from BOAC)
G-ARVA (leased, then purchased as 5N-ABD)

Sierra Leone Airways Type 1103
G-ASIW (leased from BUA)

Royal /Government Flights
A40-AB Sultan of Oman Royal Flight Type 1103
G-ARVF UAE Government Type 1101
G-ARVJ Qatar Government Type 1101

RAE MoD Experimental Fight Type 1102:
XX914 Ex G-ATDJ (Finally to RAF Brize Norton as test airframe 8777M)

RAF VC10s:

RAF VC10 C. Mk 1 Type 1106
XR 806 George Thompson VC
XR 807 Donald Garland VC /Thomas Gray VC
XR 808 Kenneth Campbell VC
XR 809 To Rolls-Royce as G-AXLR for RB.211 trials
XR 810 David Lord VC
XV 101 Lanoe Hawker VC
XV 102 Guy Gibson VC
XV 103 Edward Mannock VC
XV 104 James McCudden VC
XV 105 Albert Ball VC
XV 106 Thomas Mottershead VC
XV 107 James Nicholson VC
XV 108 William Rhodes–Moorhouse VC
XV 109 Arthur Scarf VC

RAF VC10 K. Mk 2 as Type 1112
ZA 140 ex A40-VL
ZA 141 ex-A40-VG
ZA 142 ex-A40-VI
ZA 143 ex-A40-VK
ZA 144 ex-A40-VC

RAF VC10 K. Mk 3 as Type 1164
ZA 147 ex-5H-MMT
ZA 148 ex-5Y-ADA
ZA 149 ex-5X-UVJ
ZA 150 ex-5H-MOG

RAF VC10 K. Mk 4 as Type 1170
ZD 230 ex-G-ASGA
ZD 235 ex-G-ASGG
ZD 240 ex-G-ASGL
ZD 241 ex-G-ASGM
ZD 242 ex-G-ASGP

Note* other 'ZD' airframes registered but not converted (scrapped)

Index